U·X·L

HISPANIC AMERICAN

CHRONOLOGY 2ND EDITION

U·X·L
HISPANIC AMERICAN
CHRONOLOGY 2ND EDITION

Sonia G. Benson, Nicolás Kanellos, and Bryan Ryan, Editors

THOMSON
★
GALE

Detroit • New York • San Diego • San Francisco • Cleveland • New Haven, Conn. • Waterville, Maine • London • Munich

U•X•L Hispanic American Chronology, 2nd Edition

Sonia G. Benson, Nicolás Kanellos, and Bryan Ryan, Editors

Project Editor
Carol DeKane Nagel

Permissions
Kim Davis

Imaging and Multimedia
Robyn Young

Product Design
Mary Claire Krzewinski, Michael Logusz

Composition
Evi Seoud

Manufacturing
Rita Wimberley

Cover photograph of Southern Pacific Railroad workers reproduced by permission of the Arizona Historical Society Library.

While every effort has been made to ensure the reliability of the information presented in this publication, The Gale Group, Inc. does not guarantee the accuracy of the data contained herein. The Gale Group, Inc. accepts no payment for listing; and inclusion in the publication of any organization, agency, institution, publication, service, or individual does not imply endorsement of the editors or publisher. Errors brought to the attention of the publisher and verified to the satisfaction of the publisher will be corrected in future editions.

LIBRARY OF CONGRESS CATALOGING-IN-PUBLICATION DATA

U•X•L Hispanic American chronology / Sonia G. Benson, Nicolás Kanellos, and Bryan Ryan, editors.—2nd ed.
    p. cm.
    Rev. ed. of: Hispanic American chronology. 1996.
    Summary: Examines significant social, political, economic, cultural, and educational milestones in Hispanic American history, from 1492 to modern times.
    Includes bibliographical references and index.
    ISBN 0-7876-6600-9 (hardcover : alk. paper)
    1. Hispanic Americans—History—Chronology—Juvenile literature. 2. Latin America—History—Chronology—Juvenile literature. 3. Spain—History—Chronology—Juvenile literature. 4. Portugal—History—Chronology—Juvenile literature. [1. Hispanic Americans—History—Chronology. 2. Latin America—History—Chronology. 3. Spain—History—Chronology. 4. Portugal—History—Chronology.] I. Title: Hispanic American chronology. II. Benson, Sonia. III. Kanellos, Nicolás. IV. Ryan, Bryan.
E184.S75 U95 2002

973'.0468'00202–dc21
2002007382

Printed in the United States of America
10 9 8 7 6 5 4 3 2 1

CONTENTS

READER'S GUIDE

U•X•L Hispanic American Chronology, 2nd Edition, explores significant social, political, economic, cultural, and educational milestones in the history of Hispanic Americans, those who came from Spain or the Spanish-speaking countries of South and Central America, Mexico, Puerto Rico, or Cuba. Arranged by year and then by month and day, the chronology spans from prehistory to modern times and contains more than one hundred illustrations and maps, extensive cross references, a glossary, and a subject index.

Related reference sources:

U•X•L Hispanic American Almanac, 2nd Edition, features a comprehensive range of historical and current information on the life and culture of Hispanic America. The *Almanac* is organized into fourteen subject chapters including immigration, family and religion, jobs and education, literature, and sports. The volume contains 120 black-and-white photographs and maps, a glossary, and a subject index.

U•X•L Hispanic American Biography, 2nd Edition, profiles one hundred Hispanic Americans, both living and deceased, prominent in fields ranging from civil rights to athletics, politics to literature, entertainment to science, religion to the military. A black-and-white portrait accompanies each entry, and the volume concludes with a subject index.

U•X•L Hispanic American Voices, 2nd Edition, presents twenty-one full or excerpted articles, memoirs, essays, speeches, letters, and other notable works of Hispanic Americans. Each entry is accompanied by an introduction, boxes explaining events discussed in the text, and a glossary of terms used in the document. The volume also contains one hundred black-and-white illustrations and a subject index.

Advisors

Special thanks are due for the invaluable comments and suggestions provided by U·X·L's Hispanic American Reference Library advisors:

Margarita Reichounia
Librarian, Bowen Branch
Detroit Public Library
Detroit, Michigan

Linda Garcia
Librarian, Southern Hills Middle School
Boulder, Colorado

Comments and Suggestions

We welcome your comments on *U·X·L Hispanic American Chronology* as well as your suggestions for topics to be featured in future editions. Please write: Editors, *U·X·L Hispanic American Chronology,* U·X·L, 27500 Drake Rd., Farmington Hills, MI 48331-3535; call toll-free: 1-800-877-4253; fax: 248-414-5043; or send e-mail via www.gale.com.

PICTURE CREDITS

The photographs and illustrations appearing in *U•X•L Hispanic American Chronology,* 2nd Edition, were received from the following sources:

Cover: Southern Pacific Railroad workers: **Arizona Historical Society Library.**

AP/Wide World Photos: pp. 78, 115, 144, 162, 168, 169, 171, 173, 175, 186, 188, 190, 193, 196, 197, 199; **Arizona Historical Society Library:** pp. 79, 94; **Courtesy of Arte Público Press Archives, University of Houston:** pp. 10, 23, 30, 51, 86, 97, 105, 112, 119, 128, 131, 136, 155, 176; **Bettmann/Corbis:** p. 31; **Courtesy of the Center for Puerto Rican Studies Library, Hunter College, CUNY:** pp. 91, 150; **Courtesy of CISPES:** p. 160; **Courtesy of the Cuban Archives, Florida International University:** p. 72; **Photograph by Curtis Dowell:** p. 156; **The Granger Collection, New York:** pp. 64, 66, 76, 90; **Ross Hall:** p. 127; **Latin Focus:** pp. 181, 191; **Lee (Russell) Photograph Collection, The Center for American History, The University of Texas at Austin:** p. 103; **Courtesy of the Library of Congress:** pp. 81, 120; **Courtesy of the Library of Congress, Historical American Buildings Survey, Prints and Photographs Division:** p. 41; **Courtesy of the Library of Congress Prints and Photographs Division:** pp. 4, 7, 13, 15, 21, 24, 26, 34, 36, 42, 47, 58, 60, 83, 102, 107, 110, 113, 122; **Courtesy of the Library of Congress Rare Books and Special Collections Division:** p. 12; *The Los Angeles Times:* pp. 88, 114; **Courtesy of the Ministry of Internal Relations, Caracas, Venezuela:** p. 53; **National Baseball Library and Archive, Cooperstown, New York:** p. 125; **Courtesy of the National Library, Madrid, Spain:** p. 20; **Courtesy of Replica Publications, Inc.:** p. 133; **Reuters/Bettmann:** p. 178; **Courtesy of the Smithsonian Institution:** p. 37; **Sporting News/Archive Photos, Inc.:** p. 187; **Transcendental Graphics:** p. 147; **UPI/Bettmann:** pp. 84, 100, 135, 142, 146, 158; **Courtesy of the U.S. Department of the Interior and National Park Service:** pp. 31, 61.

INTRODUCTION

A Hispanic American Chronology

Hispanic Americans are people who live in the United States who came—or whose ancestors came—from Spain or the Spanish-speaking countries of South, Central, and North America. The three major Hispanic groups in the United States are Mexican Americans, Puerto Rican Americans, and Cuban Americans. There are also significant numbers of Hispanic Americans whose origins are the Dominican Republic, El Salvador, and Nicaragua. Other countries are represented in smaller numbers.

Today Hispanic Americans are a diverse group with different homelands, customs, and even ways of speaking Spanish who, nonetheless, share a similar place in the American experience. Like every American, Hispanic Americans are the product of immigration from an old world to a new one. Yet they are unique. Through their history, Hispanic Americans have brought together three great cultures: European, African, and Native American. In one form or another, Hispanic Americans have introduced their own mixtures of these three cultures to the United States, a country that grew out of an English (Anglo) tradition.

U•X•L Hispanic American Chronology, 2nd Edition, is a history of the Hispanic American people, a compilation of significant social, political, economic, cultural, and educational milestones from the past and present. It is a history of their contact with the Anglo culture, and of the encounters between their homelands in Latin America and the United States. *U•X•L Hispanic American Chronology,* 2nd Edition, traces this history over 25,000 years. It begins in the dark caves of prehistory, crosses an Ice Age land bridge, spreads out to two continents, rides the winds of exploration, struggles through conquest and colonization, gets swept up in the wave of immigration, and explodes in today's cultural awareness. It is the story of our fellow countrymen, our neighbors, our friends, our families, ourselves.

Hispanic American Roots in Europe, Africa, and the Americas (25,000 B.C. to A.D. 1492)

The history of the Hispanic American people has its roots in Europe, Africa, and the Americas. Over 25,000 years ago, hunters left their mark on cave walls in the Pyrenees Mountains of northern Spain. These hunters foraged for food among the wild plants of the area, hunted ancient bison and other animals, and found shelter in caves. To record their world, they painted pictures of the animals they hunted. These hunters are among the earliest known inhabitants of the land now known as Spain.

As the years went by, Spain, at the westernmost tip of Europe, became the home of many more European peoples. Around 1000 B.C., Celtic warriors, hunters, and shepherds spread across Europe, building new settlements along the way. On the Iberian Peninsula (where Spain and Portugal are located), these Celts mixed with the native Iberians to form a new mixed culture. Greek traders followed around the year 600 B.C., setting up ports along the Mediterranean coast of Iberia. By the year 200 B.C., the Romans had arrived on the Iberian Peninsula. For almost six centuries, they battled to build and defend a Roman colony there. When the Roman Empire crumbled around A.D. 400, Germanic tribes from eastern Europe moved in to take control of the Iberian Peninsula. Together, all of these groups provided Spain's European heritage, a heritage shared by Hispanic Americans.

Perhaps the first Africans crossed the narrow Strait of Gibraltar to the Iberian Peninsula in 2000 B.C. These Iberians, as they are known, may have been related to the Berber people who still live in Libya, Algeria, and Morocco. They built their own villages and planted crops. One thousand years later, they mixed together with newcomers, the Celts, to create a new culture. About 500 B.C., a powerful city-state in northern Africa, Carthage, began to send armies and colonists across the Mediterranean to the Iberian Peninsula. There, the Carthaginians created colonies that lasted almost 300 years, until the Roman Empire moved in to take control.

The next major African influence on Hispanic history came in A.D. 711. At this time, a group of Muslims invaded the Iberian Peninsula and forced the mixed European culture northward toward the Pyrenees. For the next 800 years, these Moors, as they became known, shaped the culture of the Iberian Peninsula. Their mark can still be seen in the mosques, gardens, and paved streets of many Spanish cities. Africa's final contribution to Hispanic American culture began in the late 1400s. At that time, Spain joined Portugal in the African slave trade. Over the next few centuries, Spain relied on the labor of Africans to build its empire in the New World. In Spanish America, Spain's African heritage joined with the heritage of Africans forced into slavery. This heritage was passed on through the years to Hispanic Americans.

Sometime near the end of the last ice age (before 11,000 B.C.), Asian hunters followed their source of food across a land bridge between Siberia and Alaska. These first American immigrants moved slowly southward. Within a few thousand years, they had reached South America. Not long afterward, these Native Americans had tamed the Americas and begun their own cultures in their new homeland.

About 7000 B.C., some ancient Native Americans turned from hunting and gathering to farming for food. At this time, a group of people living in Central America probably developed corn from a wild plant with edible seeds. Over the next 5,000 years, farming brought people together and a village culture grew. By 1200 B.C., the Olmec culture had been founded. Soon after the Olmecs, the Mayan civilization emerged in Central America.

The Mayan civilization thrived in Mexico and Central America from around 800 B.C. to A.D. 1500. During this time, the Mayans built one of the world's most advanced civilizations. They perfected a writing system and used it to record their history, religion, and literature. They created an accurate calendar and were excellent mathematicians. Other civilizations followed the Mayas in Mexico and Central America. The most important of these was the Aztec civilization. The Aztecs were a warrior people who built an empire in Mexico. Their civilization thrived from A.D. 1325 to 1521.

Elsewhere in the Americas other Native American civilizations grew and prospered. Among the most important were the Incas of Peru and the Pueblo culture of the American Southwest. Others lived in South America, the Caribbean, and the American Southeast. These cultures influenced the Spaniards and Africans who traveled to the New World after 1492. This Native American heritage has also been passed on through Hispanic Americans.

The Meeting of Two Worlds (1492 to 1776)

Christopher Columbus was born in Italy, but he led his adopted homeland, Spain, in its greatest adventure. Seeking new routes to the rich lands of Japan and China, Columbus turned Spain's attention to the west. When he accidentally came upon a different continent in 1492, he started three centuries of Spanish exploration, conquest, and colonization in the Americas. In the Spanish Empire that grew, the Old World—Europeans and Africans—came together and mixed with the New World—Native Americans. These people of Spanish America created the cultures and traditions that we now see in the United States among Hispanic Americans.

On his second voyage to the New World, Columbus built La Isabela on the island of Hispaniola. This first Spanish settlement in the Americas was founded on January 1, 1494. Many more explorers and settlers followed during the 1500s.

Some, like Juan Ponce de Léon, Diego Velázquez, and Hernán Cortés, led the Spanish in exploring and colonizing Puerto Rico, Cuba, Mexico, and other Hispanic American homelands. Others, like Pedro Menéndez de Avilés, Alvar Núñez Cabeza de Vaca, Hernando de Soto, and Francisco Vásquez de Coronado, led the Spanish in exploring and colonizing lands that are now part of the United States.

The exploration, conquest, and colonization of Spanish America continued through the 1600s well into the 1700s. Spain spread its empire from the Caribbean and Mexico southward toward the tip of South America and northward into North America. To the south, the Spaniards met the Incas and other Native American cultures, as well as the Portuguese who were building colonies in Brazil. To the north, the Spaniards encountered the Pueblo Indians and others. They also competed with the English and French trying to found colonies in what is today the United States. California was Spain's last frontier in North America. A number of Spanish expeditions pushed northward from Mexico into the lands of the Yuma Indians. Don Gaspar de Portolá and Father Junípero de Serra led one such expedition to San Diego in 1769. Captain Juan Bautista de Anza led another expedition even farther north. De Anza founded the presidio (fort) of San Francisco on September 17, 1776. Spain had established its northernmost outpost in the New World.

American Expansion and the First Hispanic Americans (1776 to 1898)

The United States of America proclaimed its independence from England in 1776. Years of war followed before the American colonies were finally free of European control. During the 50 years after the American Declaration of Independence, many of Spain's colonies in the New World went through the same kind of experience. By the mid-1800s, independent nations in the New World had shaken free of European control and were battling among themselves for power. As the United States pushed toward its Manifest Destiny of controlling the continent from the Atlantic to the Pacific, it encountered a newly independent Mexico. Anglo Americans going west met Mexicans moving north.

Many of the first Hispanic Americans did not choose to come to the United States. It came to them. Mexico had inherited Texas, New Mexico, Arizona, California, and parts of Nevada, Utah, and Colorado from Spain. The battle for Texan independence in 1836, the Mexican War in 1845, and treaties between the United States and Mexico in the 1850s eventually won these lands for the United States. Because of these wars and treaties, many Mexicans found their homes in U.S. territory. Those who stayed became the first Hispanic Americans. Over the next 50 years, Hispanic Americans and Mexicans went back and forth across the border to work, trade, and rejoin families.

Hispanic Immigration in an Era of Revolution (1898 to 1962)

As the end of the nineteenth century approached, the United States had already celebrated 100 years as an independent democratic nation. It had spread west to the Pacific Ocean, developing its agriculture and industry along the way. It was not yet a world power, but it did have considerable influence in the Americas. The same could not be said of the lands in Spain's fallen empire in the New World. Political, economic, and social power was tightly held in the hands of a few. Mexico was ruled by the dictator Porfirio Díaz. Puerto Rico and Cuba were still colonies of Spain. The Dominican Republic lived under the terror and corruption of dictator Ulises Heureaux. Many of the nations of Central America struggled under dictators and the influence of large foreign businesses.

The situation was ripe for revolution in Latin America and for U.S. intervention. Cuba began a war for independence from Spain in 1895. Cuba had not yet achieved its goal when the United States went to war with Spain in 1898. When the war was over less than a year later, the United States had control of Cuba and Puerto Rico. In 1910, Mexicans rose up against the abuses of their own government and launched the Mexican Revolution. In the 12 years between the Spanish-American War and the Mexican Revolution, the United States was involved in political turmoil in Cuba, the Dominican Republic, Nicaragua, El Salvador, and Panama. In some cases, it sent troops to these countries; in other cases, it used diplomacy. This type of involvement continued throughout the early and mid-twentieth century.

Perhaps the most dramatic encounter between the United States and the Hispanic American homelands occurred after the Cuban Revolution of 1959, led by Fidel Castro. In 1962, the United States and Cuba—backed by the Soviet Union— became embroiled in the Cuban Missile Crisis. The crisis was the most dangerous nuclear showdown between the United States and the Soviet Union ever.

The climate of revolution had a great influence on Hispanic immigration to the United States. Political and economic unrest in these countries forced many to leave their homelands. Contact with the U.S. military and businesses gave Hispanics a taste of what the United States had to offer. To this was added U.S. labor shortages during the two world wars. As a result, during the years from 1898 to 1962, the United States saw several waves of Hispanic immigration. Mexicans came to work in the fields of the Southwest, to man factories in the Midwest, and to build railroads. Puerto Ricans became U.S. citizens in 1917. This made it relatively easy for them to travel to the Northeast to work in factories and shops. Cubans came later, most between 1959 and 1962, fleeing Castro's revolution. Other Hispanic Americans came for similar reasons. This immigration created communities of Mexican Americans, Puerto Rican Americans, Cuban Americans, and others in the Southwest, New York, Florida, and the Midwest.

The Rise of Hispanic Americans (1962 to the present)

Since the early 1960s, many of the same factors have continued to drive Hispanic immigration: political and economic unrest, close contact with U.S. troops and businesses, and U.S. labor demands. Because of this immigration, the United States has seen the emergence of Hispanic Americans as an important part of the American culture. Mexican Americans, Puerto Rican Americans, Cuban Americans, and others have begun to assert themselves. These separate groups have come together to celebrate their common heritage, to educate their fellow Americans, and to forge a Hispanic American identity. United, they have shown their economic and political power, and spread their influence to almost every corner of American life.

The rise of Hispanic Americans began on several fronts in the 1960s. In the early 1960s, young Mexican Americans, inspired by the civil rights movement, began their own movement. This Chicano Movement pushed for social and political change. It also sparked a rebirth in the arts among Mexican Americans. Chicano literature, theater, and art thrived during this time. A similar flourishing of the arts took place among Puerto Rican Americans in New York in the late 1960s. Nuyorican literature came alive during this period. In more recent years, Cuban Americans have been recognized for their artistic expression.

During the 1960s and 1970s, Hispanic Americans also made economic and political gains. In 1962 in California, César Chávez organized Mexican American farm workers to strike for better working conditions. Similar strikes were organized in other parts of the country. In 1963 in Texas, Mexican Americans founded their own political party. They won local elections and eventually found a home in the Democratic Party. Puerto Rican Americans in the Northeast and Cuban Americans in Florida have made similar political gains. Hispanic Americans also benefitted from new laws and court decisions protecting voting rights and bilingual education.

Perhaps the most visible gains by Hispanic Americans have come in business, popular culture, and the media. From 1977 to 1987, the number of Hispanic-owned businesses in the United States almost doubled from 219,000 to 422,000. Over the next decade, the number of Hispanic-owned businesses and their share of the U.S. economy continued to grow. During the same period, the Hispanic American population continued to swell. According to the 2000 U.S. Census, the Hispanic population in the United States grew to 35 million—13 percent of the population—making it the largest and fastest-growing minority group in the country. At the turn of the twenty-first century, Hispanic Americans were more visible than ever as television and movie personalities, as singers and musicians, and as sports figures. These Hispanic stars appealed not only to Hispanic audiences, but to all Americans. Finally, Hispanic Americans have made their culture and concerns known through the growth of Spanish-language newspapers, magazines, radio stations, television networks, and Web sites.

U•X•L Hispanic American Chronology, 2nd Edition, offers a fascinating walk through Hispanic American history, year by year, and sometimes month by month or day by day. Just open it to any page and relive history as if you were reading the day's headlines.

25,000 B.C. ✦ Early inhabitants of Spain.

The earliest known inhabitants of the Iberian Peninsula (present-day Spain and Portugal) were game hunters and cave dwellers. During the Ice Age, they hunted, gathered food, and found shelter in caves near the Pyrenees Mountains. In these caves, they left behind drawings of the animals they ate, and one can still see paintings of ancient bison in the caves of Altamira and Tito Bustillo in Spain.

11,000 B.C. ✦ First immigrants to the Americas.

During a period from 125,000 to 10,000 B.C., glaciers (large sheets of ice) covered much of the Northern Hemisphere. In North America, the ice sheets came as far south as the Ohio River Valley. During the most recent glacial stage of this Ice Age, so much water from the oceans became frozen over the land that sea level may have been as much as 300 feet lower than it is today. The lower ocean waters uncovered a land bridge between northeastern Asia and Alaska. This Bering Land Bridge, or Beringia, may have been 1,000 miles wide in some places. Sometime near the end of this glacial stage (before 11,000 B.C.), Asian hunters crossed the Bering Land Bridge into Alaska, following their source of food or a desire for new homelands. At first, these people were trapped in Alaska by the glaciers to the east and south.

It is not clear how many different groups of Asian hunters made the trip across the Bering Land Bridge or during how many periods they came. Some scientists who study fossil records, deoxyribonucleic acid (DNA), or languages believe that there were two major waves during this period of migration. A third wave of Asian immigration probably occurred around 3500 B.C. and included the ancestors of the Eskimo-Aleut and the Na-Dene people. Because much of the Bering Land Bridge was underwater at this point, these groups had to come by water. The Eskimo-Aleut eventually settled the Arctic regions of North America and reached Greenland by 2000 B.C. The Na-Dene settled the Pacific Northwest.

Other scientists who have examined the archaeological records and languages believe that there were far more than three waves of migration. In any case, those who crossed from Asia to Alaska were the first immigrants to the Americas.

ANIMAL MIGRATION

The Bering Land Bridge was not only a path for human migration. It also allowed animals to migrate from Asia to North America and in some cases from North America to Asia. Mammoths (Ice Age elephants), bison, deer, and bear were among the animals that crossed the land bridge from west to east. Horses and camels, which were common in North America before the most recent Ice Age, may have crossed the land bridge from east to west.

10,000 B.C. ✦ The Clovis culture.

The first widespread human culture in the Americas seems to have been that of a people called Clovis. This name comes from a site in New Mexico where their artifacts were first discovered. Archaeologists (scientists who explore the ruins left behind by ancient people) have found the distinctive stone spear points and tools of the Clovis people from the American Southwest to the Atlantic shores of Canada.

10,000 B.C. ✦ Paleo-Indians cover North America.

The glaciers covering North America began to melt around 20,000 years ago. By 10,000 B.C., two or three major routes to the south had cleared. At this time, America's first immigrants, called Paleo-Indians, began to move south to settle in areas that are now in Canada and the United States. These people were nomadic hunter-gatherers, meaning they had no permanent home, but moved to follow their sources of food and water. The Paleo-Indians hunted the large animals that lived throughout North America at that time: mammoths (Ice Age elephants), camels, and bison (or buffalo). They also gathered wild fruit and vegetables. To help them in killing and preparing their food, these people crafted spear points, axes, scrapers, and knives from stones and bones.

8000 B.C. ✦ The decline of big game hunting.

Around 8000 B.C., the climatic changes that had ended the Ice Age began to change the environment in many parts of prehistoric America. For example, much of the American Southwest and Mesoamerica (present-day southern Mexico and Central America) became hotter and drier. The lush green plants that had provided food for large animals disappeared. With these changes in climate and the onset of hunting throughout the continents, mammoths, camels, giant sloths, and other large animals became extinct. As some of their food sources disappeared, the hunters turned more to foraging (eating wild plants as well as fish and small animals for protein). During this period of history from 8000 B.C. to 2500 B.C., known as the Foraging Period, the first Americans became increasingly better at gathering and storing food. They also discovered that they could grow some of the plants they had been gathering.

8000 B.C. ✦ Native Americans in South America.

The descendants of the first American immigrants probably reached South America by 8000 B.C. They soon spread to the southern tip of South America. Along the way, they separated into many groups, each with its own culture and language. By the time Christopher Columbus arrived in the New World, Native American cultures in North and South America flourished throughout approximately one quarter of the world's land mass.

7000 B.C. ✦ The cultivation of corn.

Around this time, the Native Americans who lived in the southern part of the Mexican plateau discovered a plant that produced edible grain. They called this plant *teozintle*. These people, known as the Otomí, worked many years to improve teozintle into the plant we now know as corn (or maize). With this new source of food, the Otomí people could stop moving from place to place, stop hunting and gathering food; they could begin to build permanent homes. By 5000 B.C. the Otomís were growing a variety of crops, such as corn, squash, beans, and chiles. They were also weaving clothing from vegetable fibers. Eventually, they acquired the skills of making pottery and utensils. The cultivation and use of corn spread to other areas of Mesoamerica and had found its way to New Mexico by 3000 B.C.

7000 B.C. ◆ The rise of agriculture in the Americas.
In addition to foraging, Native American peoples began to take steps toward consistently raising their own food. Around 7000 B.C., the people of Mesoamerica began to plant and water the seeds of wild plants such as squash, beans, peppers, gourds, and amaranth (a grain). They also tamed some of the wild animals they found around them, including turkeys and small dogs. There were no large animals such as cattle or horses to tame, however. For the most part, these animals had not survived the change in climate. (The exception was the buffalo, which roamed the northern part of the continent.) Without cattle and horses, these people had no beasts of burden. For this reason, they carried things themselves.

2500 B.C. ◆ Village culture in the Americas.
With the stable supply of food that came with raising their own crops, ancient Americans began to build permanent villages and develop cultures that went with their new lifestyle. Corn and other crops allowed these cultures to grow in number and prosper. The crops also became central to many Native American customs and religions. The prosperity that came with agriculture also allowed these cultures to make advances in pottery, basketry, metalworking, architecture, and astronomy.

2000 B.C. ◆ The Iberian culture.
On several occasions, groups from Africa migrated to present-day Spain in search of a better home. Perhaps the first people to make this trip in recorded history were the Iberians. (The Iberian Peninsula—Spain and Portugal—now bears their name.) They probably traveled across the narrow Strait of Gibraltar between Morocco and Spain. The Iberians may have been related to the Berber people who still live in Libya, Algeria, and Morocco. Once in Spain, they lived in villages and practiced agriculture, but little else is known about them.

1200 B.C. ◆ The Olmec culture.
Farming villages continued to develop in the Americas. As they grew and prospered, they began to band together, trade food and other useful products, establish religious beliefs, and begin social and political organization. These were the

Mayan palace
with observatory
at Palenque,
Mexico.

first steps toward civilization. In Mesoamerica, one of the first attempts to build such a civilization was made by the Olmec people. They lived and built their religious and economic centers from about 1200 to 500 B.C. in the present-day Mexican states of Veracruz and Tabasco. Archaeologists have found evidence of the Olmec culture at sites in Tres Zapotes, San Lorenzo, Cobata, and La Venta in these two states. The Olmec left behind large stone monuments of the heads of gods and helmeted men fashioned out of basalt, a fine-grained rock. They also left behind carved jade statues, ball courts, calendars, and writing symbols. The Olmecs may have influenced more advanced civilizations that followed them, including the Mayas.

1100 B.C. ◆ Phoenician trading ports on the coast of Iberia.

The Phoenicians, superb sailors from the coast of present-day Lebanon, crisscrossed the Mediterranean Sea in search of goods to buy and sell. (They also developed an alphabet that is an ancestor to our own.) They spread their influence to the western end of the Mediterranean when they set up trading ports on the coast of Iberia. Two of the cities they founded were Cádiz and Málaga.

1000 B.C.–A.D. 300 ◆ Mayan civilization in the Preclassic Period.

The first advanced civilization to develop in the Americas was that of the Mayas. The Mayas built religious and economic centers in the jungles of what are now Mexico's Yucatán Peninsula, Belize, Guatemala, Honduras, and El Salvador. They were impressive architects, mathematicians, astronomers, artists, and writers. Mayan civilization can be divided into three periods: the Preclassic (1000 B.C.–A.D. 300), the Classic (A.D. 300–900), and the Postclassic (900–1500).

Nomadic speakers of Mayan languages first settled down into farming villages sometime between 2000 and 1500 B.C. Later, these villages gathered together around religious and trading centers. During the thirteen centuries known as the Preclassic Period, the Mayas built up their distinct culture in the lowlands of the Petén region of Guatemala and surrounding areas. Some of the earliest cities were at Cuello in Belize, El Mirador in Guatemala, and Río Bec in Mexico. In these and other cities, the Mayas developed one of the most advanced civilizations in the world. By the third century B.C., Mayan mathematicians were using zero (an advanced concept) as a place holder in numbering. (*Also see entries dated* A.D. *300–900: Mayan civilization in the Classical Period; and 900–1500: Mayan civilization in the Postclassic Period.*)

1000 B.C. ◆ The Celtic migration to Iberia.

Numerous tribes of warriors, hunters, and shepherds migrated to the Iberian Peninsula from somewhere in present-day Hungary near the Danube River. These Celtic peoples brought with them a new culture and a new language, Gaelic. They did not destroy the native Iberian people and culture, but rather mixed together with them. The result was a new and unique Iberian-Celtic culture. The influence of this culture is strongest today in northwest Spain in a province known as Galicia. There, the language and celebrations have much in common with other Celtic regions such as Brittany, Wales, Scotland, and Ireland.

600 B.C. ◆ Greek ports on the Iberian coast.

Greek traders crossed the Mediterranean Sea to set up colonies on the coast of Iberia. These coastal colonies did not mix with the Iberian-Celtic culture in the interior of the peninsula. However, they did influence the native culture by introducing new forms of transportation, mining techniques, and art forms. They also began the cultivation of grapes for wine and olives for oil.

500 B.C. ✦ **Colonies of Carthage in Iberia.**

Carthage was a great city-state founded by the Phoenicians on the coast of North Africa in present-day Tunisia. Through trade in the Mediterranean, the city grew in size and power from 900–500 B.C. During this time, the Carthaginians began to spread their culture through colonization and war. Carthage sent many colonists to the coast of Iberia over the next few centuries to set up trading towns, including Cartagena.

206 B.C.–A.D. 400 ✦ **Roman colonization of Iberia.**

As Rome grew in power during the fourth and third centuries B.C., it began to battle Carthage for control of the Mediterranean. The conflicts between these two powers were the cause of the three Punic Wars (264–241 B.C., 218–201 B.C., and 149–146 B.C.). During the Second Punic War, the great Carthaginian general Hannibal launched his invasion of Italy from Spain in 218 B.C. With more than 50,000 men and 37 elephants, Hannibal was successful in three battles in Italy. However, the Romans withstood the invasion. In 206 B.C., a Roman army defeated the Carthaginians in Spain. This was the first of many victories that would ensure the expansion of the Roman Empire onto the Iberian Peninsula. In 133 B.C., the Romans finally defeated a group of Iberian-Celtics who had resisted Roman control for six years from a stronghold in Numantia.

The Roman Empire had a great impact on what would become Spanish culture. Many Romans came with their families to Hispania (as they called present-day Spain) and settled the land. They enslaved natives and set up a plantation system based on slave labor. Their Latin language mixed with the native tongues. After hundreds of years, this Iberian Latin became Castilian, which we now call Spanish. The Romans influenced the political organization, laws, and religion of Spain. They introduced large cities, courts of law, and Christianity.

The Romans also influenced the layout of towns and the ownership of land that would become characteristic of Spanish culture both in Europe and the Americas. The typical Spanish and Spanish American town was organized around a town square or plaza. The Catholic Church overlooked the square and government buildings occupied the remaining space around the plaza. The town center also included a bathhouse, an amphitheater, and a coliseum. Roman plantations built on the Iberian Peninsula became models for the large farms and ranches later found in Spanish culture.

The Romans controlled the Iberian Peninsula until their empire began to crumble around A.D. 400. The empire eventually fell, but it left behind cities such as Seville, Córdoba, Toledo, and Salamanca.

150 B.C. ✦ **The civilization at Teotihuacán was founded.**

Among all of the marvelous cities of Mesoamerica, perhaps the most spectacular was the city of Teotihuacán, home to the Toltecs, in the central valley of Mexico near present-day Mexico City. It was founded around 150 B.C. and grew in size until it reached a population of over 120,000 people sometime after A.D. 300. It had streets, marketplaces, parks, apartments, temples, and hundreds of pyramids. The most impressive were the Pyramid of the Sun, the Pyramid of the Moon, and the Pyramid of Quetzalcoatl (the feathered serpent god of many Mesoamerican cultures). The Toltecs slowly abandoned the city sometime after A.D. 600. They may have helped found the Toltec capital at Tula, also in the central valley of Mexico.

A.D. 300–900 ◆ Mayan civilization in the Classic Period.

During the Classic Period, the Mayan civilization continued to spread throughout the southern jungles of the Yucatán Peninsula. Among the great Mayan cities of the Classic Period were Tikal in Guatemala, Copán in Honduras, and Palenque in Mexico. The classic Mayas further developed their religion and sciences. Mayan priests excelled in chronology, the study of time. Their year had 20 months of 18 days each, with 5 extra days at the end of the year. They made periodic adjustments to keep their calendars accurate. In fact, Mayan calendars were more accurate than anything developed in Europe before the 1600s. The Classic Period ended shortly before A.D. 900. No one is sure what caused the Mayas to abandon the cities of the southern Yucatán. Some think that the land no longer produced good harvests, others believe that a civil war or a war with outsiders may have caused the fall of these cities.

A relief chiseled out of stone by Mayan artists in Palenque, Mexico, during the Classic Period.

Mayan records and monuments interpreted by archaeologists provide a great deal of information about these Native Americans. At its peak, the Mayan civilization covered approximately 200,000 square miles of Mexico and Central America. In that vast area were many city-states with a shared language, culture, and religion. During the Classic Period, the Mayas raised their culture to a high level. This was reflected in their dress, customs, buildings, and arts. Mayan architecture was original and outstanding. They used burnt limestone to build their cities and pyramids. The many temples and monuments within the cities were decorated with carvings and wall paintings.

Mayan intellectual achievements included written language. They used pictures to represent words, a system called either hieroglyphics or pictographs.

Other pictures represented syllables. They carved this picture writing in wood and stone and painted it with watercolors on fiber paper. They used pictographs to write their own literature. The *Popol-Vuh,* the sacred book of the Mayas, traces the creation of man prior to 3151 B.C. The book of *Chilam Balam* is a masterpiece of Mayan literature.

409 ◆ The invasion of Spain by Germanic tribes.

As the Roman Empire crumbled, Germanic tribes from northern Europe and western Asia began to move across Europe to take control. In the fifth century A.D., Vandals and Goths invaded the Iberian Peninsula and replaced the Romans as the dominant power. The new leaders were influenced by the Iberian-Celtic-Roman culture of Spain. They eventually took on the language and religion (Christianity) of the native people. In turn, they added their influence to the culture. The Germanic tribes, for example, were warriors. Their warrior cult would strongly shape Spanish culture. This would be evident later in the Crusades and the Reconquest (both religious wars against Muslims). The warrior cult also influenced early encounters between the Spanish and Native Americans in the New World.

711 ◆ Spain under the Moors.

Spain had often attracted the attention of people from North Africa as a promising new land. The original Iberians and the Carthaginians represented two major migrations from Africa to Spain. The third group from North Africa to set its sights on Spain was a group of Muslim invaders. Tariq ibn Ziyad led 12,000 Arabs and Berbers from Morocco to Spain across the Strait of Gibraltar in A.D. 711. By that time Germanic tribes, called the Visigoths, had carved up Spain into numerous small regions, each controlled by a feudal lord. These lords spent much time fighting among themselves. By working together, the North Africans were able to defeat the Visigoths in several battles. They took the Visigoth capital of Toledo in 712 and soon pushed the feudal lords and their armies into the northern frontiers of Spain.

The Moors—as the new invaders were called—brought new leadership to the Iberian Peninsula. More importantly, they brought organization, skill, and learning to a culture mired in the Dark Ages. The Muslims had closely studied the advanced civilizations of their own time and of past times. Moorish farming techniques brought the dry land to life. Muslim architects renewed the cities with intricately decorated mosques, lush gardens, and paved streets. They built the Great Mosque of Córdoba in 786 and the Alhambra in Granada in the 1300s. The Moors introduced to Spain the secrets of making medicine and of making steel, things they had learned from the Far East. Their philosophy made Spain a center of learning. Toledo, Córdoba, and Granada were especially important cities where Muslim, Christian, and Jewish scholars were all welcome. In effect, the Moors brought progress like that experienced in Spain under the Romans. (*Also see entry dated 206 B.C.–A.D. 400: Roman colonization of Iberia.*)

900–1500 ◆ Mayan civilization in the Postclassic Period.

During the Postclassic Period, leaders from the southern Yucatán Peninsula had moved to Mayan settlements in northern Yucatán. There they began to transform the settlements into independent cities that controlled the land around them. This type of political unit is called a city-state. Among the great city-states of the Postclassic Period were Mayapán, Chichén Itzá, and Uxmal.

Mayan culture continued to make advances. By the end of the Postclassic Period, Mayan astronomers could predict eclipses and chart the course of Venus. Yet, even though its culture was advanced, Mayan government organization was simple. A hereditary ruler helped by priests and nobles directed each city-state. There was no powerful central leadership. By the fifteenth century A.D., civil wars and more powerful outsiders had caused the Mayan civilization to decline. It would be replaced as the dominant culture in Mesoamerica by other groups, namely the Toltecs and Aztecs. (*Also see entries dated A.D. 300–900: Mayan civilization in the Classic Period; and 1000 B.C.–A.D. 300: Mayan civilization in the Preclassic Period.*)

1085 ◆ The Reconquest of Spain.

While the Moors built their culture from Toledo south to the Mediterranean coast of Spain, Visigoth kings continued to control the northern regions of the peninsula. In 1085, Christian armies under Alfonso VI recaptured Toledo from the Muslims. This began a slow, steady push to the south by the Christians. For the next 400 years, Christians and Muslims fought for control of Spain. This period is known as the Reconquest.

1100 ◆ The Incan civilization began.

The Incan civilization began in the Cuzco Valley of Peru. At first, small groups of Quechua-speaking tribes came together to control this valley in the Andes Mountains, which run along the Pacific coast of South America. In the 1400s, through wars and colonization, this nucleus grew to become the most widespread of the Native American civilizations. By 1492, the Incan empire included the area of present-day Peru and Bolivia, as well as parts of Argentina, Chile, and Ecuador. In order to control their vast lands, the Incas built a system of roads and bridges that crossed mountains, jungles, and deserts. They even had their own postal service. Incan rulers also created a strong, highly organized government which directed many parts of the daily life of the society. Government workers, accountants, and engineers had great influence over the social classes, laborers, and the use of land.

A model of the ceremonial center of Tenochtitlán.

Incan culture also made many advances in the field of medical science. Incan doctors used drugs to treat illness and anesthesia to control pain during surgery. Surgeons amputated limbs and conducted brain surgery.

1325 ◆ The Aztecs founded Tenochtitlán.

The Aztecs migrated from what is present-day northern Mexico to the central plateau of Mexico in the thirteenth century A.D. Poor at first, they became subjects of the Toltec Empire at Tula. After many years spent searching for a homeland, they moved to some islands on Lake Texcoco (the site of present-day Mexico City). The Aztecs increased the farmland available on these islands by stacking fiber mats and topsoil in the shallow lakes until they had floating gardens or *chinampas*.

In 1325, the Aztec villages came together to found the city of Tenochtitlán. This Aztec capital became a magnificent city. At its peak, it had an estimated population of 200,000 people. Three causeways (raised roads) connected the island city to the mainland. It had canals for transportation and aqueducts (water channels) to bring pure drinking water to its citizens. The giant market of Tlatelolco sold fresh produce grown on the chinampas. From this capital, the Aztecs spread out to conquer the people of surrounding areas. Eventually, their empire stretched from the Pacific to the Gulf coast and south into Guatemala.

The Aztecs are best known for their warrior culture and religion. In 1487, to celebrate their military victories and to consecrate a new temple to their war god, Huitzilopochtli, the Aztec sacrificed 20,000 prisoners of war. Yet they also made contributions in the areas of art, architecture, literature, and education.

1444 ◆ The birth of Portuguese slave trade.

Under the direction of Prince Henry the Navigator, the Portuguese expanded sea exploration and trade to Africa. In 1444, Portuguese ships sailed beyond Cape Verde in present-day Senegal to the Sierra Leone coast. Within 30 years they reached equatorial Africa. On these West African shores they began to trade for gold and slaves. In 1482, they built Elmina Castle in Ghana to protect their trade. From the start, the slaves were taken to islands off the coast of Africa—the Azores and Madeira—to work on sugar plantations. The early Portuguese slave trade laid the foundation for slavery on the sugar plantations of the Caribbean, two centuries later.

1469 ◆ The union of Aragon and Castile.

With the marriage of Ferdinand of Aragon and Isabella of Castile, Spain's two largest Christian kingdoms united into one powerful force. Together, they ascended to the throne as the Catholic Monarchs of Spain in 1475. Their reign together, which lasted until Isabella's death in 1504, saw many important events and marked the end of the Middle Ages and the beginning of the Renaissance in Spain.

January 2–April 1, 1492 ◆ Spain was united.

On the second day of 1492, the Christian armies of Ferdinand and Isabella finally completed the Reconquest. They defeated King Boabdil, the Moorish ruler of Granada, forcing the Moors out of Spain once and for all. The direct influence of North African culture and the Islamic religion on Spain now came to an end. Even so, like the cultures that had gone before, the Moors left their mark on the land and people of the Iberian Peninsula. On April 1, 1492, the Spanish government signed the order to force over 200,000 Jews to leave Spain. Next, the king and queen brought local Christian nobles under their political control. With these victories, Ferdinand and Isabella were able to unite Spain—its varied land and mixed people—under one government and one church.

April 17, 1492 ◆ Support for Columbus's westward voyage.

Having united their country, Ferdinand and Isabella were free to turn to exploration and trade as a way of building Spain's power. On this date, the king, queen,

Columbus, ready to embark on his historic journey, bids farewell to his supporters, King Ferdinand and Queen Isabella of Spain.

and the Italian-born Christopher Columbus signed a contract to set the terms for Columbus's voyage. He agreed to sail west to Asia on behalf of the Spanish crown. There he would establish trade, discover new lands, and convert the native people to Christianity. In return, Columbus would be the chief admiral of the Spanish *armada* (fleet) as well as viceroy and governor of any new lands he found. He would receive one-tenth of all of the metals and gems that were found. He would also serve as judge in any legal issues raised in the new lands.

August 3, 1492–March 15, 1493 ◆ Columbus's first voyage of discovery.

Admiral Columbus set sail from the port of Palos de Moguer in southwestern Spain with three ships. The admiral directed the expedition from his flagship, the *Santa María*. The largest of the three vessels, it carried a crew of 39 men and boys. Martín Alonso Pinzón served as captain of the *Pinta* with a crew of 26. Martín's brother, Vicente Yánez Pinzón, directed the 22-man crew of the *Niña*. The *Niña* and *Pinta* were caravels, a type of ship that was smaller but faster and more nimble than the flagship. A week after leaving Spain, the ships arrived at the Canary Islands. They remained among these islands for almost a month while the captains and their crews made repairs, changed the riggings, and took on supplies.

On September 6, 1492, Columbus led the expedition westward into the unknown. On September 25, Martín Alonso Pinzón diverted the ships to check on what was thought to be land in the middle of the Atlantic Ocean, but it turned out to be a false sighting. Five weeks after leaving the Canary Islands, shortly after midnight on October 12, the crew did spot land. Columbus's ships soon arrived at a small island—either present-day Watling Island

A 1512 portrait of Christopher Columbus based on a painting by Laurens Lotto.

or Samana Cay—southeast of Florida in the Bahamas. After sunrise, the admiral, his two captains, a few Spanish officials, and some armed guards went ashore and claimed this new land for the monarchs of Spain. Columbus named the island San Salvador. On this beach, Spain first encountered the people of the New World, a small group of Arawaks.

After a brief stay, Columbus and his men continued to explore the waters of the Caribbean Sea. On October 27, the expedition made landfall on the northeastern coast of Cuba. Columbus believed he had found Japan or China. He sent some men to seek out the leader of this island and his golden cities. Instead, he found the native Arawak people living in simple huts.

On Christmas day of 1492, the *Santa María* ran aground on Hispaniola, the island on which present-day Haiti and the Dominican Republic are located. The crew used the timbers from the shipwreck to build a small fort. Thirty-nine men stayed behind to man this settlement (which Columbus named La Navidad), while the *Niña,* with Columbus aboard, and the *Pinta* set sail for Spain. They arrived back at Palos de Moguer on March 15, 1493, returning with precious metals, exotic plants (including maize), parrots, and several of the native people.

May 1493 ♦ The division of the New World between Spain and Portugal.

Soon after Columbus returned from the New World, Ferdinand and Isabella asked Pope Alexander VI to recognize Spain's authority over these new lands.

The Portuguese monarchy had also asked the pope to recognize Portugal's authority over its African discoveries. In a papal bull, or decree, Pope Alexander VI drew a line from north to south one hundred leagues west of the Azores Islands. All lands to the east would belong to Portugal and all lands to the west to Spain. In 1494, the Treaty of Tordesillas between these two countries moved the line farther west, to 370 leagues west of the Cape Verde Islands. The new line would give Portugal authority over Brazil when it was discovered five years later. The pope also gave Ferdinand and Isabella the authority to convert the people of these new lands to Christianity and to govern them.

September 25–November 28, 1493 ♦ Columbus's second voyage to the New World.

King Ferdinand and Queen Isabella had been very impressed with Columbus's first voyage. They quickly granted the admiral 17 ships and 1,200 men for a second voyage. This time, however, the expedition was to build a Spanish colony in the New World. In order to do this, the ships were loaded with horses, mules, cows, and other animals. They also carried sugarcane and many other seeds and plants. Among those making the trip were twelve Catholic missionaries whose work would include converting the native Arawaks to Christianity.

The second voyage began on September 25. Choosing a more southerly course, Columbus discovered the Virgin Islands on November 18 and Puerto Rico the next day. Both are part of the United States today. He reached Hispaniola on November 28. There he found La Navidad destroyed and no trace of his men. Some had died of disease and others had been killed by a hostile group of Arawaks.

ORIGINS OF U.S. HISPANICS

Countries or regions of origin of the nearly 22 million Hispanics in the U.S.

- Mexico — 61%
- Puerto Rico — 12 %
- Central America — 6%
- South America — 5%
- Cuba — 5%
- Spain — 5%
- Other — 4%
- Dominican Republic — 2%

Source: U.S. Bureau of the Census, 1991b,1.

1494 ♦ Columbus introduced sugarcane to the New World.

Columbus brought sugarcane with him from the Canary Islands off the western coast of Africa. Over the next three centuries, sugar became more and more important as an export from the Caribbean islands to Europe. As the sugarcane industry grew, so did the number of African slaves in the islands.

January 1, 1494 ♦ La Isabela, the first Spanish settlement in the New World.

Columbus and his *flotilla* (fleet) left La Navidad behind and arrived at a promising site on the northern coast of Hispaniola. There he decided to build

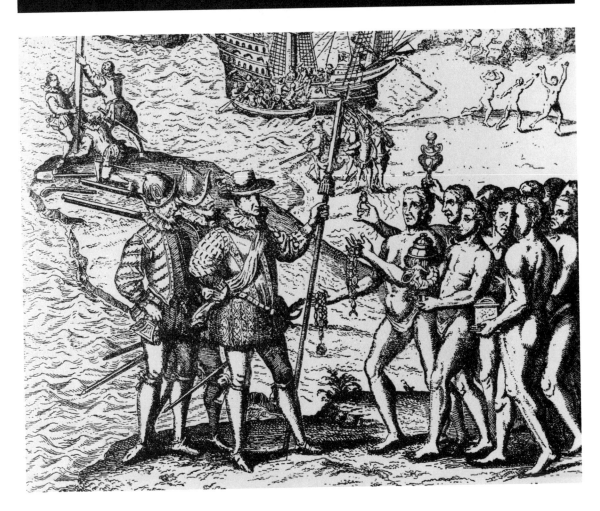

La Isabela, the first permanent Spanish settlement in the New World. The colonists built a town overlooking the ocean that included a house for Columbus, a church, a hospital, quarters for officials, and a storehouse. (The settlement lasted only until 1498.) In the spring of 1494, Columbus set sail to continue his search for Japan and China. Instead, he found Jamaica on May 5.

August 4, 1496 ◆ The founding of Santo Domingo.

Columbus left his brother Bartholomew in charge of the town of La Isabela on Hispaniola while he continued to explore the Caribbean islands. In March 1496, Admiral Columbus returned to Spain. During this time, Bartholomew led a number of expeditions from La Isabela into the interior of Hispaniola. Colonists eventually reached the southern shore. There they built the town of Santo

An engraving by Theodore de Bry depicting Columbus meeting the Indians. Note how the *conquistadors* erect crosses (a sign of Christianizing the natives), how some Indians run away from the white men, and how some Indians bring treasures as gifts.

Spanish authorities parceling out land plots to the Indians as a part of the *repartimientos,* according to the *Tudela Codex,* written in Mexico, 1536–66.

Domingo, founded on August 4. It later became the capital of the Spanish colonies in the New World.

1498 ♦ Columbus's third voyage to the New World.

On his third voyage Columbus sailed to Hispaniola and then south. On July 31, he discovered the island of Trinidad, just off the coast of Venezuela. He sighted the Venezuelan coast and the mouth of the Orinoco River, and believed them to be China and one of the four rivers of Paradise. He returned to Hispaniola in August to find that the colonists had revolted against his brother Bartholomew.

1500 ♦ The fall of Columbus.

Complaints against Christopher and Bartholomew Columbus reached Queen Isabella in Spain. Many in Hispaniola clashed with the two brothers who controlled the colony. Isabella sent Francisco de Bobadilla, the queen's chief justice and royal inspector, to investigate Columbus's dealings with the natives. In 1500, a year after his arrival in Hispaniola, Bobadilla had Christopher Columbus arrested and sent to Spain in chains. Isabella stripped Columbus of his titles.

September 16, 1500 ♦ The *encomienda*—rules for slavery among the Indians.

After the Spanish had defeated the Moors on the Iberian Peninsula, they forced the conquered Muslims to work on farms as slaves. These slaves were also forced to become Christians. This system of slavery became known as the *encomienda.* As colonies began to grow in the New World, colonists such as Nicolás de Ovando pushed to enslave and convert the native people. He and others urged Queen Isabella to extend the rules of the encomienda to include the New World. She did so on September 16, 1500. On December 20, 1503, she set down additional rules for dividing Indians among the discoverers, *conquistadors* (conquerors), and colonists. These rules of division were called *repartimientos.* These two sets of rules greatly influenced the colonization of Spanish America as well as the culture and people in the colonies. They helped create a Catholic, *mestizo* (people of mixed Spanish and Native American ancestry), Spanish-speaking society throughout these lands.

September 3, 1501 ✦ African slavery was permitted in the New World.

On this date, Queen Isabella authorized Nicolás de Ovando to transport slaves from southern Spain to Hispaniola. This marked the official beginning of African slavery in the New World. The queen gave permission to transport only African slaves who had been Christianized. Since it was the Catholic monarchs' duty to Christianize the New World, neither Jews nor Muslims, free or enslaved, were allowed in the Spanish colonies.

In the first days of colonization, the Spanish had planned to enslave and Christianize the native peoples of the Caribbean. But the Indians were neither culturally nor physically accustomed to the hard work imposed by the Spaniards. Forced labor in mines and on plantations—as well as new diseases brought from Europe—killed more and more of the Native American population.

The Spanish wanted a hardier work force in order to extract the riches of the New World. African slaves seemed the solution. Early reports assured the crown that Africans adapted very well to the climate and environment as well as the hard labor in the Indies. By 1511, the Casa de Contratación (Contract House) informed King Ferdinand that one black slave was doing the work of four Indians. The group added that it was necessary to bring more slaves from Guinea, on the west coast of Africa.

There is no accurate way to judge the number of slaves imported from Africa to Spanish America over the next three centuries. Just before the slave trade was abolished and many of the colonies gained their independence, approximately 70,000 slaves were being imported per year.

May 1502 ✦ Columbus's fourth voyage to the New World.

Columbus had lost the favor of Queen Isabella, but she was still willing to give him another chance—a fourth voyage. With four ships and 150 men, he sailed from Spain in May of 1502. When he reached the Caribbean, he discovered the island of Martinique and explored the Lesser Antilles and Puerto Rico. Next, he headed for Hispaniola, where he was denied permission to land by the Spanish authorities on the island. He then sailed west and explored the coast of Central America.

For eight months, Columbus continued his search for China. Eventually he headed back to Hispaniola, but was shipwrecked off Jamaica en route (on the way). Finally, in 1503, rescuers from Hispaniola arrived. In November 1504, Columbus returned to Spain. Two years later, he died in the Spanish city of Valladolid. He had opened up a New World but he died a forgotten man, not knowing the importance of his exploration.

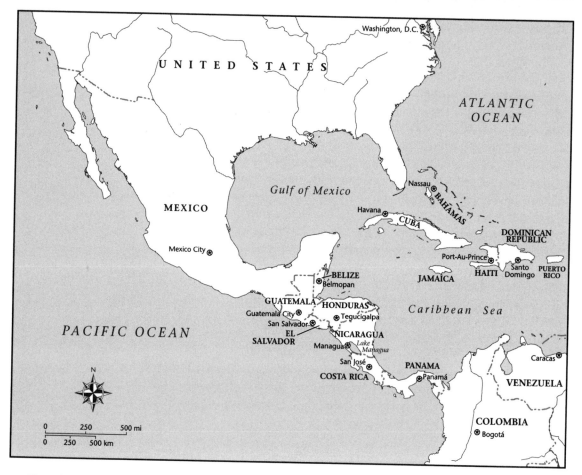

Map of Mexico and Central America.

1503 ♦ The birth of Spanish American architecture.

The church of San Nicolás de Bari in Santo Domingo was built from 1503 to 1508. With this building, Spanish American architecture—religious, civil, and military—began to take form.

February 14, 1503 ♦ Spain organized its New World Trade under the Contract House.

In 1495, the port of Cádiz was the only port allowed to serve the trade from the Indies. In 1501, the Spanish crown decided that anyone who wished to leave for the Indies had to be licensed. On February 14, 1503, Queen Isabella created the Casa de Contratación in Seville to enforce these orders. In 1543, this contract house began collecting a duty (tax) on all trade with the Indies. The Contract House soon became the customs office, the court, the post office, the admiralty, the naval school, and the market for people and goods into and out of Spanish America. The first head of the Contract House was Amerigo Vespucci.

1505 ✦ The first elementary school in the Americas.

Santo Domingo was the site of the first school for the children of Spanish colonists. From then on, elementary schools were part of Catholic convents, where children were taught reading, writing, arithmetic, and religion. Later, Catholic missions included schools for the children of Native Americans and *mestizos*.

1508 ✦ The conquest of Puerto Rico.

Juan Ponce de León (1460?–1521) first traveled to the Indies in 1493 on Columbus's second voyage. His name then appears in colonial records in 1504, when he took part in a campaign against the native village of Higuey in Hispaniola. As a reward, he was promoted to lieutenant and he settled in the village of Salvaleón, Hispaniola. In 1508, he sailed from Hispaniola in a small caravel to San Juan Bautista (later named Puerto Rico). There he established friendly relations with the chieftain, Agüeybana. During the next year, Ponce de León and his men defeated the native Taino people who resisted Spanish settlement. He then established himself as the governor of Puerto Rico over other Spaniards seeking the position.

1508 ✦ Cuba was proven to be an island.

Christopher Columbus made landfall in Cuba on both his first and last voyages. Even so, he never proved if Cuba was an island or part of the continent. Sebastián de Ocampo was the first to circumnavigate (sail around) Cuba and prove that it was an island.

1508 ✦ The first sugar mill in the Americas.

Sugarcane was the first Old World crop grown in the New World for trade by the Spaniards. Originally from India, this plant was taken first to Hispaniola and then to the rest of the Americas for cultivation. The first sugar mill was built in 1508 or 1509 on Hispaniola. The first samples of sugar were sent to Spain about 1515. By 1523, there were 24 mills operating on the island.

1509 ✦ Early outposts on the mainland.

The Spanish founded their first settlements on the mainland of the Americas on the Gulf of Darién near the border between present-day Panama and Colombia. Alonso de Ojeda founded New Andalusia on the eastern part of the gulf. He became the first governor of that area. Diego de Nicuesa led the settlement of Castilla de Oro (Golden Castle) on the western part of the gulf. The Gulf of Darién became the center for the conquest and colonization of South America.

Diego de Velásquez de Cuéllar.

1509 ✦ **The first Spanish settlement in Jamaica.**

Juan de Esquivel led a small group of Spaniards who set up cattle ranches near what is today St. Ann's Bay, Jamaica. The settlement remained small and never became important to the Spanish crown.

1510–12 ✦ **The conquest of Cuba.**

In 1508, Sebastián de Ocampo sailed around Cuba and started to spread tales that there was gold and silver to be found there. Two years later, Diego Velásquez de Cuéllar was sent to lead a group of 300 Spanish soldiers in the conquest of Cuba. Velásquez had sailed to Hispaniola on Columbus's second voyage. In over 15 years on that island, he had become rich and famous among the colonists. (*Also see entry dated 1508: Cuba was proven to be an island.*)

Velásquez's army landed on Cuba at Puerto Escondido, where it encountered Arawak warriors. The Arawak were led by Hatuey, who was already familiar with the Spanish on Hispaniola. He led the warriors on Cuba in several deadly raids against the Spanish. But, in the end, the Spanish defeated the Arawak because their weapons were better. Hatuey was captured by Velásquez, condemned to death, and burned at the stake. Today, Hatuey is remembered in Cuba as its first hero, a symbol of the island's resistance against foreigners.

After defeating the Arawak warriors, Velásquez worked to take control of the Arawak population in Cuba and set up Spanish settlements. In 1512, he directed the building of the town of Nuestra Señora de la Asunción de Baracoa. In 1514, Velásquez founded Santiago in the southeastern part of the island to provide access to Hispaniola. Within the next few years, Velásquez conquered the entire island, became its governor, and founded Havana. Under his control, Cuba replaced Hispaniola as the base for further exploration and conquest of the New World.

1511–12 ✦ **Early efforts to save the Native Americans of the Caribbean.**

A campaign to end the abuse and exploitation of the native people of the New World began in 1511. Dominican Friar Antonio de Montesinos launched the effort in a sermon in Santo Domingo, Hispaniola. He then took the Dominican cause directly to the Spanish throne. As a result of his and other petitions, King

Spaniards beating Indian slaves. Engraving by Theodore De Bry for the German edition of Bartolomé de las Casas' *Breve relacion de la destuccion de las Indies.*

Ferdinand's advisors produced the Laws of Burgos in 1512. These laws, the first European colonial code, set down principles to guide Spanish treatment of Native Americans. Among these principles were the ideas that Indians were free men, not slaves, and they were to be converted to Christianity by peaceful means, not by force.

In 1512, the Jeronymite Fathers of Hispaniola decided that in order to save the Arawak from disease and abuse, they would gather the remaining native population into missions (centers for religion and education). Similar missions were soon built in many other parts of the Spanish Empire.

1511 ✦ The Catholic Church in Spanish America.

Pope Julius II established the Diocese of San Juan Bautista (Puerto Rico) and named Alonso Manso the first bishop for the island. This made Manso the first bishop for the Americas. This same year, two bishops were also installed in Hispaniola. In 1513, a bishop was sent to Darién; in 1522, to Mexico; in 1529, to Colombia; and in 1534, to Peru. By the end of the 1500s, there were five arch-bishops and twenty-seven bishops in Spanish America. By the end of the colonial period, there were ten archbishops and thirty-eight bishops.

1511 ◆ Spanish justice in the New World.

The first Spanish court, the *audiencia* (tribunal), was established in Santo Domingo. Because the New World colonies were so far from the central government in Spain, the court also performed administrative and political tasks. A second audiencia was set up in New Spain (Mexico) in 1525. Eventually, eleven more New World courts were founded during the height of the Spanish Empire.

1511 ◆ The Taino rebellion.

The native Taino people rebelled against the Spanish in Puerto Rico in an attempt to regain their freedom, land, and culture. The Spaniards put down the rebellion with victories in the battles of Yauco and Yagueca. With the help of the Carib Indians, the Tainos continued to resist the Spanish through small skirmishes (brief fights).

1513 ◆ Early education for Native Americans.

By order of a royal edict, selected Indians were to be taught Latin. Schools for Native Americans would later become important, especially in Mexico and Peru. In these colonies, Latin, religion, painting, sculpture, and skilled trades were eventually taught to the native people.

1513 ◆ The first school in Puerto Rico.

The first school in Puerto Rico was founded at the Cathedral of San Juan by Bishop Alonso Manso. This school, *Escuela de Gramática* (grammar school), offered Latin, history, science, art, philosophy, and theology free of charge to its students. Primary schools were soon set up at churches.

February 4, 1513 ◆ The Gulf Stream discovered.

On his voyage to Florida, Juan Ponce de León's pilot, Antonio de Alaminos, dis-covered the ocean current known as the Gulf Stream. This current, it was later determined, runs from the Florida Strait into the Bahama Channel. From there, it continues past the coast of the Carolinas into the open ocean. It eventually forks northward to Norway and eastward to the Azores. Once the entire course of the current was charted, it would change trade routes from the Indies. Havana would become a major port and Florida would become a common stopping place for return voyages to Spain.

March 27, 1513 ◆ Ponce de León's discovery of Florida.

Having returned to Spain in 1512, Juan Ponce de León came to an agreement with the Spanish crown to search for and settle the island of Bimini. This island was famous among the native people of the Caribbean because it had a "fountain of youth," which could supposedly make those who drank its waters young again. Ponce de León may have hoped to find this fountain, but he likely had other reasons for his voyage.

Ponce de León's initial plans to make the voyage in 1512 were delayed. He was needed to command a fort in Puerto Rico. The following spring, he resumed his quest. He obtained the ships and supplies that he would need and on March 3, 1513, he set sail from San Germán, Puerto Rico. The expedition sailed on three caravels—small, sturdy, wooden ships well suited to the task of exploration. The three ships were called the *Santiago,* the *Santa María de la Consolación,* and the *San Cristóbal.*

The expedition sailed north-northwest. On March 14, it reached San Salvador, Columbus's first discovery. After making repairs and gathering supplies, Ponce de León directed the three ships to the northwest. On March 27, Easter Sunday of 1513, he sighted the Florida mainland. He sailed along the coast until April 2, looking for a place to land. Sometime during the following week, he went ashore to take possession of the newly discovered land. There is no clear record of the landing place. Some historians believe that it was between the St. Johns River and present-day St. Augustine. Others believe that it was at Cape Sable. Ponce de León named the new land La Florida. He may have been referring to the beauty of the land's plant life, or he may have chosen the name because Easter Sunday is known as *Pascua Florida* in Spanish.

Medallion with a likeness of Juan Ponce de León.

In April, the expedition first sailed north, then south, along the coast of Florida. During the month of May, the three ships rounded the southern tip of the peninsula and sailed north along its Gulf coast. In June, the Spaniards discovered some islands off the southern Florida coast. There they stopped to make some repairs to the *San Cristóbal.* Throughout his voyage, Ponce de León believed that Florida was an island—not Bimini, but a large new island. From time to time along their voyage, the Spaniards tried to make contact with the natives of Florida. Each time the attempts ended in battle. Having found no fountain of youth, no gold, and no place to settle easily, Ponce de León decided to return to Puerto Rico.

On June 15, the Spaniards set sail through the Florida Keys. One week later, they came upon some small islands. Because his group was able to capture 170

An engraving by Theodore De Bry illustrating slaves working in a sugar mill in all of the different processes. In De Bry's *Americae*, 1590.

turtles there, Ponce de León named the islands the Tortugas ("turtles" in Spanish). Two days later, he sent Antonio de Alaminos and one of the caravels to continue the search for Bimini. Ponce de León returned to Puerto Rico on October 10, 1513, to report the large new island that he had discovered and named La Florida. Alaminos returned four months later. He had discovered the small island of Bimini, but he had not found the fountain of youth.

September 25, 1513 ♦ The Spanish discovery of the Pacific Ocean.

Vasco Núñez de Balboa was a Spanish adventurer whose life was a series of ups and downs. Because his family had lost its wealth in Spain, Núñez de Balboa went to work at an early age. Attracted by the opportunity for riches and adventure, he left for the Americas in 1501. In Hispaniola, he started a farm worked by Indians, but it was a total failure. In 1510, he escaped his debts by stowing away on a caravel bound for Panama. In battle and exploration, Núñez de Balboa made a name for himself. He eventually became governor of colonies in Central America. On September 29, 1513, his overland expedition arrived at the shores of the Pacific Ocean (which the Spaniards called the South Sea). He claimed for Spain all lands touched by the waters of the South Sea. After a few years of political fighting, Núñez de Balboa lost his governorship and was reduced to poverty again. In 1517, he was found guilty of treason and executed.

1518 ◆ The Catholic Church permitted direct slave trade.

In this year, a special commission from the Catholic Church gave permission for traders to transport slaves directly from the west coast of Africa to the New World. The need for slaves had become greater than the need to maintain the Christian purity of the colonies. In 1518 alone, 40 new sugar plantations were founded in Hispaniola based on African slave labor.

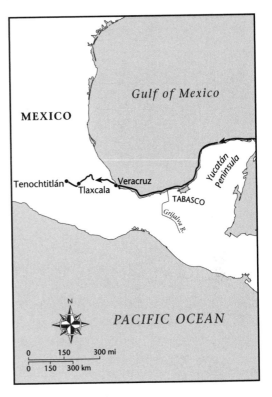

Map of Cortés's conquest of Mexico.

1519–22 ◆ The first voyage around the world.

On September 9, 1519, Portuguese navigator Ferdinand Magellan (1480?–1521) set sail from Spain to prove Columbus's theory. The Spanish expedition of five ships sailed along the coast of Africa, then crossed the Atlantic to the coast of Brazil. Magellan and his men spent much of 1520 searching the eastern coast of South America for a passage through to the Pacific Ocean. One of the ships was lost when it ran aground and another was lost to mutiny, but three of the ships reached the Pacific Ocean on November 28. Magellan eventually succeeded in crossing the Pacific to discover the Mariana Islands and on March 26, 1521, the Philippines, but died soon after in a battle with the native people of those islands on April 27. Battles and disease had already claimed many of his men, and the hard journey had weakened another ship so much that it was abandoned. Of the two remaining ships, only one completed the journey around the world. The *Victoria,* under the command of Juan Sebastián de Elcano, returned to Spain in September of 1522.

1519–20 ◆ The conquest of Mexico.

Voyages by Columbus (in 1502), Francisco Hernández de Córdova (in 1517), and Juan de Grijalva (in 1518) were the first to sail along the Gulf Coast of Cen-

Cortés entering
Tenochtitlán.

tral America and Mexico. Each of these expeditions brought back reports that
there were large civilizations inland. In 1518, Diego Velásquez de Cuéllar, the
governor of Cuba, sent Hernán Cortés (1485–1547) and an army of more than
500 to find these civilizations. Cortés sailed from Santiago de Cuba to the
Yucatán Peninsula and along the Mexican coast. Along the coast, the Spanish
expedition encountered and fought with a number of groups of native Mexicans.
They defeated many and made alliances with others. One chief offered Cortés
several young women as a gift. One of these women, Malinche, became Cortés's
mistress and interpreter.

In April of 1519, Cortés and his men arrived at a bay on the east coast of Mexico. There, the expedition went ashore and founded the city of Veracruz. Contact with the local natives brought more stories of the civilization inland, the
Aztecs. Cortés made plans to lead his men to the Aztec capital, Tenochtitlán (present-day Mexico City). To ensure that none of his men would desert, Cortés
ordered that the ships be sunk.

In time, the Spanish force set out for the interior of Mexico. Along the way, the Spaniards met and battled the natives of Cholula. Later, they encountered the people of Tlaxcala. Cortés convinced the Tlaxcalans to join him. The Spanish and Indian armies finally arrived in Tenochtitlán on November 8, where the Aztec people welcomed the Spanish leader and his followers into the city. Many of the Aztecs, including the emperor, Moctezuma, believed that Cortés was Quetzalcoatl, an important Aztec god. Aztec legends told that some day this blond, blue-eyed god would return from the sea. Cortés took advantage of this situation to take control of the city by forcing the emperor to do his bidding.

Velásquez de Cuéllar became convinced that Cortés had grown too powerful. So, in 1520, the governor sent another Spanish expedition to arrest and replace Cortés. Cortés met the group at the coast and convinced them to join him instead. The Aztecs in Tenochtitlán took advantage of Cortés's absence to launch a rebellion. When the *conquistador* (conqueror) returned, he tried to regain control of the city through Moctezuma. However, the rebels, lead by Moctezuma's brother Cuitlahuac, killed the emperor and forced the Spaniards out. The Spanish would call this defeat on July 1, 1520, *La Noche Triste* ("The Sad Night").

Cortés rallied the defeated Spaniards and Tlaxcalans. The following year, they returned to lay siege to Tenochtitlán. They did not allow anything in or out of the city from the end of May to August. After almost three months of siege, the Aztecs were weakened. Cortés took the opportunity to attack both Tenochtitlán and neighboring Tlatelolco. The Spanish weapons and European diseases introduced earlier devastated the cities. Cuitlahuac, the hero of the Aztec rebellion, died not in battle, but rather in a sickbed.

After Cuitlahuac's death, Cuauhtémoc—a Tlatelolcan—took command. Despite his efforts, he and the defenders of Tenochtitlán were forced out of the city on August 13, 1521. He was executed by the Spanish on February 26, 1525, for planning a rebellion. Following their victory, Cortés and his men leveled Tenochtitlán. In its place, they built a European city they called Mexico City. (*Also see entry dated 1325: The Aztecs founded Tenochtitlán.*)

1519 ✦ Pineda explored the Gulf Coast.

Alonso Alvarez de Pineda sailed around the western tip of Cuba, then north to the Gulf Coast of Florida. He followed the coast around to Veracruz in Mexico. Along the way, he claimed present-day Texas for Spain.

1521 ✦ Ponce de León's return to Florida.

After his discovery of Florida, Ponce de León returned to Spain to make a report to the officials who oversaw Spanish exploration in the New World. He also made new proposals to the crown. He was granted new rights and appointed captain general of a fleet to fight against the Carib Indians. In 1521, Ponce de León set out from Puerto Rico to take possession of Florida for Spain. His expedition of two ships brought enough men and livestock to build a settlement. It also brought Catholic priests to Christianize the Native Americans. The ships explored the Gulf Coast of Florida up toward Tampa Bay, but the attempt to start a settlement ended in failure. The Spanish were pushed back in a battle with the Florida Indians and Ponce de León returned to Cuba suffering from an arrow wound that soon took his life.

1522 ◆ African slave revolts.

African slaves revolted on Hispaniola and escaped to the interior, setting up their own communities.

1523 ◆ The education of Native Americans in Mexico.

The Franciscan monks who had come to Mexico believed that schools for Native Americans would help them appreciate Spanish culture. Pedro de Gante, a Flemish monk, founded Mexico's first school for Native Americans at Texcoco. The school served from 500 to 1,000 Indian boys every year and offered such subjects as Spanish, manual arts, artisanry, and the decoration of churches. Later, schools were set up for the sons of Indian chieftains and for Indian girls. Many Spanish landholders and some religious orders opposed schools for Native Americans. As a result, by the end of the century most of these schools had closed. Only the sons of powerful families continued to receive schooling.

1523 ◆ The turkey came to Europe.

The *uexolotl,* or turkey, was first domesticated and raised for food by the Aztecs. After the Spanish conquest of the Aztec Empire, traders introduced this bird to Europe.

1524–25 ◆ Gómez explored the Atlantic Coast.

Portuguese navigator Esteban Gómez had sailed with Magellan's expedition to find a passage through South America to the Pacific Ocean. (*Also see entry dated 1519–22: The first voyage around the world.*) But, once in the treacherous unexplored strait (which became known as the Strait of Magellan), he had led a mutiny to return to Spain. Despite his mutiny, he sailed again for the Spanish crown in 1524. This time, he led a voyage from Florida up the Atlantic Coast to present-day Maine. Along the way, he explored the mouths of the Delaware, Hudson, and Connecticut rivers. Similar voyages were made by Giovanni da Verrazano for France and John Cabot for England. As a result, these three European powers would compete to explore and settle the regions north of Florida.

1527–36 ♦ The odyssey of Cabeza de Vaca.

Alvar Núñez Cabeza de Vaca (1490–1557) joined the expedition of Pánfilo de Narváez to explore and settle the land between Florida and the Rio Grande river in present-day Texas. The expedition of several ships and almost 600 men left Spain on June 27, 1527. It traveled first to Hispaniola, where more than 100 men deserted. On the short passage from Hispaniola to Cuba, two ships were lost in a hurricane.

After wintering in Cuba, Narváez led about 400 men on the remaining ships to Tampa Bay, Florida, where they anchored on April 12, 1528. The Spaniards searched for gold among the Native Americans of western Florida, but found none. Instead, they were attacked by hostile Indians. Tired and hungry, Narváez and the remaining men built five makeshift boats to sail to Mexico. Narváez, Cabeza de Vaca, and about 240 other men began the long voyage around the Gulf Coast. Along the way, Narváez and his boat were lost. The four remaining boats were destroyed by a hurricane off the coast of Texas.

Cabeza de Vaca and about 80 other men survived the storm, but only 15 of them survived the winter of 1528–29. The surviving Spaniards were taken captive by Native Americans in the area, where illness and attempted escapes eventually claimed the lives of all but Cabeza de Vaca and three others. They lived among the Indians for a time, with Cabeza de Vaca serving as a medicine man. After being separated and then reunited, the four escaped in September of 1534. They began a march across Texas, New Mexico, Arizona, and northern Mexico

A painting of the Virgin of Guadalupe by Juan de Villegas.

that did not end until February 1536, when they came upon a group of Spanish soldiers. Their return to Mexico City stirred up many rumors, including one that they had found the legendary Seven Cities filled with gold and silver.

1531 ◆ Our Lady of Guadalupe.

According to the Catholic faithful, one morning in December on the hill of Tepeyac outside Mexico City, the Virgin Mary appeared to Juan Diego. Diego was a Native American who had been converted to Catholicism. The Virgin, in the form of Our Lady of Guadalupe, had Native American features. She appeared where a temple to the Aztec goddess Malintzin had been. Through a miracle, she caused her image to appear on Diego's poncho. This image is guarded today at the Shrine of the Virgin of Guadalupe, which was built on the site of the vision. This image is also duplicated in the thousands of churches named for the Virgin of Guadalupe that exist throughout Mexico.

Francisco Pizarro

The appearance of the Virgin of Guadalupe to Juan Diego led to the conversion of many Native Americans in Spanish America to Catholicism. She has become very important to the religious life of Mexicans, especially those of Native American heritage. She is the patron saint of Mexico and a symbol of the Mexican Catholic Church. She was also a symbol of Mexican nationalism during various independence movements.

1532–35 ◆ Pizarro's conquest of the Incas.

Francisco Pizarro (1476–1541) led an expedition of three ships from Panama down the Pacific Coast of South America in search of the Incan Empire and its riches. He took with him 3 brothers, 183 men, and 37 horses. The Spanish went ashore near the present-day border between Ecuador and Peru and founded San Miguel. From there they headed inland where Pizarro found the Incan Empire in the middle of a civil war. He took advantage of the situation and tricked Emperor Atahualpa with promises of friendship. Pizarro then took Atahualpa captive, accepted a ransom of silver and gold (but broke his promise to free the emperor), and killed him. The Spanish soldiers and horsemen killed thousands of Incas. Pizarro and his men completed the conquest of the Inca Empire by 1535. He founded the city of Lima in 1535 as the capital of the conquered lands. In June 1541, Pizarro was assassinated by followers of Diego de Almagro, a Spaniard who also sought to control the region.

1533 ◆ Colombian gold.

Pedro de Heredia led an expedition to Colombia that discovered much more gold than either Cortés in Mexico or Pizarro in Peru. Colombia soon became the chief source of gold for the Spanish Empire.

1533 ◆ The first printing press in the Americas.

The printer Esteban Martín was the first to bring a printing press to Mexico City. By the mid-1500s, seven printers were operating there, printing contracts and public notices. They published religious books, literary works, dictionaries, scientific books, and grammars of the native languages of Mexico.

1536 ◆ The viceroyalty of New Spain.

Spain's first province in the New World was founded to cover the area of the conquered Aztec Empire in Mexico. It brought together several Spanish colonies under the administration of a single viceroy, the direct representative of the king. The province was called New Spain, because it was meant to be an extension of Spain. Its capital was Mexico City.

1538 ◆ The first university in the Americas.

The Dominicans, an order of Catholic monks, established the first university in the New World in Santo Domingo. St. Thomas Aquinas University had already served as a Dominican college for a number of years. It is still functioning today as the Autonomous University of Santo Domingo.

1539–43 ◆ De Soto's exploration of the American South.

A Spanish expedition led by Hernando de Soto (1500–42), then governor of Cuba, explored much of the American South. De Soto led over 600 Spaniards from Havana up the Gulf Coast of Florida, north through Georgia and the Carolinas, and over the Smoky Mountains to Tennessee. From there, he turned the group south into Alabama, then west to Mississippi. Continuing northwest, De Soto came upon the largest river that he had ever seen in May 1541. He named it *Río Grande de la Florida* (Great River of Florida). Today, it is known as the Mississippi River. During his journey, De Soto lost almost half of his men to disease and battles with the Native Americans. He himself fell ill and died on May 21, 1542, in present-day Arkansas. The expedition, under the direction of Luis de Moscoso, continued into Texas, then down through Louisiana to the Gulf Coast. From there, they sailed along the coast to Tampico, Mexico, arriving in September 1543.

1539 ◆ Potatoes were introduced into Spain.

Potatoes were first cultivated by the Native American people of present-day Peru. Pizarro and his men found them an important part of the Incan diet. Some of the

Spaniards returning from the conquest of the Incas brought these vegetables to Spain. From Spain, potatoes spread to many parts of the world. They would later become a very important source of food for people living in areas with a cool climate, such as northern Europe.

1540–42 ✦ Coronado's exploration of the American Southwest.

Francisco Vásquez de Coronado (1510–54) set out from Nueva Galicia in north-western Mexico in search of the Seven Cities of Cíbola. Spanish legend told of cities of gold and silver built by Portuguese bishops in a land across the Ocean Sea (Atlantic Ocean). Native American reports and early Spanish exploration north of Mexico led many to believe that the cities were located in the American Southwest. Coronado led an expedition of several hundred Spaniards and Native Americans into this area.

The Seven Cities of Cíbola, turned out to be adobe villages built by the Zuñi people of New Mexico. Reports by the Pawnee people of Texas of a rich land to the north, called Quivira, also turned out to be exaggerated. However, Coronado's expedition did explore much of the American Southwest. It explored the Sonora Valley of Arizona, the area around Albuquerque (New Mexico), north-western Texas, Oklahoma, and parts of Kansas. One of his scouting parties discovered the Grand Canyon on August 25, 1540. Coronado and his men also encountered many Native American groups, including the Zuñi, Hopi, Pueblo, and Pawnee. Some of these meetings were peaceful, but many ended in battle. Coronado failed to return to Mexico with gold and silver, but he prepared the way for future settlement of the American Southwest.

1541–42 ✦ Orellana discovered the Amazon River.

Francisco de Orellana led an expedition through northern Peru into present-day Ecuador. There, the Spaniards found the Napo River in December 1541. Following this river, they came to the Amazon, which they traveled until they arrived at its mouth at the Atlantic Ocean in August 1542. A member of the expedition, Friar Gaspar de Carvajal, wrote the first European description of the river.

1542–43 ✦ Early exploration of the California coast.

Juan Rodríguez Cabrillo was a Portuguese sailor chosen by Antonio de Mendoza, the Mexican viceroy, to sail north along Mexico's west coast in search of treasure. On September 28, 1542, Cabrillo came upon an excellent port—present-day San Diego, California. The expedition continued north but found no gold or silver. After Cabrillo died, Bartolomé Ferrelo directed the ship north to the Oregon coast. His crew threatened by disease, Ferrelo returned to his home port on April 14, 1543.

Bartolomé de las Casas, "Defender of the Indians."

1542 ✦ The New Laws of the Indies.

Bartolomé de las Casas (1474–1566) was a *conquistador* (conqueror) and land-holder who became a Dominican friar and champion of Native American rights. After battling and enslaving the native people of Hispaniola for several years, Las Casas finally could no longer ignore the abuse he and other Spanish colonists inflicted on the Indians. He began to speak out both in the Indies and in Spain. His work earned him the official position of "Protector of the Indians." His efforts as a priest and writer eventually contributed to the passage of *Las Leyes de Indias* ("The Laws of the Indies") in 1523. These laws continued the effort to improve the condition of Native Americans that had been started by the Laws of Burgos. (*Also see entry dated 1511–12: Early efforts to save the Native Americans of the Caribbean.*)

Las Casas continued to push for better protection for Indians until King Charles V proclaimed *Las Nuevas Leyes de las Indias* ("The New Laws of the Indies") in 1542. These laws were designed to end the *encomienda* and to prohibit forcing Indians to work in mines and to dive for pearls. (*Also see entry dated September 16, 1500: The* encomienda—*rules for slavery among the Indians.*) If they did work, they would have to be paid. The laws made Native Americans free vassals (a person owing homage to a superior) of the Spanish crown. Despite Las Casas's efforts, the laws did little to change the actual condition of the native people. Most of the land and power was already in the hands of Spanish plantation owners and Catholic Church leaders who did not agree with Las Casas.

1550 ✦ A new form of slavery for Native Americans.

The New Laws of the Indies had outlawed the *encomienda* form of slavery for Indians. Even so, Spanish colonists found ways around the laws. In 1550, they revived the *repartimientos*—a form of encomienda. Under this policy, Native Americans were seized and forced to work on plantations, in mines, and in building churches and roads. The Spanish treated them cruelly and separated their families.

1551 ✦ The king chartered universities in the New World.

King Charles V called for the establishment of the University of Mexico in Mexico City and the University of San Marcos in Lima, Peru, to provide higher education for these viceroyalties. The University of Mexico opened its doors in 1553 and the University of San Marcos opened in 1572. Modeled after universities such as the one in Salamanca, Spain, these New World universities offered courses in the humanities, theology, law, and medicine. Latin was the official language used in classes. The University of Mexico grew in stature and, during the 1600s, boasted 23 professors. Most taught law and theology. Others taught medicine, surgery, anatomy, astrology, rhetoric, and languages, including Aztec and Otomí.

1551 ✦ Slavery became a money-making venture for the Spanish crown.

King Charles V needed funds to sustain his wars in Europe, so, he began selling licenses for the importation of slaves to the New World colonies. The first year he sold 123,000 licenses. For the next two centuries, selling these licenses

---

SLAVES REBELLED

While the Native Americans fell victim to the *repartimientos* in 1550, African slaves began to rebel, overthrowing their masters and fleeing to the backlands of Venezuela.

A nineteenth-century engraving of a panoramic view of Mexico City, showing the cathedral at center.

became a lucrative (profitable) source of revenue for the crown. But there was even more money to be made in slavery. On June 6, 1556, the crown began taxing the importation of slaves to the New World.

1562 ◆ Destruction of Mayan books.

Catholic bishop Diego de Landa ordered the burning of numerous Mayan books. These books were a collection of the Mayas' knowledge in mathematics, philosophy, astronomy, history, and religion. By destroying the books, the Spanish bishop deprived the world of the wisdom of one of the most advanced civilizations of the Americas and the world. (*Also see entries dated 1000 B.C.–A.D. 300: Mayan civilization in the Preclassic Period; A.D. 300–900: Mayan civilization in the Classic Period; and 900–1500: Mayan civilization in the Postclassic Period.*)

1563 ◆ The Cathedral of Mexico.

Spain began building its largest church in the Americas and one of the largest churches in all Christianity. The Cathedral of Mexico in Mexico City was influenced by Renaissance architecture and is reflective of the cathedrals located in Andalusia, southern Spain.

September 1565 ◆ St. Augustine founded.

The French founded Fort Caroline at the mouth of the St. John's River in Florida in 1564. In response, King Philip II of Spain sent Pedro Menéndez de Avilés to force the French out of Florida and establish a Spanish settlement. Menéndez's expedition arrived at Florida on August 28, the feast day of St. Augustine, and located a good site for a settlement. After a week of searching for and battling the French, Menéndez returned to build a fort at St. Augustine. The Timicua Indians of the area welcomed these first Spanish settlers and offered them shelter in huts. From this base, the Spanish succeeded in defeating the French in several battles. These were the first steps toward securing Florida for Spain. The village of St. Augustine, which grew up near the original fort, became the oldest permanent European settlement in what is today the mainland United States.

1570 ◆ The Spanish Inquisition in the New World.

The first Catholic Church court was established in Lima, Peru, to judge people accused of religious crimes, including blasphemy (cursing or slander), bigamy (having more than one spouse), heresy (religious opinions that contradict established beliefs), and witchcraft and enchantment (the practice of sorcery and the casting of spells). Such courts were later set up in Mexico City in 1591 and Cartagena, Colombia, in 1610. The church did not carry out punishment, but left that to government officials.

An illustration of the smallpox epidemic among the Aztecs as a result of contact with the Spaniards.

1573 ◆ Missions in Florida.

An order of Catholic monks, the Franciscans, arrived in Florida to build a mission (a church and other buildings to serve as a religious center). Over the next century, the Franciscans would build several missions from St. Augustine north to North Carolina and west to present-day Tallahassee, Florida.

1580 ◆ The growth of the Spanish Empire.

King Philip II of Spain took control of Portugal and added this country and all of its overseas colonies in Africa, Asia, and South America to his empire. The most important of these was Brazil. This meant that the Spanish Empire stretched as far as Baja California to the west and the Philippines to the east. In the same year, Juan de Garay built a permanent settlement at Buenos Aires, extending the empire as far south as present-day Argentina. The Spanish Empire now touched every continent except Australia and Antarctica.

1580 ✦ Puerto Rican Indians suffered from disease and slavery.

Diseases brought by the Spaniards and the hardships of forced labor nearly wiped out the native people of Puerto Rico. Sugar plantation owners on the island began to use African slaves as workers.

1590 ✦ De Fuca explored the Pacific Coast.

Juan de Fuca navigated his ships to the northern coast of present-day Washington State. Spanish maps soon included the Strait of Juan de Fuca as a possible northern route from the Atlantic to the Pacific. His discovery turned out to be an entrance to Puget Sound, the inlet on which present-day Seattle, Washington, is located. The search for this "Northwest Passage" would continue for three centuries.

1598 ✦ Colonizing began in New Mexico.

On February 7, Juan de Oñate left Santa Bárbara, in southern Chihuahau, Mexico, with hundreds of men and their families. Traveling north to present-day El Paso, Texas, then up the Rio Grande, the expedition reached New Mexico. On July 11, Oñate directed the Spaniards to build the settlement of San Juan de los Caballeros. From this base, Oñate and his men set out to explore the regions around the settlement to discover riches. The expedition failed to discover gold or silver, but the settlement continued to grow. In 1608, New Mexico became a province of New Spain (Mexico).

1598 ✦ Early drama in the United States.

Captain Marcos Farfán de los Godos, an amateur playwright, was a part of Oñate's expedition to New Mexico. He wrote a play about the settlement effort and some of the Spanish soldiers performed it for the settlers. This was the first play in a European language written and performed in the present-day United States. The soldiers also performed *Los moros y los cristianos* ("The Moors and the Christians"), a popular folk play in Spain and its colonies. This play told the story of the Reconquest, the long struggle of the Spanish people to win the Iberian Peninsula back from the Muslim Moors.

1600 ✦ Mission schools in the United States.

By 1600, the Spaniards had established the first schools in the what is now the United States. These schools became a regular part of the missions (centers for religion and education) that Catholic monks built in present-day Florida, Georgia, and New Mexico.

1610 ✦ Santa Fe was founded.

Don Pedro de Peralta established Santa Fe as a new capital for New Mexico. It thus became the oldest of the capital cities in the current United States.

1612 ✦ The first Native American language books in the United States.

A Franciscan missionary named Pareja living in present-day Georgia translated books from Spanish into Timicuan, the language of a group of native people from the Atlantic coast of Florida and Georgia. (*Also see entry dated September 1565: St. Augustine founded.*) Pareja continued translating books into Timicuan until 1627.

1642 ✦ The first library in Puerto Rico.

The Convent of San Francisco was the site of the first library on this island.

1670 ✦ The Treaty of Madrid.

Spain recognized England's presence in the Caribbean and accepted its settlements in the Americas for the first time when the two countries signed the Treaty of Madrid. The treaty prohibited trade between Spanish and British colonies without a special license. These and other laws led to little contact between Spanish and English settlers. However, illegal trade became common. Smuggling was especially widespread between New England and Caribbean islands.

San Miguel Mission, Santa Fe, New Mexico.

1675–80 ✦ Pueblo rebellions in New Mexico.

Fed up by the growing number of Spanish settlements in their traditional homeland, the Pueblo Indians began to attack the Europeans. After five years of slow gains against the Spanish, Pueblo leader Popé and his followers took control of Santa Fe on August 9, 1680. The Pueblo force then pushed the Spaniards and many Christianized Indians south to a place just north of El Paso. There, the refugees founded Ysleta. The Pueblo victory was short-lived, however. A few years later, Governor Diego de Vargas succeeded in regaining northern New Mexico for Spain.

1681 ✦ Reorganizing the Spanish American laws.

By 1635, Spanish officials had issued almost 400,000 laws to govern New World colonies. In 1681, the government issued the *Recopilación de las leyes de las*

Indias ("Compilation of the Laws of the Indies"). This reorganization reduced the number of colonial laws to 6,400.

1687–1711 ◆ Jesuit missions in Arizona.

Catholic priest Eusebio Kino, a missionary in the Jesuit order, led the Spanish into present-day Arizona. In 1687, Father Kino took over the mission effort in an area of northern New Spain that included present-day Sonora, Mexico, and southern Arizona. He immediately began to set up missions (centers for religion and education). Over the next 24 years until his death, Father Kino rode on horseback throughout the region, founding missions and teaching the Native Americans European farming techniques. Of the 24 missions that he founded, several were in southern Arizona. They included San Javier del Bac (near present-day Tucson), Nuestra Señora de los Delores, Santa Gertrudis de Saric, San José de Imuris, Nuestra Señora de los Remedios, and San Cayetano de Tumacácori.

1690–93 ◆ Early Spanish settlement in Texas.

In order to stop the French from taking control of the land along the northern border of New Spain (Mexico), Spain sent expeditions into present-day Texas. In 1690, Spanish commander Antonio de León, Father Massanet, and Father Fontcubierta founded San Francisco de los Tejas near the Nueches River. Texas became a separate Spanish province in 1691, and Domingo de Terán de los Ríos arrived to serve as governor. He set up eight missions among the Native Americans in eastern Texas. However, fear of Native American attacks forced the Spaniards to abandon Texas two years later.

THE STRUGGLES OF A WOMAN SCHOLAR

Sor Juana Inés de la Cruz (1651–95) was one of the greatest figures of Spanish American literature. Though a gifted child, Juana Inés de Asbaje was not admitted to the university because it did not allow women. She disguised herself as a man to get around the rules. Fed up with the court and society, she became a nun in the Carmelite Order in 1667 and became known as Sor Juana Inés de la Cruz. She wrote religious and secular plays as well as letters on the rights of women, but it is her lyric poetry for which she is known as one of the great Hispanic poets.

1696 ◆ Pensacola, Florida, was founded.

In an effort to keep the French from moving into their large Florida colony, the Spanish set up a settlement at Pensacola in the northwestern part of present-day Florida.

1697 ◆ Hispaniola was divided.

Spain spent much of the 1600s trying to extend its influence in Europe. At the same time, it had to defend its New World possessions from other European intruders, especially the French. There were several wars and treaties between Spain and other European countries. In 1697, several European powers signed the Treaty of Ryswick (Ryswick is a South Holland province in the Netherlands). In this treaty, Spain gave France the western third of the island of Hispaniola, a colony that later became known as Haiti. The Spanish portion later became the Dominican Republic.

1700 ✦ Operas in the New World.
By the end of the seventeenth century, operas and other forms of musical theater were regularly performed in Mexico City and Peru. A number of these operas had been composed in the New World.

1701–13 ✦ The War of Spanish Succession.
When King Charles II of Spain died in 1700, he had no son to succeed (follow) him on the throne. This plunged the country into a power struggle that spread to several other European countries. Charles had chosen Philip of Anjou, grandson of France's King Louis XIV, to become king and unite Spain and France. England, Austria, the Netherlands, and others feared the power of a combined Spain and France. These countries supported another candidate for king, either Archduke Charles of Austria, or Joseph Ferdinand of Bavaria. The war eventually spread to the New World, where British and French forces fought. In 1713, the Treaty of Utrecht ended the war. Philip of Anjou did become king of Spain, but Spain and France were not permitted to unite. As Philip V, he started the Bourbon Dynasty in Spain. The House of Bourbon ruled Spain until 1808. It returned to rule Spain from 1813 to 1868 and then again from 1874 to 1931.

Fort San Carlos, near Pensacola, Florida.

1716 ✦ The Spanish return to Texas.
The French continued to push west from Louisiana toward the northern reaches of New Spain, present-day Texas. In order to stop this expansion and to convert Native Americans to Christianity, Spanish expeditions returned to Texas to build missions (centers for religion and education). Over the next 30 years, several missions were built along the San Antonio River in southeastern Texas.

1717–48 ✦ Battles for European power.
Spain spent much of the first half of the eighteenth century caught up in battles for land and power in Europe. It fought Austria, Britain, France, and others during this period.

1717 ✦ African slavery grows in Spanish America.
England's South Sea Company obtained permission to bring African slaves into Spanish lands in the Americas. It would transport slaves to the Indies at a rate of

Unloading slaves in Havana harbor, Cuba.

4,800 per year for 30 years, a total of 144,000 slaves. France's Company of the Indies was also active at this time.

1718 ✦ San Antonio was founded.

Martín de Alarcón led a Spanish expedition into southeastern Texas where he built a *presidio,* or fort. A group of Catholic monks from the Franciscan order accompanied the expedition and founded a mission (center for religion and education), San Antonio de Valero. In March of 1731, 15 families (56 people) from the Canary Islands arrived on the banks of the San Antonio River to settle a town near the presidio and mission. They named their settlement San Fernando de Bexar. It became an important trade center and, in 1773, it became the capital of Spanish Texas. The town later became known as San Antonio.

1722 ◆ **Early newspapers in the Americas.**

La gaceta de México ("The Mexico Gazette") was the first newspaper published in the New World. Soon, other newspapers appeared in Guatemala, Lima, Buenos Aires, and colonial settlements.

1728 ◆ **The University of Havana.**

Cuba's first university, the University of Havana, was founded.

1760 ◆ **Large-scale ranching began in Texas.**

Captain Blas María de la Garza Falcón obtained a grant to 975,000 acres of land in Texas. He named his land Rancho Real de Santa Petronila. In time, this ranch would become the King Ranch, the largest cattle ranch in the United States.

1762 ◆ **The British occupation of Havana.**

During the great European power struggle of the Seven Years' War, the British occupied Havana, Cuba, for ten months. (*Also see entry dated 1763: France gave the Louisiana Territory to Spain.*) This was the first time that Cubans could legally have contact with soldiers and traders from the British North American colonies. They began to discover the benefits of trade outside of the Spanish Empire. This contact influenced future relations between Cuba and the United States, especially in the area of trade.

During the first half of the nineteenth century, trade between Cuba and the United States expanded. Cubans moved to New Orleans, New York, and Philadelphia in order to conduct business. Other Cubans came to the United States to attend college, and the United States became a refuge for Cuban revolutionaries who sought independence for their homeland. These close ties with the United States led many Cubans and some U.S. politicians to push to make the island a part of the United States.

1763 ◆ **France gave the Louisiana Territory to Spain.**

From 1756 to 1763, a great war occupied the major powers of Europe. During the Seven Years' War, as it was called, France joined Austria, Russia, and Sweden against Britain and the German states of Prussia and Hanover. Spain joined the French at one point. The Peace of Paris, signed in 1763 by Britain, France, and Spain, ended their hostilities. Britain had won Canada and all of the French territories east of the Mississippi and also received Florida from Spain. However, France gave Louisiana and its lands west of the Mississippi to Spain to keep them out of British hands, giving New Spain a huge new area of land.

1767 ◆ **The Jesuits were forced out of the Spanish Empire.**

Fearing the growing power of the Jesuit order of Catholic monks, King Charles III moved to expel them from Spanish lands. (*Also see entry dated 1687–1711:*

Junípero de Serra.

Jesuit missions in Arizona.) The King's minister, the Count of Aranda, prepared precise, secret orders for the viceroys and governors. Without warning, Jesuits were removed at specific dates and times from their universities, colleges, and convents. They were not allowed to take anything with them but a few personal objects. Together, all of the Jesuits were shipped to Italy. With the Jesuits gone, the Franciscans became the primary missionaries in Spanish America.

Because the Jesuits were popular in the colonies, their removal caused protests in Mexico, Peru, Chile, and Argentina. The protests were put down by the Spanish military. The actions of the Spanish crown and military fueled the desire of some colonists for independence from Spain.

1769–70 ◆ Early Spanish settlements in California.

In early 1769, José de Gálvez outfitted two ships to leave from Mexico to carry supplies for the planned colonization of Alta (Upper) California, the present-day state of California. Two parties of Spaniards, one led by Gaspar de Portola, also left Mexico to make the journey by land. On July 3, the chaplain of the expedition, Father Junípero de Serra, founded a Franciscan mission (center for religion and education) at San Diego. The Spanish also built a *presidio* (fort) at the site. In June of 1770, Portola and Father Serra sailed north from San Diego to found a mission and presidio at Monterey.

1770–1800 ◆ The growth of slavery in Cuba.

At least 50,000 Africans were transported to Cuba between 1770 and 1790. In nearby Haiti, a slave revolt led by Toussaint L'Ouverture in 1791 destroyed that colony's sugar industry. As a result, even more slaves were transported to Cuba to help fill Europe's need for sugar.

1773–89 ◆ Spanish exploration of the Canadian coast.

Spanish expeditions began to explore the Canadian coast up into Alaska. Along the way, the Spaniards made contact with Russians exploring south from their outposts in Alaska. The Spaniards later built a base at Nutka on the coast of Vancouver Island—the only European outpost between San Francisco and Alaska. Later, the Spanish also set up short-lived settlements in Valdez and Córdoba in present-day Alaska.

In 1789, Spanish soldiers arrested several English sailors who arrived at Nutka. This action raised protests and threats from the British government. With the Nutka Convention of 1789, the Spanish abandoned the base. The convention allowed all nations to trade on the coast of "Columbia," but no nation would be allowed to build any settlements.

1774 ✦ A trail to California.
Pedro de Garcés, a Spanish Franciscan missionary, blazed the first overland route from Mexico to California.

1776 ✦ San Francisco was founded.
In October 1775, Captain Juan Bautista de Anza led an expedition of 240 Spaniards, 700 horses, and 350 cattle out of northern Mexico into California. De Anza was carrying out the orders of Don Antonio María Buscareli, the viceroy of New Spain, to build a *presidio* (fort) in northern California. After stopping over at missions (centers for religion and education) in San Gabriel and Monterey, De Anza's expedition reached San Francisco, the large bay discovered by previous scouting parties. The presidio of San Francisco was founded on September 17, 1776, becoming Spain's northernmost outpost.

1779 ✦ Spanish support for the American Revolution.
France had joined the Americans in their war for independence in 1778. Spain followed a year later. France gave the Americans cannons, guns, bombs, other arms as well as money in an effort to defeat its British rivals. It also attacked the British outpost of Gibraltar on Spain's southern coast.

1780–82 ✦ The Incan rebellion.
José Gabriel Condorcanqui (1740?–81), an Incan chief known as Tupac Amaru and a direct descendant of the Incan rulers, led a two-year rebellion against the Spanish in Peru. Tupac Amaru had a grand vision of regaining lost Incan lands and of returning government power to the Indians. He put together a force of almost 6,000 poorly armed Indians. In the early months of the rebellion, he met with great success. He won control of much of southern Peru, most of Bolivia, and some of Argentina. His army then marched on Cuzco (now in Peru), where Tupac Amaru's force was first defeated. He then regrouped and returned with a force of 50,000 Indians. Again he was defeated, but this time Tupac Amaru was forced to watch the execution of his wife and sons. In 1781, he himself was executed, and his body parts were stuck on poles and displayed in villages that had supported him. The rebellion was completely defeated by 1783. (*Also see entries dated 1100: The Incan civilization began; and 1532–35: Pizarro's conquest of the Incas.*)

1781–83 ◆ Spain regained Florida.

In 1781, Spanish Brigadier General Bernardo de Gálvez captured Mobile (Alabama) and Pensacola (Florida) from the English. The Spanish attack helped George Washington and the American armies by forcing the British Colonial Army to fight on two fronts. The Spanish also opened a route to supply Washington's army with money, food, and weapons. A year later, the Spanish forced the British out of the rest of Florida. The victory returned the region to Spanish control after 20 years under the British. In 1783, the treaty that ended the American War for Independence recognized the Spanish claims to Florida.

1781 ◆ Los Angeles was founded.

Felipe de Neve, governor of Alta California, headed south from Monterey to establish the *Pueblo de Nuestra Señora la Reina de los Angeles de Porciúncula*. The settlement later became known as Los Angeles.

1790–1830 ◆ Spanish settlements grew in Arizona.

The threat of attack by Apaches on Spanish colonists in Pimería Alta (northwestern Mexico and southern Arizona) decreased during this period. Spanish soldiers succeeded in fighting the Indians, and colonists succeeded in establishing treaties with them. Over 1,000 Spanish settlers came to live in the Santa Cruz Valley.

1793 ◆ The weakening of the Spanish Empire.

Spain was drawn into a war with France, still caught up in its own revolution. The war, which lasted until 1795, weakened Spain's Bourbon monarchy and caused the loss of some New World colonies to France. The greatest loss was the Louisiana Territory.

DID YOU KNOW?

As the Spanish Empire weakened, so did the French. In fact, the King and Queen of France, Louis XVI and Marie Antoinette, were beheaded at the guillotine in 1793 for treason at the start of the French Revolution's Reign of Terror.

1795 ◆ A new border between the United States and Spanish America.

The United States and Spain signed the Pinckney Treaty. The treaty recognized the 31st parallel as the southern boundary of the United States. (This line is still the border between Alabama and Florida.) It also granted U.S. boats free navigation of the Mississippi River and rights to trade at New Orleans.

1795 ◆ Territory lost to the British.

Spain made peace with France and joined it in battles against England. British victories gave Britain control of Belize and the island of Trinidad.

1798 ✦ **Early immigration laws in the United States.**

The Alien Acts of 1798 passed by Congress gave the president the power to expel any alien he deemed dangerous. Thomas Jefferson, then the vice president, opposed these measures. The Alien Acts expired under their own terms in 1800, during Jefferson's presidency. The Naturalization Act of 1798 raised the number of years an immigrant had to live in the United States to be eligible for citizenship. The government had required immigrants to live in the United States for five years; under the new law, they had to live in the United States fourteen years.

1800 ✦ **Life in New Spain.**

Agriculture was important to the economy and society of northeastern New Spain. Small towns were surrounded by large, sprawling *haciendas* (ranches) with huge herds of cattle and sheep. This livestock and other farm products brought a lot of profit to the colonists and, in turn, to Spain. The farm products developed by the Native Americans and introduced to the world by Spain included corn, potatoes, sweet potatoes, tomatoes, manioc, new types of nuts and melons, vanilla, cacao (chocolate), quinine, coca, ipecac, sarsaparilla, rubber, and tobacco. Mexico also introduced the Spaniards to the turkey.

The Spaniards, in turn, brought numerous livestock and crops with them to the New World. Farm animals included sheep, hogs, chickens, goats, and cattle. For the most part, the Spaniards depended on Indian labor to plant and care for the food crops. It also depended on Indian and then African labor to build and tend its sugar industry. Sugarcane was among the first crops introduced to the New World when Columbus brought it to the Caribbean in 1494, and it became Spain's chief export throughout the Colonial Period. Coffee, another cash crop, was introduced in the eighteenth century.

Hacienda owners (left) and administrator (right).

By 1800, mining was the second most productive activity in New Spain. At the time, Spain and Portugal were producing 90 percent of the world's precious metals. Spanish American industry was third in importance. Colonial industry was built on the craftsmanship of the Native Americans, who wove cotton and wool and used beautiful and durable dyes. Their woodwork, stonework, and metallurgy were also prized. But the textile (cloth) industry was by far the most widespread and successful industry. Mexico and Peru built many cotton and wool mills.

Napoleon Bonaparte.

1800 ◆ **Spain returned the Louisiana Territory to France.**
In the Treaty of San Ildefonso, Spain agreed to cede (turn over) Louisiana to France. In return, France agreed not to give or sell the territory to any country but Spain. Napoleon Bonaparte, who had become the consul of France the year before, had a plan for Louisiana. He saw it as way to rebuild a French empire in the New World. He would make Louisiana a dukedom and settle it with 200,000 people. It would supply the agricultural base for France's New World colonies. Haiti would supply a naval station in the Caribbean. But in 1802, African slaves on Haiti started a successful rebellion that put an end to Bonaparte's plans.

1803 ◆ **The Louisiana Purchase.**
By 1800, the United States stretched from the Atlantic to the Mississippi, from the Great Lakes to Georgia. Spain continued to hold Florida, which at the time included the Gulf Coasts of Alabama and Mississippi. American traders used the Mississippi River to transport goods to the Gulf of Mexico, but France had control of the final miles of the river in Louisiana. President Thomas Jefferson and Congress wanted to secure a trade route to the gulf. Jefferson instructed Robert R. Livingston, the U.S. minister to France, and James Monroe to offer to buy New Orleans and part of West Florida.

Napoleon had turned his attention to battles in Europe. He did not want a conflict with the United States and he needed money to pay for his military campaigns in Europe. When the United States offered to buy New Orleans, France offered the whole Louisiana Territory instead. Livingston and Monroe accepted and signed a treaty in May 1803. The United States paid about $15 million for enough land to almost double its size. The Territory of Orleans and the Louisiana District (as the land became known) stretched from the Mississippi River to the Rocky Mountains, from the Gulf of Mexico to British lands in Canada. The United States now shared a long border with Texas, New Mexico, and other parts of New Spain.

1804–06 ◆ **The Lewis and Clark expedition.**
President Thomas Jefferson convinced the Congress to fund the expedition of Meriwether Lewis and William Clark to explore the Louisiana Territory. Lewis and Clark set out from St. Louis on May 14, 1804. They followed the Missouri River northwest into Montana. They crossed the Rocky Mountains and later took the Snake and Columbia rivers to the Pacific Ocean. When they returned to St. Louis two years later, they had enough information to open up the Louisiana Territory to settlement. Settlement by Anglos (those of north-European ancestry) along the northern border of New Spain worried the Spanish.

1805 ◆ **The Battle of Trafalgar.**

In the wars for power in Europe, Spain joined into alliance with France against the British. Napoleon, who had made himself emperor of France, ordered Spain to put its navy under French control. His goal was to use the combined fleet to invade England. Instead, Lord Horatio Nelson led the British fleet to victory on October 21. Off the coast of Cape Trafalgar in southwestern Spain, Nelson's 29 ships destroyed about 35 ships directed by Admiral de Villeneuve of France. Because of this defeat, Spain had no navy to protect itself or to hold its New World colonies together.

1806 ◆ **Puerto Rico's early newspapers.**

Publishers had a difficult time starting newspapers in Puerto Rico because the Spanish crown controlled licenses to publish. *La Gaceta de Puerto Rico* ("The Puerto Rican Gazette"), a government paper, was the first newspaper published in Puerto Rico. It lasted until 1898. In 1810, the Spanish *Cortes* (legislative body) made it even more difficult to start a newspaper when it created the *Junta Suprema de Censura* (Supreme Censorship Commission). But it only lasted until 1814. Puerto Rico's second newspaper, *Diario Económico de Puerto Rico* ("The Puerto Rican Economic Daily"), was founded on March 8, 1814, by Alejandro Ramírez. Its third paper, *El Cigarrón* ("The Cigar"), was founded later that year.

By 1820, ten or more printing presses existed in Puerto Rico. It was then that newspapers began to spread. The first real daily newspaper, *Diario Libertad y de Variedades* ("The Liberty and Variety Daily") began publishing on December 6, 1821. But the Cortes once again restricted printing and publishing with the 1820 *Ley de Imprenta* ("Law of the Printing Press"), and newspapers disappeared until 1839. In 1874, General Laureano Sanz became governor of the island and enforced strict censorship. He actively persecuted publishers and editors, and put an end to the liberal press.

1807–08 ◆ **Bonaparte's invasion of Spain and Portugal.**

Continuing his grab for power in Europe, Napoleon sent French armies to take control of the Iberian Peninsula. Portugal fell in 1807 and its king fled to Brazil. King Ferdinand VII of Spain surrendered power in 1808. Napoleon named his brother, Joseph Bonaparte, to the Spanish throne.

1808 ◆ **The U.S.'s first Spanish-language newspaper.**

Several Spanish-language newspapers were circulated in the American Southwest while that region was a part of New Spain and Mexico. But the first Spanish-language newspaper inside the United States was probably *El Misisipí* ("The Mississippi"). This newspaper was first published in New Orleans, Louisiana, by William H. Johnson and Company. The four-page paper focused on commerce and trade. It was written primarily in Spanish but included English translations of some articles and of all the advertisements.

1810–11 ◆ The first Mexican independence movement.

Miguel Hidalgo y Costilla (1753–1811), a parish priest in the town of Dolores, Mexico, led a grassroots movement for independence. He declared Mexico's independence from Spain from the pulpit of his church on September 16, 1810. His cry for freedom was *¡Qué viva la Virgen de Guadalupe y qué mueranlos gachupines!"* ("Long live the Virgin of Guadalupe and death to the Spaniards!"). He led masses of Indians, *mestizos* (people of mixed Indian and Spanish ancestry), and Creoles (Spanish Americans) in battle. He appealed to Native Americans to regain their lands and culture. "My children, will you be free? Will you make the effort to recover from the hated Spaniards the lands stolen from your forefathers three hundred years ago?" he asked them. Hidalgo journeyed to Guadalajara, where he organized a government, abolished slavery, and began to redistribute the land to the Indians.

Hidalgo and his followers took several cities. But when he marched on Mexico City, he was defeated by royalists. In March 1811, Hidalgo was captured, tried, and convicted by a military court. He was also expelled from the priesthood and was executed by a firing squad on July 31. Hidalgo's independence movement weakened the Spanish hold on Mexico. In response, the Spanish pulled back from frontier outposts in the American Southwest. In Mexico today, Hidalgo is still considered the "father of his country."

Miguel Hidalgo y Costilla.

1810 ◆ South Americans rebelled against European rule.

After Napoleon occupied Spain, he sent his own representatives to take control of the Spanish viceroyalties (or colonies) in the Americas. The Spanish colonists in the South American viceroyalties refused to recognize Napoleon's representatives and began to plan wars of independence from France. The Creole colonists (Spaniards born in the New World) claimed that they wanted to return to Spanish rule. But their goal would soon include freedom from Spain also. In this year, colonists in Caracas (now in Venezuela), Santiago (now in Chile), and present-day Argentina and Uruguay set up *juntas* (committees) to rule in the name of the Spanish King Ferdinand VII, who had been jailed by Napoleon.

1811 ✦ Declarations of independence in South America.

On May 14, 1811, Juan Pedro Caballero led a successful coup d'état (forceful overthrow of the government) and won independence for Paraguay from Spain. On June 17, a national congress named a five-person *junta* (committee) to govern Paraguay. But it was not until October 12, 1813, that Paraguay was declared a republic. On July 7, 1811, the leaders of the Venezuelan independence movement declared independence from European powers. They chose Francisco de Miranda (1750–1816) to lead the government. Miranda had already fought in both the American Revolution and the French Revolution before he directed the Venezuelan rebel armies. Similar declarations followed later in the year in New Granada (Colombia).

January 11, 1811 ✦ The No-Transfer Resolution.

The wars in Europe were weakening Spain's hold on Florida. As a result, President James Madison proposed that the United States temporarily take control of Florida to keep it from falling into the hands of another European power. Spain declined the offer. But, in a secret session, the U.S. Congress decided that it could not permit any part of Florida to pass from Spain to another foreign power. The decision was known as the "no-transfer resolution." It stated that the United States would take control of east Florida if it was threatened by a foreign power.

January 22, 1811 ✦ Texas sought independence from Spain.

The Mexican war for independence from Spain spread to Texas. Militia captain Juan Bautista de Casas took up arms and arrested governor Manuel de Salcedo and the commander of the Spanish auxiliary troops, José Bernardo Gutiérrez de Lara. The rebellion was put down, however, by royalist troops sent from Veracruz and Tampico in eastern Mexico. Texas was again under the control of the Spanish throne by March 1811.

November 5, 1811 ✦ A call for Central American independence.

José Matías Delgado, a priest, gave the first call for Central American independence in San Salvador (now in El Salvador). It was not until 1821, however, that independence was achieved, first as part of Mexico (1821) and then as a separate Central America (1823). (*Also see entries dated 1821: Mexican independence; and 1823: Independence for Central America.*)

November 6, 1813 ✦ A second declaration of Mexican independence.

Father José María Morelos y Pavón picked up where Hidalgo had left off and declared independence from Spain once again at a congress that he had organized in Chilpancingo. A constitution was drafted and proclaimed in 1814. In 1815, Morelos was defeated by the royalists. He was tried, convicted, removed from the priesthood, and executed on December 22, 1815.

June 1, 1814 ◆ Paraguay became a dictatorship.

Paraguay had been the first colony to win its independence in 1811. On June 1, 1814, the congress of Paraguay elected José Gaspar Rodriguez Francia the supreme dictator. Francia was named "Perpetual Dictator of the Republic." From 1814 to 1840, Paraguay closed its doors to the rest of the world— foreigners were not permitted to enter, no mail was allowed into the country, and the only foreign trade was for weapons. Paraguay's leaders hoped to protect the country from the disorder in other Spanish American colonies fighting for their independence.

1816 ◆ A declaration of independence for Argentina and Uruguay.

A congress of leaders from the United Provinces of the River Plate (Argentina and Uruguay) declared independence from Spain on July 29.

1817–24 ◆ Simón Bolívar and the liberation of Gran Colombia.

Simón Bolívar (1783–1830) had failed twice to win independence for Venezuela. In 1817, he began a successful campaign for independence. He led his army of revolutionaries to a final victory in New Granada (now Colombia) in 1819 and Venezuela in 1821. Bolívar's lieutenant-general, Antonio José de Sucre, defeated the Spanish in Quito (now in Ecuador) in 1822. After these conquests, a congress was held at Angostura, Venezuela, proclaiming the birth of the Republic of Gran Colombia. Gran Colombia included present-day Venezuela, Ecuador, and Colombia. Bolívar was named president, and served in this post until 1830.

Portrait of Simón Bolívar.

1817–18 ✦ Independence for Chile.

José de San Martín (1778–1850) crossed the Andes Mountains from Argentina with an army of revolutionaries to liberate Chile from the Spanish in February of 1817. San Martín was born in Argentina and raised in Spain. As an officer in the Spanish army, he fought against Napoleon's armies in Spain and Africa. In 1812, he returned to Argentina to fight for independence. He became one of South America's great liberators, freeing both Argentina and Chile from colonial rule. A year after the military victory, Bernardo O'Higgins (1778–1842) declared independence from Spain and became the country's first political leader.

1817 ✦ Slavery reforms in Spanish America.

In this year, the first census taken in Cuba revealed that there were 291,000 whites, 224,000 slaves, and 115,000 free persons of color on the island. The same year, Spain outlawed slave trade in Cuba and all of its colonies north of the equator. It also signed a treaty with England that set guidelines for enforcing these anti-slavery laws. But slave traders continued to smuggle slaves. As a result, the number of slaves imported to the Caribbean continued to rise steadily in the 1820s and 1830s. Another treaty with England signed in 1835 again emphasized the desire of both nations to end the slave trade. But the trade to Cuba was not effectively ended until 1865. Many Cubans were against slavery on humanitarian grounds, but they also feared that the sugar industry could not stay alive without slave labor. Whites also feared living in an independent country where the majority of people were black, such as Haiti. Many whites preferred to remain a colony of Spain where blacks were powerless.

1819 ✦ Spain turned Florida over to the United States.

The United States had long wanted control of Florida. (*Also see entry dated January 11, 1811: The No-Transfer Resolution.*) For 30 years, the United States had been taking steps to secure Florida under its doctrine of Manifest Destiny. (Manifest Destiny was the belief that the United States should expand its territory and influence throughout North America.) Through military action or settlement, Americans had slowly gained control of Baton Rouge (Louisiana) in 1794, Mobile (Alabama) in 1814, Pensacola (Florida) in 1818, and Amalia Island in 1819. In 1819, General Andrew Jackson led a U.S. military force into Florida and captured two Spanish forts. Unable or unwilling to hold onto Florida, Spain gave up the territory.

1819 ✦ The United States and Spain agreed on their borders.

The Adams-Onís Treaty was negotiated by U.S. Secretary of State John Quincy Adams and Spain's Luis de Onís. It settled disputes between the United States and Spain over lands in North America. The treaty set the border between the United States' Louisiana Territory and Spanish Texas at the Sabine River, which is the present-day boundary between Louisiana and Texas. Farther west, the northern border of Spanish territory followed the 42nd parallel all the way to the Pacific. (The 42nd parallel still marks the northern borders of Utah, Nevada, and California.) The treaty also formally gave Florida to the United States. In return, the United States agreed to pay the $5 million in claims by American citizens against the Spanish government. The treaty went into effect in 1821.

1820–23 ◆ A revolution in Spain.

Democratic forces succeeded in forcing King Ferdinand VII from power. They restored the Spanish constitution that had been established in 1812. The revolution lasted until 1823 when the French invaded Spain and returned Ferdinand to his throne.

1820 ◆ Anglo settlers in Texas.

Anglo-American frontiersman Stephen Long led a revolt against the Spanish in Texas. Long's revolt was similar to others seeking independence for Mexico. But because of his ties to the United States, it also threatened to open up Texas to American control. In response to this threat, Spain made an agreement with Moses Austin, a Catholic from Missouri. Austin could settle Anglo-Catholic families in Texas, as long as they became Spanish citizens. Spain needed settlers in Texas, even foreigners, to keep its claim to the territory. Anglo-Catholics were still arriving when Mexico (including Texas) gained its independence in 1821.

1821 ◆ More slavery reforms in Spanish America.

Spain outlawed the slave trade in all of its colonies south of the equator.

1821 ◆ Mexican independence.

Mexico finally won its independence from Spain when liberals, Freemasons, and conservative Creoles (Spanish Americans) united to support the Creole Agustín de Iturbide. Iturbide and his army triumphantly entered Mexico City in September. He offered Mexicans three guarantees: union, religion, and independence. Iturbide's *Plan de Iguala* (Iguala Plan) called for equality for all citizens, including Native Americans and *mestizos* (people of Spanish and Native American descent). However, the plan supported the Catholic Church and praised the culture and achievements of Spaniards in the Americas while condemning Hidalgo's independence movement. (*Also see entry dated 1810–11: The first Mexican independence movement.*) It also ignored the needs of Native Americans and the achievements of their civilizations before the arrival of Columbus. The power of independent Mexico was solely in the hands of Creoles and mes-

José de
San Martín.

tizos. Indians continued to be abused and ignored. Iturbide had himself crowned Emperor of Mexico in 1822.

Independent Mexico included settlements in coastal California, southern Arizona, south Texas, southern Colorado, and most of New Mexico. It inherited a long border with the United States that continues to affect the two countries up to the present.

July 28, 1821 ◆ Peru's declaration of independence.

After liberating Argentina and Chile, José de San Martín invaded Peru from the sea and captured Lima from the Spanish. (*Also see entry dated 1817–18: Independence for Chile.*) He declared the independence of Peru on this date. He was proclaimed the "Protector" of Peru. In 1822, San Martín met secretly with Simón Bolívar in Guayaquil, Ecuador, to discuss the future government of the independent South American countries. That same year, San Martín turned his armies over to Bolívar to complete the wars for independence.

1822–44 ◆ Haitian control of Santo Domingo.

The island of Hispaniola, divided between the French colony of Haiti and the Spanish Dominican colony, went through many changes in the early part of the 1800s. (*Also see entry dated 1697: Hispaniola was divided.*) France took control of the island at the beginning of the century. (*Also see entry dated 1800: Spain returned the Louisiana Territory to France.*) African slaves in Haiti overthrew the French in 1802, but the Dominicans remained under the control of Napoleon until 1809 when they forced the French off the island. At that point, the Dominicans tried to start a free republic but failed and fell again under the rule of Spain. They finally proclaimed independence as Spanish Haiti in 1821. The country sent ministers to Simón Bolívar, seeking to join Gran Colombia. But the president of Haiti, Jean Pierre Boyer, led his army into Santo Domingo and declared it part of Haiti in 1822. Haiti imposed a brutal rule of military, cultural, and racial oppression from 1822–44.

1822 ◆ The first Hispanic American was elected to Congress.

Joseph Marion Hernández was elected to the U.S. Congress to represent Florida and the Whig Party. No other Hispanic American held national office for the next 30 years. In the entire nineteenth century, only 11 Hispanics were elected to Congress, 9 of them from New Mexico.

March 8, 1822 ✦ **The United States recognized Spain's independent colonies.**

U.S. support for the independence movements in Spanish America grew during the wars in Central and South America. Many saw these revolutions as similar to the American Revolution. On March 8, President James Monroe recommended that Congress recognize the Spanish American colonies that had declared their independence from Spain. These included the United Provinces of the River Plate (Argentina and Uruguay), Chile, Peru, Gran Colombia, and Mexico. Monroe stated that these new nations also deserved protection from European invaders.

1823 ✦ **California's Mission Trail.**

Father Junípero Serra (1713–84) was a part of the expedition to Alta California (now California) that had founded a mission (center for religion and education) at San Diego in 1769. (*Also see entry dated 1769–70: Early Spanish settlements in California.*) He went on to set up 8 more missions before his death. His fellow Franciscans carried on his work and built another 12 missions.

1823 ✦ **More Anglo settlers in Texas.**

Texan Erasmo Seguín, a delegate to the Mexican national congress, persuaded that body to pass an act that would bring more Anglo settlers to Texas. Between 1824 and 1830, thousands of Anglo families entered east Texas. Some acquired free land and others bought land much more cheaply than they could have in the United States. By 1830, Texas had 18,000 Anglo inhabitants and their African slaves, who numbered over 2,000.

1823 ✦ **Independence for Central America.**

In 1821, when Mexico declared the independence of New Spain, the viceroyalty also included Central America. However, the captain-general of Guatemala quickly declared its own independence from New Spain/Mexico. The United Provinces of Central America included the present-day countries of Guatemala, Honduras, El Salvador, Nicaragua, and Costa Rica. On July 1, 1823, the provinces reaffirmed their freedom from Mexico. The group became the *Confederación de Repúblicas Centroamericanas* (Central American Federation), of which José Manuel Arce of Guatemala was named president. Political, economic, and social conflicts weakened the federation and it started to break apart in 1838.

THE FAMOUS MISSION TRAIL

By 1823, California's Mission Trail included 20 missions stretching from San Diego to San Francisco: San Diego de Alcalá (1769), San Carlos de Monterrey (1770), San Antonio de Padua (1771), San Gabriel Arcángel (1771), San Luis Obispo de Tolosa (1772), San Francisco de Asís (1776), San Juan Capistrano (1776), Santa Clara de Asís (1777), San Buenaventura (1782), Santa Bárbara (1786), La Purísima Concepción (1787), Santa Cruz (1791), San José de Guadalupe (1797), San Juan Bautista (1797), San Miguel Arcángel (1797), San Luis Ray (1798), Santa Inés (1804), San Rafael Arcángel (1817), and San Francisco Solano (1823).

Illustration of the execution of Mexican emperor Agustín de Iturbide, by an anonymous artist.

1823 ✦ **The United States set its sights on Cuba.**

U.S. Secretary of State John Quincy Adams informed the Spanish government that the United States aimed to annex (add) Cuba to the Union.

March 19, 1823 ✦ **The fall of the Emperor of Mexico.**

Mexico's Emperor Agustín de Iturbide was overthrown by democratic forces opposed to his monarchy. He went into exile, but was captured while returning to Mexico, and was executed by a firing squad on July 19, 1824, in Padilla, Tamaulipas. (*Also see entry dated 1824: Democracy for Mexico.*)

December 2, 1823 ✦ **The Monroe Doctrine.**

With the end of the Spanish Revolution in 1823, the Spanish crown turned its attention to regaining its American colonies. The United States had already defended its independence against the European powers. It now wanted to be clear that it would also defend its independent neighbors from attack. In his annual message to the U.S. Congress, President James Monroe sent this message to the European powers. The Monroe Doctrine, as it was called, stated that the Western Hemisphere was off limits to further European expansion and political ideology.

1824 ✦ A Central American constitution.

The Central American Federation already had abolished all noble and royal titles. It also had reduced the power of the Catholic Church. In 1824, the federation drafted the Constitution of 1824, one of the most liberal constitutions in all of the Americas, which was dedicated to "liberty, equality, security, and property." It outlawed slavery and guaranteed individual liberties. It created a federal congress to be elected along with an executive branch, a separate senate, and a separately elected supreme court. The constitution also declared that Roman Catholicism was the official state religion.

1824 ✦ Democracy for Mexico.

After Augustín de Iturbide's brief reign as emperor, Mexico started a period of democracy. Guadalupe Victoria was elected Mexico's first president. He served at that post until March 21, 1829.

1824 ✦ The end of Spanish rule in Central and South America.

Simón Bolívar and Antonio José de Sucre continued their liberation of Peru and present-day Bolivia. Sucre's victory over the Spanish army at Ayacucho, Peru, signaled the end of Spanish rule in Central and South America. Independence had come to all of Spanish America, except Cuba and Puerto Rico. (These countries would have to wait until 1898.) Independence was followed by almost 30 years of social and political turmoil, including dictatorships, civil wars, and new revolutions.

1824 ✦ Music education in Mexico.

The first conservatory of music in the Americas was founded by José Mariano Elízara in Mexico City.

1825 ✦ Independence for Bolivia.

Bolivia had been a part of Peru under the Spanish. But after his victory over the Spanish, José de Sucre founded a new republic, named after Simón Bolívar. The new nation declared its independence on August 6, with Sucre becoming its first president.

1825 ✦ Puerto Ricans traveled abroad for a higher education.

The Spanish government did not provide higher education in Puerto Rico, so young Puerto Ricans began to travel to Santo Domingo, Cuba, Venezuela, Mexico, and the United States to study medicine, engineering, and other professions. Spain was afraid that these students would learn American ideals of liberty and democracy. As a result, it began to enforce the Royal Decree of 1799, which prohibited study in the United States. The Spanish made a list of 200 Puerto Rican and Cuban students studying in the United States who were forced to return home.

Antonio López de
Santa Anna.

1825 ✦ **Spain stifled Cuban and Puerto Rican independence.**
Ferdinand VII of Spain gave unlimited powers to the governors of Cuba and Puerto Rico to repress the independence movements.

1826 ✦ **The Congress of American Republics.**
Simón Bolívar convinced Gran Colombia, Peru, Mexico, and the Central American Federation to come together in Panama to discuss matters of interest to the New World's new nations. The United States did not attend. The countries discussed building a common defense force and creating an Assembly of Federated States, but little was actually accomplished.

1828 ✦ **Uruguay separated from Argentina.**
During a dispute between the United Provinces of the River Plate and Brazil, Brazil invaded and occupied the northeastern part of the country (present-day Uruguay). When the conflict ended, the United Provinces were divided into Uruguay and Argentina. Uruguay declared independence this same year.

1829 ✦ **Slavery was abolished in Mexico.**
President Vicente Guerrero and his republican government put an end to slavery in Mexico. The abolition of slavery was not enforced in Texas.

1830 ✦ **The end of Gran Colombia.**
Simón Bolívar dreamed of bringing together all of the Spanish colonies in South America into a "United States of South America," but his dream came to an end in 1830. Both Venezuela and Ecuador withdrew from the union to become separate nations. Bolívar stepped down as president and died soon after on December 17 near the present-day city of Santa Marta, Colombia. At the end, he believed his efforts for unity had been wasted. His famous last words were reported to have been: *"Aquellos que hemos servido a la Revolución hemos arado en el mar"* ("Those of us who have served the Revolution have plowed in the sea").

1833 ✦ **Santa Anna became president of Mexico.**
Antonio López de Santa Anna (1794–1876) was a powerful figure in nineteenth-century Mexico. In 1829, he stopped an invasion of Mexico by the Spanish. In 1832, he returned Mexico to its people two years after a coup d'état (forceful

overthrow of the government) had removed President Vicente Guerrero from office. In 1833, he was elected president. At first, he moved to make democratic reforms, but in 1835 he changed his direction and moved toward military rule. He removed the governors from the Mexican states and replaced them with military officers. Although he was temporarily forced out of power on two occasions, Santa Anna served as dictator over Mexico for most of the next twenty years.

The Alamo, San Antonio, Texas.

1834 ◆ Cuba suffered under military rule.

General Miguel Tacón was appointed captain-general of Cuba. Tacón had suffered many defeats in South America's wars of independence, and neither he nor the Spanish crown wanted to lose the last Spanish colonies. As a result, Tacón kept a tight grip on Cuba, holding all of the government power in his own hands. Seventy-five percent of the money that the Cuban government collected was used to support the military on the island. Under this military rule many Cubans, especially Creoles (Spaniards born in the New World), were imprisoned and exiled. Cubans lost the right to carry weapons, to vote on delegates to the Spanish *Cortes* (legislative body), and the right to information regarding the government. Education suffered as well, as many teachers were barred from classrooms for political reasons.

April 21, 1836 ◆ Texan independence from Mexico.

Anglo-Texans resisted Santa Anna's military rulers and his new laws. Santa Anna took matters into his own hands and personally led a large army north to San Antonio, Texas. There he surrounded the Texans, who had turned the Alamo Mission into their fortress, eventually killing all of the resisters. Among the dead Texans were Colonel William B. Travis, Davey Crockett, and Jim Bowie. Six weeks later, the tide turned. On April 21, Anglo-Texans defeated the Mexican forces at the Battle of San Jacinto (near present-day Houston) and took Santa Anna prisoner. The Texans declared their independence from Mexico and forced Santa Anna to accept their demands.

The conflict came to an official end with the Treaty of Velasco, signed by Texas President David G. Burnet and Mexican President Santa Anna, on May 14, 1836. The 1836 Constitution of the Republic of Texas made citizens of all those living in Texas at the time of the rebellion. The rights of citizenship would be forfeited by people who had supported the Mexican side. Many from the

Anglo-Texan majority ignored the constitution. They attacked their Hispanic neighbors, regardless of their loyalties during the war, and forced them off their property. As a result, many Hispanic Texans crossed the border and returned to Mexico.

1837 ♦ The first railroad in Spanish America.

Spain began building the first railroad in Spanish American in Cuba, between Havana and Guines. The railroad connected sugar plantations, sugar mills, and shipping ports.

1838–65 ♦ Guatemala's first dictator.

The *caudillo* (grassroots leader) Rafael Carrera (1814–65) became the first of many dictators of Guatemala. Carrera, of Native American heritage, could not read, but he was a shrewd military strategist. He succeeded in keeping peace and security, building roads, improving farming, honestly managing the nation's money, and reducing the national debt but he did not tolerate opposition. He also continually intruded in the politics of El Salvador, Honduras, and Nicaragua to put conservatives in power. In addition to his political goals, Carrera had religious goals for his country. One of his main missions was to make Guatemala a devoutly Catholic country. Many Native Americans even believed Carrera was their messiah. He ruled over Guatemala for 27 years until his death in 1865.

1838–60 ♦ Cuba became the world's major sugar producer.

During this 22-year period, Cuba was the world's largest producer of sugar. In 1850, sugar accounted for 83 percent of Cuban exports. By 1860, the island was producing 500,000 tons per year.

May 30, 1838 ♦ The breakup of the Central American Federation.

The congress of the Central American Federation gave each of its individual members the right to develop its own government. The federation gradually fell apart. Between 1838 to 1841, members formed the independent countries of El Salvador, Nicaragua, Costa Rica, Guatemala, and Honduras.

1840–70 ♦ Immigration to Cuba.

The need for paid labor grew in Cuba during the early nineteenth century. To meet these demands, 125,000 Chinese were brought to Cuba between 1840 and 1870. They worked as sugarcane cutters, railroad builders, and servants in the cities. European immigration, primarily from Spain, also increased during this period. Newly arrived Spaniards worked in the retail trades and operated small general stores called *bodegas*. Immigration during this period created the ethnic and social diversity that can be found today in Cuba.

1840 ◆ Spain tightened its grip on Puerto Rico.

Because Spain feared the growth of an independence movement in Puerto Rico, it took steps to control the island. Foreigners were prohibited from entering Puerto Rico, and mustaches and beards were not allowed because it was believed that they were the fashion among revolutionaries.

January 14, 1840 ◆ A civil war for Texas and Mexico.

In San Patricio, Texas, General Antonio Canales, Juan N. Seguín, and a group of Texans and Mexicans declared the independence of the Republic of the Río Grande. This new country would be made up of southern Texas and the Mexican state of Tamaulipas. In the following months, Canales's forces succeeded in capturing Laredo, Texas, a number of border towns, and Ciudad Victoria, Mexico, the capital of Tamaulipas. However, in the battle for Saltillo, most of Canales's troops went over to the Mexican government side. The remaining soldiers were forced to withdraw to Texas. Canales finally surrendered to the Mexican government in November.

1841 ◆ Texas invaded New Mexico.

In June of this year, Texas President Mirabeau Buonoparte Lamar sent an armed group of merchants to New Mexico to start a revolt against the Mexican government. He hoped to unite New Mexico with the Texas Republic, but the expedition had only bad luck. The 300 Anglo and Hispanic Texans, led by General Hugh McLeod, encountered hostile Indians and prairie fires, and often lost their way. When they reached New Mexico, they surrendered to Governor Manuel Armijo's soldiers. Some were executed in Santa Fe and others were marched on foot to prison in Mexico City. Eventually, these *filibusteros* (mercenaries), were released from prison.

1844–99 ◆ Dictators in the Dominican Republic.

From 1844 until the turn of the century, just three men controlled the government of the Dominican Republic. The first two, Pedro Santana and Buenaventura Báez, worked together. They alternated terms as president of the republic. By the 1850s, however, they had become enemies. Santana took control and held power most of the time until his death in 1864. Báez then returned to power until his death in 1882. After Báez, Ulises Heureaux led a brutal reign of power from 1882 until 1899. (*Also see entry dated 1882–99: The Dominican Republic's brutal dictator.*)

March 1845 ◆ Texas joined the United States.

United States President John Tyler signed the resolution to annex (add) Texas. (In December, Texas became the 28th state.) The move angered the Mexican government and it broke off diplomatic relations with the United States. A conflict soon arose between the two countries over their official border. Texas and the

The storming of the palace of Chapultepec on September 13, 1847, during the Mexican War.

United States claimed that the Rio Grande was the southern border. Mexico argued that the Nueces River, a few hundred miles to the north, was the actual border.

1846–48 ◆ The Mexican War.

The United States declared war on May 13, 1846, due to disputes between itself and Mexico over Texas and New Mexico. President James K. Polk sent General Zachary Taylor and his army to the north bank of the Rio Grande. American General Winfield Scott marched to Mexico City, which surrendered on September 14, 1847. The United States defeated Mexico in 1848 and forced it to sign the Treaty of Guadalupe Hidalgo. Under the treaty, signed on February 2, Mexico gave up half of its land area, including Texas, California, most of Arizona and New Mexico, and parts of Colorado, Utah, and Nevada. (In 1855, the Supreme Court ruled that the treaty did not apply to Texas.) The border between the United States and Mexico was set at the Rio Grande and Gila rivers. In return, the United States offered peace and $18 million. The treaty also guaranteed that Mexicans who now found themselves in the United States would keep their property, civil rights, and freedom of religion. Mexicans within the U.S. border had one year to choose U.S. or Mexican citizenship. Seventy-five thousand Mexicans chose to remain in the United States.

1846 ◆ California's Bear Flag Revolt.

In California, conflicts between Anglos and Hispanics had been growing for some time. On June 10, one month after the United States had declared war on Mexico, Anglo settlers seized a herd of 150 horses being driven south to the Mexican militia. Four days later, thirty armed Americans, led by William B. Ide and Ezekiel Merritt, took General Mariano Vallejo as prisoner of war. At Sonoma, Ide and other Americans declared independence from Mexico. They raised an improvised flag with a grizzly bear (hence the name of the revolt) and a star. Following a battle on June 24, John C. Fremont merged his troops with the "bear flaggers." The combined forces marched to San Francisco. On July 1, they took over the *presidio* (fort), which was in ruins. The United States, at war with Mexico, joined the conflict on the side of the Anglos. On July 7, in Monterey, the United States proclaimed that it had annexed (added) California to its territory.

DID YOU KNOW?

Kit Carson, famed American trapper, guide, and Indian agent, was involved in the Bear Flag Revolt. He also played a part in the Civil War (1862–65), commanding the 1st New Mexico Volunteers against the Indians.

1848–54 ◆ Early U.S. attempts to obtain Cuba.

In 1848, President James K. Polk of the United States made an offer to Spain to purchase Cuba for $100 million. Spain responded that the island was not for sale. In 1852, England and France invited the United States to join in an agreement

California gold rush miners, circa 1850s.

never to seek control of Cuba, but American leaders in Washington refused. After President Franklin Pierce took office in 1853, he sent ministers to Europe to offer Spain $130 million for Cuba. The offer, which became known as the Ostend Manifesto, also warned Spain that if it refused to sell, the United States might force Cuban independence from Spain, which would make it easier for the United States to annex Cuba. The Ostend Manifesto caused a great deal of controversy. Spain and other European countries accused the United States of imperialism (extending authority of a nation over a foreign country). American politicians from the North saw the offer as an attempt to add another slave state to the Union. These early efforts to obtain Cuba failed. Further attempts were interrupted by the American Civil War (1861–65).

1848–51 ◆ Failed attempts to free Cuba.

Narciso López, a Spanish officer of Venezuelan nationality, hoped to start a war of independence in Cuba. He organized three invasions of Cuba from U.S. shores in 1848, 1850, and 1851. All failed. López was eventually hanged.

1848 ✦ The California gold rush began.

Discovery of gold at Sutter's Mill and elsewhere lured a flood of Anglo settlers to the California Territory. So many settlers arrived that California became a state in 1850. Settlement in Arizona and New Mexico occurred at a slower pace, and they did not become states until 1912.

1848 ✦ The Costa Rican constitution.

Unlike its neighbors in Central American, Costa Rica tried to build peace at home and abroad. Its constitution of 1848 abolished the army and substituted a small civil guard. Aside from some minor clashes during its history and a period under the dictatorship of Tomás Guardia (1870–82), Costa Rica became a peaceful country, free of internal and external wars.

1848 ✦ The resettlement of Mexicans.

Mexico sent commissioners to California, New Mexico, and Texas to help families move to Mexico. The commissioners offered land and equipment to those who chose to move south of the new border. Three thousand did. In 1855, Mexico again tried to regain its citizens living in California by offering land in Sonora. Even in the late 1870s, the Mexican government encouraged people to come back to Mexico. No more than 2,000 Mexicans chose to move to Mexico as a result of these efforts.

September 5, 1848 ✦ Puerto Rican education suffered under Spanish rule.

Spain never created a public education system in Puerto Rico. On this date, General Juan Manuel de la Pezuela, the Spanish governor of Puerto Rico, turned down a request to start the Colegio Central, a secondary school. He said that "education had lost the Americas, and that ... it behooves young people to go to Spain to study." When he was told that the majority of young Puerto Ricans could not afford to go to Spain, he responded, "It is enough for the poor to learn reading and writing, Christian doctrine, and a trade."

1850 ✦ The Compromise of 1850.

The U.S. Congress passed a series of laws to address the growing divisions over the slavery issue and disputes over the land acquired in the Mexican War. The compromise allowed California to be admitted to the Union as a free state and New Mexico as a territory. New Mexico was denied statehood because a majority of its residents were Hispanic. Texas was given $10,000 to compensate it for territory east of the Rio Grande that was given to the New Mexican Territory.

1850 ◆ The Foreign Miners Tax Law.

Californians were determined to keep foreigners from joining the Gold Rush. Angry groups drove Mexicans out of the gold fields. The first California Assembly asked the U.S. Congress to bar all foreigners from the fields. On May 20, California's state legislature passed the Foreign Miners Tax Law, charging a tax of $20 per month on all foreign miners, to discourage them from mining in California. Most people ignored the law because it was difficult to collect the tax and to protect those who had paid it. Instead, Anglos increased their violence against Mexicans. Many Mexicans were murdered or lynched. In 1851, the tax was repealed. By then, Spanish-speaking people had already been driven from the mines and immigration had decreased greatly.

1850 ◆ Plans for a Central American canal.

The United States and Great Britain signed the Clayton-Bulwar Treaty, stating that the two countries would jointly control any railroad or canal built across Central America from the Gulf to the Pacific. A zone around the railroad or canal would be neutral and would charge the same toll for both countries. No Central American nation signed the treaty or was even consulted. (*Also see entry dated 1901–03: Treaties and laws cleared the way for a Central American canal.*)

1851 ◆ The California Land Act.

During the Bear Flag Revolt of 1846, the United States took over California. After this takeover, the biggest issue for *Californios* (Hispanic Californians) was land ownership. These former Mexican citizens had to prove what land they had owned before the revolt. They also had to defend their claims against newly arrived Anglos who wanted to settle these lands. The U.S. Congress passed the California Land Act to help Californios prove and defend their claims. However, the law did not work well and many Californios lost their land.

1853 ◆ The Gadsden Treaty.

Even after the end of the Mexican War, the United States wanted to increase the amount of land it held along the Mexican border. One reason was so that it would have a good route for a railroad to the Pacific Ocean. In 1853, the U.S. representative to Mexico, James Gadsden, reached an agreement with General Antonio López de Santa Anna, who had returned to power in Mexico. Through the Gadsden Treaty, Mexico sold the region from Yuma along the Gila River to the Mesilla Valley to the United States for $10 million. This added the southern parts of Arizona and New Mexico to the United States.

1855–64 ◆ Mexico moved toward democracy.

In 1855, Benito Juárez (1806–72), a Zapotec Indian lawyer and politician, led a popular march from Acapulco to Mexico City. There the rebels overthrew the

Mexican dictator Santa Anna and his government. Over the next decade, Juárez and other reformers took steps to move Mexico toward a democracy with greater rights for its citizens.

1855 ✦ "Greaser Laws" in California.

The California Anti-Vagrancy Act, aimed at the customs of *Californios* (Hispanic Californians), prohibited bear-baiting, bullfights, and cockfights. The laws were called "greaser laws" because "greaser" was a negative term Anglos used for their Hispanic neighbors.

1855 ✦ Los Angeles's first Spanish-language newspaper.

El Clamor Público ("The Public Clamor") was founded by Francisco P. Ramírez. Throughout its lifespan, the newspaper protested discrimination against Mexicans and *Californios* (Hispanic Californians). It fought against measures to force Hispanics out of the mines and off the ranches of southern California. The newspaper closed shop in 1859.

William Walker.

1856–57 ✦ An American president for Nicaragua.

In 1855, liberals (those favoring political progress and reform) in Nicaragua invited a mercenary (soldier for hire) from Tennessee, William Walker, and his 57 soldiers of fortune to help them defeat the conservatives (those resistant to political change). They defeated the conservatives in 1856 and burned their capital city, Granada. At first, Walker allowed a liberal leader to serve as president while he kept control of the army. But in July 1856, he named himself president of Nicaragua. As head of the country, he legalized slavery and made English the official language. The United States did not recognize Walker's presidency and withdrew its diplomats from Nicaragua. A year later, however, President Franklin Pierce tried to use the Nicaragua issue in his reelection bid. To gain votes from Americans who supported slavery and Manifest Destiny, he recognized Walker's government. When Democrats refused to nominate Pierce at their convention, he withdrew recognition. With the support of the British and the combined armies of the Central American countries, Walker was driven out of Nicaragua in 1857. He returned in 1860, but was captured by the British and executed in Honduras on September 12.

Benito Juárez.

June 25, 1856 ✦ Mexico limited the power of the Catholic Church.

Mexico passed the Lerdo de Tejada Law, forcing the Catholic Church to sell all lands and properties not used for religious purposes. The church sold its cultivated land to sharecroppers, and uncultivated land to the Indians. The government set fees for weddings and baptisms and secular cemeteries were founded. At first, this redistribution put land in the hands of small farmers. However, wealthy ranchers soon bought or stole much of the land.

1857 ✦ The Cart War in Texas.

Anglo businessmen attempted to force Mexican teamsters (wagon drivers) out of south Texas. These actions violated the guarantees offered by the 1848 Treaty of Guadalupe Hidalgo. (*Also see entry dated 1846–48: The Mexican War.*) Seventy-five people eventually died in this "Cart War."

1857 ✦ A new constitution for Mexico.

Under the leadership of the populist reformer Benito Juárez, Mexico adopted a new constitution, which remained in effect until 1917. The constitution was an important step toward greater democracy. It guaranteed freedom of speech and freedom of the press and prohibited monopolies and hereditary titles. It established a republican form of government and separated church and state.

1858–60 ✦ Mexico's War of Reform.

Conservatives opposed most of the reforms passed by President Benito Juárez and his government, and launched a civil war to regain power from the reformers. Known as the War of Reform, or the Three Years' War, this civil war lasted until 1860. In the end, Juárez and his supporters prevailed.

1858 ✦ The return of the Nicaraguan Republic.

After defeating its American-born dictator, William Walker, Nicaraguans united to make their nation a republic. They created a government with a legislature of two houses and a president elected to a single four-year term. The conservative Tomás Martínez was elected the first president of the republic. The conservatives stayed in power for 35 years. (*Also see entry dated 1856–57: An American president for Nicaragua.*)

1859–60 ◆ Conflict on the Texas-Mexico border.

For two years, Juan Nepomuceno Cortina led a guerrilla war on Anglo settlements in Texas's Lower Rio Grande Valley. Cortina's rebellion was a response to Anglo abuses against Mexicans.

1859 ◆ The cigar industry attracted Cubans to the United States.

Protectionist tariffs in the United States made it expensive to import Cuban cigars, but not expensive to import the cigar tobacco. As a result, cigar factories were built in Florida, Louisiana, and New York to make genuine Cuban cigars. Many working-class Cubans followed the industry to jobs in the United States. Later tariffs, such as the McKinley Tariff of 1890, continued to raise the cost of importing cigars. Eventually, almost all cigars sold in the United States were made in U.S. factories using Cuban tobacco. Tampa, Florida, became a center for the cigar industry and the home of many Cubans.

July 12, 1859 ◆ Mexico's Reform Laws.

In the middle of the civil war in Mexico, Benito Juárez's government decreed the Reform Laws. (*Also see entry dated 1858–60: Mexico's War of Reform.*) These laws nationalized the holdings of the church and dissolved orders of Catholic monks. They made marriage a civil contract and required registration of weddings, births, and deaths. They also decreed freedom of worship and regulated religious festivities.

1861–64 ◆ A brief return of Spanish rule in Hispaniola.

Afraid that Haiti would again attempt to take control of his nation, Dominican President Pedro Santana asked Spain to return as colonial ruler. Spain reoccupied the Dominican Republic, but its abuses angered many Dominicans. Opponents of Spanish rule led revolts throughout the colony in 1863 and 1864. In 1865, Spain decided to give up the Dominican Republic.

1862 ◆ The Homestead Act.

This law, passed by the U.S. Congress, allowed squatters in the West to settle and claim vacant lands. These lands were often owned by Mexican Americans.

1864–67 ◆ The French Intervention in Mexico.

In 1861, Benito Juárez announced that Mexico would not pay the debt it owed to foreign countries, angering, among others, the French. In 1864, French Emperor Napoleon III sent troops to invade and occupy Mexico. After the French victory, Napoleon III made Archduke Maximilian of Austria the Emperor of Mexico. Benito Juárez set up a Mexican government in the north of the country and fought back. Juárez and his Mexican patriots succeeded in forcing out the French in 1867. Maximilian was executed the same year.

Carlos Manuel
de Céspedes.

1865–81 ◆ Education reforms in Puerto Rico.
With the *Decreto Orgánico,* ("Organic Decree"),
Spain finally established public education in Puerto
Rico. It required each town to set up its own
schools with public funds. The decree also gave the
government the power to create a normal school
(teachers' college) to prepare teachers, but such a
school was not established until 1890. The governor was responsible for appointing teachers, but
school administration was directed by a *Junta
Superior de Instrucción Pública,* a board of public
instruction. The system authorized by the Decreto
Orgánico broke down within a year because of the
social, economic, and political conditions on the
island. Over the next decade, there was little direction given to education. One Puerto Rican governor, Laureano Sanz, believed the goal of education
was to teach loyalty to Spain, so he hired only
teachers brought from Spain.

1865–70 ◆ The Triple Alliance War in South America.
In the early 1860s, dictator Francisco Solano López built up the Paraguayan military. In 1864, Paraguay asked Argentina for permission to cross through its
northern territory in order to attack Brazil. Argentina refused. In 1865, the triple
alliance of Argentina, Brazil, and Uruguay began a bloody war with Paraguay.
The Triple Alliance War lasted until 1870, when General Solano López's forces
were attacked and he was killed in Cerro Corá, Paraguay. As a result of the war,
Paraguay lost part of its national territory.

1866 ◆ American baseball was introduced to Cuba.
In 1866, sailors from an American ship in Matanzas harbor invited local Cubans
to play baseball. Together they built a baseball diamond at Palmar del Junco and
played while the ship remained in the harbor. By 1874, Cuban teams had been
started and were playing each other regularly.

1868–78 ◆ Cuba's Ten Year War with Spain.
Carlos Manuel de Céspedes (1819–74) was a black lawyer, poet, and general
who believed in the ideals of individual freedom and liberty expressed in the
French Enlightenment. On October 10, 1868, he proclaimed Cuba's independence. He set up a revolutionary government at Yara, on the eastern part of the
island. He freed his slaves and led an uprising of all races and classes against the
Spanish. The majority of the rebel groups accepted Céspedes as the president of

an emerging republic. Rebel forces took control of more and more cities. On April 10, 1869, the revolutionaries presented a new constitution. Bayamo, a city in southern Cuba, became the capital of the independent republic.

The war with Spain raged for ten years. Eventually, divisions among the rebels weakened their forces. Céspedes and his government were replaced on October 27, 1873. In 1878, the Spanish forced a peace plan on the Cubans, the Pact of El Zajón. Spain's victory caused many Cubans to leave for Europe and the United States to continue to plot independence. One such plot began to take shape as early as October 1878. The defeated rebel general Calixto García issued a manifesto in New York inviting all Cubans to unite to fight against Spanish tyranny.

1868 ♦ Hispanic Americans won protection under the U.S. Constitution.

The Fourteenth Amendment to the U.S. Constitution was ratified. Section One of the amendment stated "All persons born or naturalized in the United States, and subject to the jurisdiction thereof, are citizens of the United States and of the State wherein they reside. No State shall make or enforce any law which shall abridge the privileges or immunities of citizens of the United States; nor shall any State deprive any person of life, liberty, or property, without due process of law; nor deny to any person within its jurisdiction the equal protection of the laws." Among its other effects, this amendment confirmed that all people of Hispanic origin born in the United States were U.S. citizens, protecting their rights and property.

1868 ♦ The U.S. attempt to annex the Domican Republic.

With the help of Dominican dictator Buenaventura Báez, President Ulysses S. Grant tried to annex the Dominican Republic to the United States. Grant's plan was rejected by the United States Senate.

September 17, 1868 ♦ Puerto Rico ended slavery for newborns.

Spain decreed that after September 17, all children born to slaves in Puerto Rico would be free.

September 23, 1868 ♦ A call for Puerto Rican independence.

In the late 1860s, Ramón Emeterio Betances and Segundo Ruiz Belvis planned Puerto Rico's independence while in exile in New York and Santo Domingo. They won the support of the middle class and Afro-Cubans who lived in the coffee-growing region of Lares, Puerto Rico. *El Grito de Lares*, both the rallying call and name for the movement for Puerto Rican independence, was declared on September 23, 1868. The disorganized rebels were easily defeated by the Spanish. Only 1,000 had joined the independence force in Lares. Betances's ship, transporting men and weapons, was seized at the island of St. Thomas.

Many of the rebels were killed and the survivors dispersed in the mountains. Hundreds of suspects were jailed by the Spanish military during the weeks that followed. Eighty of the prisoners soon died from a yellow fever epidemic in the prison. In 1870, Spanish officials in Puerto Rico granted amnesty to those who had participated in the Lares rebellion.

Although the rebellion had failed, it was an important event. It called international attention to the colonial repression in Puerto Rico. It is seen in Puerto Rican history as the first great heroic act for Puerto Rican independence.

1869 ✦ Proposals for a Nicaraguan canal.

U.S. President Ulysses S. Grant announced that the United States would build a canal in Nicaragua from the Gulf of Mexico to the Pacific Ocean. In 1871, President Rutherford B. Hayes repeated the proposal. By the end of the century, Americans were clamoring to create a canal, citing numerous commercial, military, and nationalistic reasons.

1870–1934 ✦ Guatemalan laws caused the Mayas to suffer.

During the 1870s under President Justo Rufino Barrios, Guatemala passed laws that seized land from the native Mayas. The displaced Mayas then were forced to work on the coffee plantations set up on their confiscated land. In 1884 alone, more than 100,000 acres of Maya-owned land became privately owned. Hundreds of thousands of Mayan farmers became coffee pickers and peons (poor farm laborers). These and similar actions in southern Mexico created problems that have remained to the present, most recently expressed in the Zapatista revolt of 1994. (*Also see entries dated January 1, 1994: Zapatista uprising in southern Mexico.; and August 1995: Zapatista ceasefire.*)

By 1905, Guatemala's coffee industry controlled 14 percent of the world trade and brought in 85 percent of the country's revenues. Barrios's laws remained in force until 1934. At that time, dictator Jorge Ubico replaced them with vagrancy laws. These laws forced all farmers who owned less than two hectares (five acres) of land to do manual labor for 100 days per year. This law ensured cheap labor during the coffee and sugar harvests on the big plantations.

1870–1900 ✦ The rise of the Banana Republics.

During the 1870s, bananas (originally from Asia) were introduced as a cash crop to Costa Rica. The "miracle" fruit was soon planted throughout Central America and became an important export. By the turn of the century, the banana trade was dominated by the United Fruit Company, a giant Boston-based corporation. This crop became so important to Central America that the republics came to be called "Banana Republics." (*Also see entry dated 1890: The king of the Banana Republics.*)

1870 ✦ **Slavery reforms in Cuba and Puerto Rico.**
In a continuing effort to end slavery in its Caribbean colonies, the Spanish government freed the slaves that it owned in Cuba and Puerto Rico.

1871 ✦ **The first Hispanic professional baseball player in the United States.**
In 1871, the National Baseball Association, a professional baseball league, was founded. The same year, Esteban Bellán, a black Cuban, was recruited from Fordham College in New York City to play for the Troy Haymakers. Bellán played three years in the major league. By the turn of the century, social changes in the United States barred blacks from the major leagues. As a result, Hispanic blacks became regular players in the U.S. Negro leagues. White-looking Hispanics, however, were allowed to play in the major leagues. Teams went to great lengths to prove the racial purity of their Hispanic players. In 1911, the Cincinnati Reds prepared legal documents to prove that their new Cuban players, Armando Marsans and Rafael Almeida, were of pure Castilian (Spanish) heritage.

CUBAN BASEBALL

Professional baseball in Spanish America is almost as old as it is in the United States. In 1878, the *Liga de Béisbol Profesional Cubana* (Cuban Professional Baseball League) was founded, just seven years after the National Baseball Association was founded in the United States.

1871 ✦ **An organization for Cuban immigrants.**
The Instituto San Carlos was founded in Key West, Florida, as a mutual aid society for Cuban immigrants. However, it quickly grew into the most important exile center for Cubans plotting the island's independence from Spain.

1872 ✦ **Puerto Rican civil rights.**
Puerto Rican representatives in the Spanish *Cortes* (legislative body) finally won equal civil rights for the colony in 1872.

March 22, 1873 ✦ **Slavery ended in Puerto Rico.**
Slavery was finally abolished in Puerto Rico by the Spanish *Cortes*. The move gave freedom to 29,182 slaves. The newly freed slaves, however, were not given political rights such as the vote until five years later.

1875 ✦ **A Hispanic governor for California.**
Romualdo Pacheco became the first and only Hispanic governor of California since the state joined the United States.

1875 ✦ **U.S. immigration law was clarified.**
In *Henderson v. Mayor of New York,* the U.S. Supreme Court ruled that only the federal government had the power to regulate immigration.

Porfirio Díaz.

1876 ✦ Mexico under Porfirio Díaz.

After losing the Mexican presidential election, General Porfirio Díaz (1830–1915), a hero in the Mexican war against the French, led an army against Mexican government forces. Díaz overthrew the government and was recognized by the congress as president. As dictator, Díaz increased foreign investment in Mexico, built railroads, and improved the mining, metallurgy, and textile industries. However, corruption also grew among government officials and businessmen. The Laws of Reform were ignored and the rich prospered while the poor suffered. The abuses of the Díaz regime led to the Mexican Revolution of 1910. Díaz was overthrown by the revolutionaries in 1911, and he died four years later in exile.

1877 ✦ The Salt War.

Anglo politicians and profiteers (people who demand exhorbitant profits, as on inferior products) tried to take over the communal salt mines outside El Paso, Texas. The move to control the essential mineral angered the Mexicans and Mexican Americans living in the area. The conflict that followed became known as the "Salt War." Many died and much property was destroyed.

May 21, 1878 ✦ The end of the Ten Years' War.

A complete ceasefire brought an end to Cuba's Ten Years' War for independence. The Pact of El Zajón marked the end of the Cuban independence movement, and Cuba returned to colonial rule.

1879–83 ✦ The War of the Pacific.

Until 1873, Bolivia stretched from the mountains to the Pacific Ocean. During a mining dispute in 1879, Chile invaded Bolivia to protect its nitrate mining interests in southwest Bolivia. In response, Bolivia and its ally Peru began the War of the Pacific with Chile. Chile won in 1883 when its forces captured the city of Lima. As a result of the war, Bolivia lost the territories that gave it an outlet to the sea. Since then, Bolivia has been landlocked.

August 29, 1879 ✦ Independence failed again in Cuba.

General Calixto García organized another Cuban independence movement while in exile in New York. (*Also see entry dated 1868–78: Cuba's Ten Year War with*

Spain.) The *Guerra Chiquita* (Little War) began in Cuba on August 29, 1879. The Spanish responded forcefully. García was captured eight months after landing on the shores of Oriente Province and the rebellion was gradually put down. By September of 1880, Spain had completely defeated the rebels.

1882–99 ♦ The Dominican Republic's brutal dictator.
One of the most brutal dictatorships in the history of the Americas was that of the Dominican Republic's Ulises Heureaux. Heureaux led a 17-year reign of terror marked by corruption and murder. After draining the treasury of the republic's money, Heureaux tried to refill it by forcing loans out of leading citizens, printing unsupported paper money, and floating bonds issued in Europe. He was assassinated in 1899.

1886 ♦ Slavery ended in Cuba.
Cuba resisted anti-slavery forces for a long time because its sugar industry was dependent on slave labor. However, in the late 1800s, Cuban businessmen realized the need to update their production methods. With modernization and growth, sugar producers found that wage labor was cheaper than slave labor. In 1886, economic, social, and political forces came together to end slavery in this Spanish colony.

1889–90 ♦ The First International Conference of the American States.
The United States held the First International Conference of the American States in Washington, D.C. The attending nations passed a number of resolutions, including one to create the International Union of American Republics (later named the Panamerican Union) to be headquartered in Washington, D.C. This organization was the forerunner of the current Organization of American States (OAS). The OAS includes many agencies, organizations, conferences, and services throughout the hemisphere.

The United States initially called for the conference to encourage a trade agreement for the Western Hemisphere. At the time, the United States had a trade deficit with Latin America of $100 million. Latin American countries commonly exported raw materials to the United States, but then imported manufactured goods from Europe. The United States hoped to lower trade barriers, encourage the purchase of American manufactured goods, and create other avenues into the Latin American market. This strategy failed, but it did result in the creation of an important organization for cooperation in the hemisphere.

1889 ♦ Costa Rica achieved full democracy.
Costa Rica became the first Central American republic to achieve full democracy. In 1889, it held its first elections with full freedom of speech and of the press, and an honest counting of votes. Throughout the twentieth century Costa Rica has had

José Martí.

one of the most stable and democratic governments in the Americas. There have, however, been occasional threats to this political stability, including the failed dictatorship of Federico A. Tinoco from 1917 to 1918 and the revolution of 1932.

1890 ◆ The king of the Banana Republics.

Minor Cooper Keith, an American adventurer and entrepreneur, completed a railroad from the Pacific Ocean to Limón, the capital of Costa Rica at the time. The railroad cost about $8 million and took 4,000 lives. After building the railroad, Keith decided that the railroad needed freight to haul. His solution was to increase banana production. Keith was among the first to see the banana as a valuable cash crop. He started up numerous plantations in Costa Rica, to Guatemala, and El Salvador. In 1899, he combined 20 small banana companies into the United Fruit Company. For this and his other business ventures in Central America, he came to be know as "the uncrowned king of Central America."

1891 ◆ Unity in the Cuban independence movement.

Cuban poet and rebel leader José Martí (1853–95) had spent years organizing Cuban exiles in the United States. On January 5, 1891, he convinced 27 Cuban separatist clubs to approve his *Partido Revolucionario Cubano* (Cuban Revolutionary Party), a new unified independence movement. In late March, the party's program was ratified by other separatist organizations in the American South, New York, and Philadelphia. In April, the program was published in the first issue of the party's official newspaper *La Patria* ("The Fatherland"), which was printed in New York.

The official goal of the party was to obtain the complete independence of Cuba and to "promote and aid that of Puerto Rico." It further stated that the ultimate goal was the establishment in Cuba of "a new and honestly democratic nation." Martí first tried to gain broad approval for the party and make it the leader of the Cuban independence movement. Only then did he approach the generals who would be necessary for military support. Martí convinced Antonio Maceo, Máximo Gómez, and other generals to accept the authority of the party to lead the movement. In August 1892, Máximo Gómez was chosen as the leader of the military. The revolutionaries began preparating for another war for Cuban independence. (*Also see entry dated 1895: Cuba's second war for independence.*)

An *Alianza Hispano Americana* parade, Tucson, Arizona.

1893 ◆ Nicaragua's dictator Santos Zelaya.

José Santos Zelaya was elected to the presidency of Nicaragua. Soon after the election, he rewrote the constitution to allow him to serve 16 years. With Santos Zelaya in office, Nicaragua built a railroad to connect its major cities, increased its number of schools, diversified its agriculture, and modernized its army, becoming the largest military power in Central America. Even so, Santos Zelaya was a brutal leader who used his position to make himself and his friends richer and more powerful. Santos Zelaya used this power to stir up revolutions in neighboring countries. Pressure from both the United States and the other Central American republics forced Santos Zelaya into exile in 1909.

1894 ◆ The *Alianza Hispano Americana*.

The *Alianza Hispano Americana* ("Alliance of Hispanic Americans") was an early civil rights organization for Hispanics. It was founded in Tucson, Arizona,

79

and quickly spread throughout the Southwest. By 1930, it had grown to include more than 10,000 members. After World War II, the organization became very active in protecting the civil rights of Mexican Americans. Today, it still counts over 300 chapters in its membership.

1895 ✦ Cuba's second war for independence.

José Martí and his Cuban rebels tried to launch their war for independence on January 12 from the United States. However, U.S. officials halted the ships and seized their supplies. The rebels tried again in February. On February 24, Martí and his *Partido Revolucionario Cubano* (Cuban Revolutionary Party) opened the final war for independence. In response, Spain sent Captain General Valeriano Weyler with instructions to put down the rebellion at all costs. Weyler began a brutal campaign, forcing peasants into the cities, destroying their crops, and killing their livestock in order to starve out the rebels. With support from communities in New York, Key West, and Tampa, the rebels were able to continue the war. Weyler's brutality caused the United States to protest to Spain and prepare to join the war. (*Also see entry dated 1891: Unity in the Cuban independence movement.*)

1897–98 ✦ Home rule for Cuba and Puerto Rico.

Spain was concerned about the possibility of U.S. involvement in the independence movements in Cuba and Puerto Rico. To end the war before the United States could enter, the Spanish crown issued a royal decree on November 25, 1897, giving Cuba and Puerto Rico autonomy and home rule. General Valeriano Weyler was withdrawn from Cuba and his campaign ended. On January 1, 1898, the decree became official. So did the Law of Universal Suffrage. Cubans and Puerto Ricans were now allowed to legislate all of their own public affairs through their own bicameral (two houses) congress, their own government, and cabinet of secretaries.

1898–1920 ✦ Guatemala's dictator Manuel Estrada Cabrera.

Manuel Estrada Cabrera took control of Guatemala in 1898. His 22 years in power were characterized by theft, murder, looting of the public treasury, repression of the Indians, and neglect of the army. He was overthrown in 1920.

1898 ✦ The Spanish-American War.

On February 15, one and a half months after Spain granted self-rule to Cuba, an American battleship, the USS *Maine,* was mysteriously blown up in the Havana harbor, killing numerous Americans. The ship had been sent to Cuba to protect the lives and property of U.S. citizens.

On April 11, U.S. President William McKinley refused to recognize the Cuban revolutionary government. The United States Congress, however, declared that it supported Cuban independence on April 19. The United States also pledged, in the Teller Amendment, that it had no intention of taking over

A painting of Theodore (Teddy) Roosevelt and his Rough Riders fighting the Battle of San Juan Hill during the Spanish-American War, 1898.

Cuba. On April 21, the United States declared war on Spain. Congress used the destruction of the USS *Maine* as one of its reasons. The American rallying cry during the war became "Remember the *Maine*."

On April 30, U.S. Commodore George Dewey launched an attack on the Spanish fleet in Manila Bay in the Philippines. The Spanish forces were easily destroyed. On June 20, American forces (including Lieutenant Colonel Teddy Roosevelt and the Rough Riders) invaded Cuba near Santiago. The Spanish surrendered on July 16. On July 25, U.S. forces invaded Puerto Rico. General William Thomas Sampson bombarded San Juan harbor and the American army moved in to occupy the island. The seaport of Ponce fell three days later. The United States had won decisive battles on land and destroyed much of the Spanish fleet in Cuba, Puerto Rico, and the Philippines. Spain and the United States signed a truce in Washington, D.C., on August 12. The war had lasted just over three months. On December 10, Spain signed the Treaty of Paris, giving Cuba its independence and transferring Puerto Rico and the Philippines to the United States for the sum of $20 million.

1899 ◆ New political parties for Puerto Rico.

The *Partido Obrero Socialista* (Socialist Workers Party) was founded in Puerto Rico by Santiago Iglesias Pantín. He introduced the program of the Socialist Party of the United States into the new U.S. colony. Iglesias Pantín supported the annexation of Puerto Rico by the United States to further the cause for social democracy. The party never won an election by itself but enjoyed significant support. The *Partido Republicano* (Republican Party), was also founded this year by José Celso Barboso. The party supported immediate U.S. statehood for Puerto Rico.

1899 ◆ Puerto Rican education under the United States.

The United States government named a commission made up of two Puerto Ricans and two Anglo-Americans to study public education on the island. As a United States colony, public education in Puerto Rico progressed rapidly. In 1899, Puerto Rico had 380 public elementary schools for males and 158 for females. Secondary education was offered at the Provincial Institute, which followed the Spanish system of education. In 1899, an island-wide board of education was established. In 1900, the *Escuela Normal Insular* (Island Normal School), or teacher's college, was founded in Fajardo. It moved to Río Piedras in 1903 and became the University of Puerto Rico.

January 1, 1899 ◆ U.S. control of Cuba and Puerto Rico.

After the last of the Spanish military forces left Cuba and Puerto Rico, the United States established a military government on each island. The United States explained that a period of transition was necessary before the islands could govern themselves. The islands were once again colonies of a world power.

1900–12 ◆ Mexican labor built railroads in the Southwest and West.

At the start of the century, American railway companies began recruiting Mexican workers in El Paso, Texas. The Southern Pacific Railroad and the Atchison, Topeka and Santa Fe Lines were the most active recruiters. By 1908, about 16,000 Mexicans were working on the railroad in the Southwest and West. The number of Mexican workers reached its peak between 1910 and 1912.

April 12, 1900 ◆ Puerto Rico founded a civilian government.

The U.S. Congress passed the Foraker Act on April 12. This law allowed Puerto Rico self-rule under U.S. control. Puerto Ricans could elect their own House of

Representatives, but could not have a vote in Washington. The newly founded *Partido Republicano* (Republican Party) won the elections of 1900 and 1902. The party pushed for the island's rapid admission to United States as a state.

1901–03 ✦ Treaties and laws cleared the way for a Central American canal.

In 1901, the Hay-Pounceforte Treaty with Great Britain was signed and approved by the U.S. Congress. It permitted the United States to build and protect a canal across the Central American isthmus (a narrow piece of land). It replaced the Clayton-Bulwar Treaty of 1850. (*Also see entry dated 1850: Plans for a Central American canal.*) At the time, there were two proposed routes for the canal, one through Nicaragua and one through Panama, then part of Colombia. The Walker Commission recommended that the United States pursue the Nicaraguan route, which would cost about $189 million to build. The Panama route would cost about $149 million to build, plus $109 million to buy the rights and property already owned by the New Panama Canal Company of France. The New Panama Canal Company, fearing it would miss its chance to make any money, dropped its price to $40 million, and the Walker Commission subsequently changed its recommendation to the Panama route. If this effort was not successful, the United States would turn to Nicaragua. In the 1903 Hay-Herrán Treaty with Colombia, the United States sought the right to build a canal in a six-mile-wide zone across Panama. In return, the United States would pay Colombia $10 million and give it an annual subsidy of $250,000. The Colombian legislature rejected the treaty.

Political cartoon satirizing the United States' Theodore Roosevelt promoting Panamanian independence and pushing Colombia out of the way of canal negotiations.

1901 ✦ American labor included Puerto Ricans.

The *Federación Libre de los Trabajadores* (Workers Labor Federation) of Puerto Rico joined the American Federation of Labor (AFL), the United States' largest labor union. By accepting Puerto Ricans, the AFL changed its policy of excluding non-whites. The AFL hoped to increase its influence on the island and reduce the impact of cheap Puerto Rican labor on the mainland work force.

1901 ✦ Cuba was promised limited independence.

After the Spanish-American War, the United States set up a military occupation force to prepare the island for independence. Cubans believed that this was

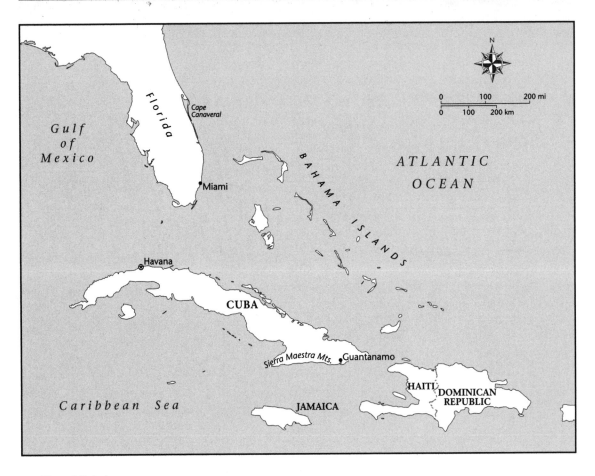

Map of Cuba's Guantanamo Bay.

a temporary measure and that they soon would have complete independence from Spain and the United States. However, the Platt Amendment to the U.S. Army Appropriation Act of 1901 limited Cuban independence. It prevented Cuba from signing treaties with other countries that were unacceptable to the United States, and it prevented Cuba from borrowing more money than the United States found reasonable. It also gave the United States the right to build a naval base on Cuba and to send troops to protect life, liberty, and property.

The United States also required that Cubans include the limits of the Platt Amendment in their constitution of 1901. Only when these limits were in place would the United States turn the government over to the Cubans. On December 28, Tomás Estrada Palma was elected president of Cuba under the new constitution.

1902 ◆ The Reclamation Act.
The Reclamation Act, passed by the U.S. Congress, helped manage American

natural resources, especially in the West. By giving the government control of many forests and rivers, the law took land away from many Hispanic Americans.

May 1902 ◆ A Cuban declaration of independence.

Cuba declared its independence from Spain and the United States. Military Governor Leonard Wood turned over the government to President Tomás Estrada Palma and returned to the United States. During his four-year term, President Estrada Palma had a number of successes. In 1903, he signed a trade agreement with the United States. Under this pact, Cuban sugar received a 20 percent reduction in tariffs—an arrangement which lasted until the Castro era. (*Also see entry dated January 1, 1959: Castro replaced Batista.*) He also convinced Washington to surrender claims to all naval bases except Guantanamo Bay and another smaller site. The United States gave up this second site in 1912, but it still holds Guantanamo Naval Base today.

March 12, 1903 ◆ The University of Puerto Rico was founded.

The University of Puerto Rico was founded by expanding the Normal School in Río Piedras. Over the years, it has expanded beyond being just a college for teachers. It opened a College of Liberal Arts (1910), an Agricultural and Mechanical College (1911), a Law School and School of Pharmacy (1913), a School of Education (1925), a Business Administration School (1926), and a School of Social Work (1934).

June 1903 ◆ Copper mine strikes in Arizona.

Mexican and Mexican American workers led one of the earliest and most important copper mine strikes in the Southwest. The Clifton-Morenci Strike failed to win labor reforms, however. Most Anglo workers did not join the walkout.

November 1903 ◆ A canal for an independent Panama.

On November 3, Panamanian rebels declared independence from Colombia. Three days later, the United States recognized the new government of Panama. On November 18, the new government signed the Hay-Bunau-Varilla Treaty with the United States, giving the U.S. the right to build a canal across Panama, including sanitation facilities at each end of the canal. It also gave the United States the right to send troops to Panama to maintain order. The treaty tied Panama's foreign policy to that of the United States and limited the debt that Panama could owe.

1904 ◆ The *Partido Unión* was founded in Puerto Rico.

Under the leadership of Luis Muñoz Rivera, a patriot for independence, the *Partido Unión* (Union Party) was founded in Puerto Rico. The party saw three courses for Puerto Rico: United States statehood, autonomy, or a dependent

Luis Muñoz
Rivera.

republic. The party stayed in power from 1904 to 1924 and focused on maximizing self-rule. One of its major successes was the passage of the Jones Act by the United States Congress in 1917. This law made Puerto Ricans U.S. citizens. (*Also see entry dated 1917: Puerto Ricans became U.S. citizens.*)

December 1904 ✦ The Roosevelt Corollary reinforced the Monroe Doctrine.

In his annual address to the U.S. Congress, President Theodore Roosevelt restated the Monroe Doctrine. In reference to the revolution in the Dominican Republic, Roosevelt reminded European powers that the United States would not tolerate their armed involvement in the Americas. He also suggested that the United States would step in to supervise the internal affairs of unstable countries in the Western Hemisphere.

1905 ✦ American intervention in the Dominican Republic.

Ulises Heureaux, the dictator of the Dominican Republic, was assassinated in 1899. (*Also see entry dated 1882–99: The Dominican Republic's brutal dictator.*) Heureaux's death left the government in chaos, and the country heavily in debt, mostly to European countries. To get their money back, a number of European governments made plans to intervene in the Dominican economy. In 1905, the United States stepped in to keep the Europeans out of the Americas, taking over the collection of import and export taxes, which were used to pay the republic's debts. American fiscal and political control increased gradually until 1916. At this time, President Juan Isidio Jiménez resigned, leaving the country without a government. The United States set up an American military government to control the country. This intervention in the Dominican Republic was the first example of the "Roosevelt Corollary" in action. (*Also see entry dated December 1904: The Roosevelt Corollary reinforced the Monroe Doctrine.*)

1906–09 ✦ American occupation of Cuba.

After Tomás Estrada Palma's reelection as Cuban president, opponents began an armed revolt. After negotiations and arbitration failed, Estrada Palma and his vice president resigned, leaving Cuba without a head. Various Cuban parties encouraged the United States to intervene under the provisions of the Platt Amendment. (*Also see entry dated 1901: Cuba was promised limited indepen-*

dence.) The U.S. occupation lasted from 1906 to just after the supervised elections of 1909.

1907 ◆ Instability in Central America.

After building up Nicaragua's army, President José Santos Zelaya invaded Honduras and replaced its president. He then prepared to invade El Salvador. The United States felt that these and other problems in the region threatened its plans for the Panama Canal. In November 1907, U.S. president Roosevelt and Mexican president Porfirio Díaz called for a general peace conference in Washington, D.C., out of which emerged the General Treaty. It stated that the United States and Mexico would not recognize governments that came to power through coup d'etat. It banned the Central American governments from interfering in each other's internal affairs. It also established the Central American Court of Justice.

1909–33 ◆ U.S. intervention in Nicaraguan politics.

To avoid an invasion by the United States, President José Santos Zelaya resigned from the presidency. (*Also see entry dated 1893: Nicaragua's dictator Santos Zelaya.*) This was the first of a series of Nicaraguan governments that the United States forced out of power. The Nicaraguan Congress selected one of Zelaya's men, José Madriz, to succeed as president. Madriz was not acceptable to the United States, however, and it refused to recognize his government. Rebels eventually overthrew Madriz. Juan Estrada became president and the United States became heavily involved in reconstructing the government. Estrada's successor, Adolfo Díaz, was so weak that in August of 1912, he requested that United States military occupy Nicaragua. The Marines soon landed on the Pacific coast.

American troops occupied Nicaragua until January 1933 (except for an 18-month period from August 1925 to January 1927). During these two decades, the United States organized Nicaragua's national finances, supervised budget expenditures, collected customs revenues, managed the national bank and the railroad, and supervised elections.

> **DID YOU KNOW?**
>
> Not only was Theodore Roosevelt the organizer of the Rough Riders and the 26th president of the United States, he also:
> - was the fifth cousin of Franklin Delano Roosevelt, our 32nd president
> - won the Nobel Peace Prize in 1906 for his role in ending the Russo-Japanese War with the Treaty of Portsmouth
> - organized a new political party, the Progressive Party, and was its candidate for president in 1912

1910–31 ◆ Political unrest in Cuba.

Despite Cuba's independence (overseen by the United States), it suffered political unrest for more than two decades. In 1910, there was an attempted revolution in Havana headed by General Guillermo Acevedo. Vicente Miniet led

Brothers Ricardo and Enrique Flores Magón in Leavenworth Federal Penitentiary in 1922.

another attempt in 1911. In August 1911, Cuban war veterans demanded that pro-Spanish officials and bureaucrats be removed from the government. In 1912, the Colored Independents launched an armed protest. This group called for more political power for blacks, who had been important in the independence movement and wars. In 1917, the liberals revolted in protest of dishonest elections. In August 1931, they also tried to overthrow dictator General Gerardo Machado.

1910–17 ◆ Mexican immigration to the United States.

The Mexican Revolution caused a great deal of social upheaval in Mexico. It also caused great disorder and social transformation in U.S. border states. Many Mexicans fled from the war in their homeland to find refuge in the American Southwest. Well-educated Mexicans left for political reasons and joined the leaders of the Hispanic communities in the major cities of Texas, New Mexico, Arizona, and southern California. Many more Mexicans left for economic reasons and joined the American work force. These new Mexican American workers changed the working classes in many industries in the United States. This large-scale immigration of Mexicans into the United States has continued into the present.

November 10, 1910 ◆ The Mexican Revolution began.

Government corruption under President Porfirio Díaz led to a revolution. Rebels devised the *Plan de San Luis,* which called for the Mexican Revolution to begin at 6:00 P.M. on November 20. The plan declared the elections void and Porfirio Díaz's government illegitimate. (*Also see entry dated 1876: Mexico under Porfirio Díaz.*) It named Francisco I. Madero the president of the United Mexican States. Not until May 1911, however, did the revolutionary forces defeat the forces of the dictator Díaz. A peace treaty signed on May 21 forced the dictator to flee to Europe. Madero made his triumphant entry into Mexico City on June 7. He was elected with 98 percent of the vote to the presidency of a newly democratic Mexican Republic on October 1. He took office on November 6.

Porfirio Díaz held power for 34 years. During this time, he helped take land and power away from Native Americans and Mexican peasants and put it in the hands of the rich. The revolution sought social justice. Madero pushed nationalism, democracy, land reform, and a reduction in the power of the Catholic Church. Anarchists (those who rebel against authority, order, or ruling power)

Ricardo and Enrique Flores Magón also organized workers on both sides of the U.S.-Mexican border.

The revolution under Madero achieved military and political victories easily. Socio-economic changes took longer. The new government still had opponents among the conservatives and in the federal army. There were also numerous revolutionary uprisings around the country by those who either did not recognize Madero's government or were pressing for greater economic and social reform.

1912 ◆ The Institute for Tropical Medicine was founded in Puerto Rico.

Puerto Rico's finest medical school began as the Institute for Tropical Medicine. In 1926, the institute became the School for Tropical Medicine of the University of Puerto Rico. It was affiliated with the Columbia University School of Medicine in New York City. In 1949, it was reorganized as the School of Medicine of the University of Puerto Rico, again in association with Columbia University. In 1966, the school became the Campus for Medical Sciences of the University of Puerto Rico. It brought the schools of medicine, dentistry, and health sciences together under one roof.

1912 ◆ Mexico protested violence against Mexican Americans.

In the Southwest, many Mexican Americans lived and worked alongside Anglo-Americans. Because of competition for land and jobs, there was often a great deal of tension between the two groups. In the late 1800s and early 1900s, the violence against Mexican Americans steadily increased. By 1912, murders and lynchings (hangings) had become commonplace in Texas and California. In this year, the Mexican ambassador to the United States formally protested the violence against Mexicans and Mexican Americans.

1912 ◆ New Mexico became a state.

New Mexico became a U.S. territory in 1850. There were several attempts to achieve statehood, but they all failed. The majority of New Mexico's population was Mexican American. These Hispanics held considerable political and economic power, and feared U.S. statehood would reduce that power. (California, which had more Anglos than Hispanics, was admitted as a state in 1850, without having to pass through a territorial stage.) (*Also see entries dated 1846: California's Bear Flag Revolt; and 1850: The Compromise of 1850.*) Although the Mexican American population was still the largest group, by 1912 their economic and political power had decreased. New Mexico joined the Union as the 47th state.

1912 ◆ Puerto Ricans founded a new independence party.

The *Partido de la Independencia* (Independence Party) became the island's first pro-independence party under U.S. rule. Among the founders of the party were writers Manuel Zeno Gandía, José de Diego, and Luis Llorens Torres.

Mexican revolutionary leader Francisco "Pancho" Villa with his troops in Mexico, 1914.

1912 ✦ **The U.S. Marines were sent to Cuba.**

A group of black Cubans called the Colored Independents started a violent revolt on the island. (*Also see entry dated 1910–31: Political unrest in Cuba.*) The U.S. government sent in the Marines to restore order. Cuban President Máximo Gómez protested, but the U.S. action was allowed under the Platt Amendment. (*Also see entry dated 1901: Cuba was promised limited independence.*)

1913–14 ✦ **The counterrevolution in Mexico.**

Opponents of President Francisco I. Madero continued to organize their armies. (*Also see entry dated November 10, 1910: The Mexican Revolution began.*) In February 1913, with the support of Henry Lane Wilson, the U.S. ambassador to Mexico, General Victoriano Huerta seized power. Madero and his vice president, Pino Suárez, were imprisoned. Later in the month, both men were executed by a firing squad. Huerta held the presidency for less than a year and a half. His government was itself opposed from within Mexico by Venustiano Carranza,

Customer buying
La Prensa.

Francisco "Pancho" Villa, and Emiliano Zapata. Huerta was also opposed by the newly elected American president, Woodrow Wilson, who sent U.S. troops to invade Veracruz on April 21, 1914. Carranza eventually forced Huerta out of power on July 15. Carranza's government was recognized by the United States on October 17.

1913 ✦ *La Prensa* was published in New York City.

José Campubrí, a Spaniard, offered a Spanish-language newspaper to serve the Puerto Rican, Cuban, and other Hispanic immigrants to the New York City area. Campubrí owned *La Prensa* until he sold it to Fortune Pope in 1957. (*Also see entry dated 1963:* El Diario de Nueva York *and* La Prensa *merged.*)

1914–17 ✦ The Mexican Revolution continued.

Under the leadership of Venustiano Carranza (1859–1920), Mexico turned back toward democracy. Despite another brief period of civil war, Carranza's government was able to push for reforms like those of Benito Juárez and Francisco I. Madero. On January 6, 1915, the Carranza administration passed a law to return lands to communities and gave peasants the right to own land. Even so, during the next five years, only 427,000 acres were parceled out to some 44,000 peasants. Carranza also returned numerous *haciendas* (ranches) that had been confiscated during the revolution to their owners. On September 16, 1916, Carranza called for a Constitutional Congress. On October 22, Mexico held elections to name the delegates to the Constitutional Congress. President Carranza accepted the new constitution in 1917. The Constitution of 1917 laid the foundation for the modern Mexican state.

August 3, 1914 ◆ The Panama Canal opened.

Soon after the first ship cleared the newly constructed Panama Canal, Panama's population became dependent on the jobs and business it generated. The canal brought a lot of money to the country, but it still had its opponents. One of the earliest disputes arose over the failure of the United States to return to their home countries the Jamaican and West Indian workers who had helped build the canal. Another dispute concerned discrimination in the Canal Zone. Employees in the Canal Zone were divided into "gold" and "silver" categories, with gold workers being U.S. citizens, and silver workers all others. Those on the gold list were paid twice as much money for the same amount of work. They also enjoyed special treatment in their daily activities, such as separate windows at the post office. Panamanians resented this separation. Many Panamanians also resented the control that the United States had over their country. (*Also see entries dated 1850: Plans for a Central American canal; 1901–03: Treaties and laws cleared the way for a Central American canal; and November 1903: A canal for an independent Panama.*)

February 20, 1915 ◆ The *Plan de San Diego.*

The Supreme Revolutionary Congress of San Diego (Texas) plotted a general uprising among Mexican Americans living near the border with Mexico. The goal was to create a separate republic, with possible future union to Mexico. The uprising never took place, however. The written *Plan de San Diego* was found on a Mexican American arrested in January 1915. The paper revealed a plan to kill all Anglo-Americans over the age of sixteen, except for the elderly. The plan's discovery, coupled with the continuing turmoil of the Mexican Revolution, caused the United States to increase the troops and border patrols in the area. It also led to increased violence against Mexicans and Mexican Americans. (*Also see entry dated 1914–17: The Mexican Revolution continued.*)

1916–22 ◆ The U.S. military occupied Cuba.

Cuba continued to be disrupted by armed revolts and political unrest. As a result, the United States sent the navy and marines to Cuba to restore order, an action allowed under the Platt Amendment. (*Also see entry dated 1901: Cuba was promised limited independence.*) U.S. forces, there to protect sugar mills, mines, and railroads (especially during World War I), eventually occupied a large portion of the island. But the occupation went beyond what was permitted by the Platt Amendment. Almost 2,600 marines were stationed in Oriente and Camaguey until 1922.

1916 ✦ New Mexico's first Hispanic governor.
Ezequiel Cabeza de Vaca became the first Mexican American elected governor of the state of New Mexico.

1916 ✦ Political unrest in Costa Rica.
After Federico A. Tinoco seized the presidency of Costa Rica, a number of American businesses called for the United States to recognize his government. These businesses included the United Fruit Company and the Canal Zone. President Woodrow Wilson refused. Instead, U.S. naval commander L.B. Porterfield took his ship to the port of Limón on the Costa Rican coast and threatened to land the marines. Tinoco resigned. Julio Acosta won the elections that followed. He was immediately recognized by the United States.

1916 ✦ The United States continued to pursue a Nicaraguan canal.
Even though the Panama Canal had opened two years earlier, the United States wanted to protect its rights to build a canal through Nicaragua. The Bryan-Chamorro Treaty, ratified by the U.S. Senate in 1916, gave the United States rights to a route that included Lake Nicaragua and the San Juan River. In return, the United States would pay $3 million. Many Nicaraguans were angered when the United States used the $3 million to pay some of Nicaragua's debts instead of giving the money directly to Nicaragua.

Costa Rica protested the treaty because it was not consulted even though it shares the San Juan River with Nicaragua. El Salvador protested the U.S. naval bases in the Bay of Fonseca permitted by the treaty, which threatened El Salvador's territory. Costa Rica and El Salvador took the United States and Nicaragua to the Central American Court of Justice. The court decided in favor of Costa Rica and El Salvador, but the United States refused to honor the decision. In 1918, the United States helped to destroy the court which it had helped to establish through the General Treaty of 1907. (*Also see entry dated 1907: Instability in Central America.*)

1916 ✦ Wilson sent the marines to the Dominican Republic.
In 1911, Dominican president Ramón Cáceres was assassinated. Between 1911 and 1916, chaos reigned. Presidents came and went, taking with them as much of the nation's money as they could. U.S. president Woodrow Wilson sent in the marines to bring order to the Dominican Republic. The Americans insisted on new financial and military reforms as well as supervision of the next presi-

Mexican workers at an Arizona mine, circa early 1900s.

dential election. U.S. general Harry Knapp reorganized the government to carry out the reforms, created a U.S.-style court system, and established a national guard to act as a police force. Over time, the country's transportation, communications, and educational systems were modernized. The U.S. occupation had many opponents and there were numerous armed revolts. The marines finally left in 1924, after Horacio Vásquez was elected. Some Americans remained to control the Dominican Republic's finances.

March 9, 1916 ◆ Pancho Villa raided the United States.

General Francisco "Pancho" Villa's troops attacked the town of Columbus, New Mexico. The attack killed 17 American citizens. Villa hoped to punish and embarrass the United States for supporting his rivals in the Mexican civil war.

He succeeded. An American force under Brigadier-General John J. Pershing chased Villa for almost a year, but failed to catch him.

1917–19 ✦ World War I brought Mexican workers to the United States.

World War I created a great demand for labor in the United States. European countries involved in the war needed products made in America. New workers that might have immigrated from Europe could not come. When the United States entered the war, American workers left to fight. Thousands of Mexican workers were brought north to work in factories and to construct railways in the Midwest.

1917 ✦ Puerto Ricans became U.S. citizens.

The Jones Act, passed by the U.S. Congress, extended U.S. citizenship to all Puerto Ricans. (*Also see entry dated 1904: The* Partido Unión *was founded in Puerto Rico.*) It also created two Puerto Rican houses of legislature whose representatives were elected by the people. English was decreed the official language of Puerto Rico. The law also allowed the United States to enlist Puerto Ricans as soldiers to serve during World War I.

1917 ✦ Puerto Ricans fought for the United States in World War I.

During World War I, a majority of Spain's former colonies joined the Allies. The only exceptions were those nations that remained neutral: Chile, Paraguay, Colombia, Venezuela, El Salvador, and Mexico. Puerto Rican soldiers fought for the first time under the United States flag.

January 16, 1917 ✦ Germany's plot to make Mexico an ally.

A telegram (known as the "Zimmermann Telegram") from the German government to President Venustiano Carranza of Mexico was intercepted and revealed to the U.S. government. The Germans offered to return the southwestern part of the United States to Mexico in return for Mexico's support for Germany's war effort. The idea of a German-Mexican alliance led many more Americans to mistrust Mexicans and Mexican Americans.

February 1917 ✦ The Immigration Act.

The United States Congress enacted the Immigration Act. This new law was aimed at reducing the number of immigrants from southern and eastern Europe, but it also slowed immigration from Mexico. All immigrants were now required to pay a head tax and show their ability to read. For those contracted by employers, their stay in the United States was limited to six months.

May 1917 ✦ The Selective Service Act.

The Selective Service Act became law in the United States, requiring American men between the ages of 21 and 30 to register for the military draft. It also

An *orquesta típica* in Houston, Texas.

required Mexican citizens living in the United States to register with their local draft boards, even though they were not eligible for the draft.

May 1, 1917 ◆ The end of the Mexican Revolution.

The Mexican Revolution officially ended when General Venustiano Carranza was elected president of Mexico under a new constitution. The Constitution of 1917 was the product of a constitutional convention of six sessions in 1916 and 1917. It is still in force today. (*Also see entries dated November 10, 1910: The Mexican Revolution began; and 1914–17: The Mexican Revolution continued.*)

1919 ◆ Adolfo Luque became the first Hispanic to play in baseball's World Series.

Adolfo Luque was a dark-skinned Cuban who broke into the major leagues in 1914 with the Boston Braves. During his career, Luque faced many challenges on and off the field because of his color. He was jeered at and called names. He weathered the storm and had one of the longest careers of any Hispanic baseball player. He pitched in relief and as a starter for the Boston Braves, the Cincinnati Reds, the Brooklyn Dodgers, and the New York Giants.

In 1919, as a member of the Cincinnati Reds, Luque became the first Hispanic to play in the World Series. He pitched in two games as the Reds beat the Chicago White Sox. (This series was famous for the "Black Sox Scandal," in which Chicago players were banned from baseball for losing games on purpose). Luque also pitched in the 1933 World Series for the New York Giants. He was credited with winning the decisive game of that series. During his best year, 1923, he led the National League for Cincinnati in wins (27), earned run average (1.93), and shutouts (6).

1920s ◆ The *orquesta típica* came to the United States.

The first orchestras dedicated to playing the typical dance music of Mexican Americans were probably organized in El Paso or Laredo, Texas, in the 1920s. Built around the violin, these *orquestas típicas* were a vital part of weddings, birthdays, and festivals in the Mexican American community. The orchestras and their music continued to evolve over the next several decades. Tex-Mex music (orchestra music mixed with polka) and *La Onda Chicana* (The Chicano Wave—Tex-Mex music fused with jazz and rock) grew out of this tradition.

Vaudeville actress Beatriz "La Chata" Noloesca with Pedro "Ramirin" Gonzalez.

1920s ◆ The rise of Hispanic theater.

As Hispanic American communities continued to grow in the Southwest, Florida, and New York, they began to build theaters and stage both serious and popular drama. San Antonio and Los Angeles attracted touring theater troupes from Mexico and at times boasted their own theater companies. In Tampa, Florida, theaters featured actors and opera singers from Cuba and Spain. New York City attracted artists from Cuba, Spain, Mexico, and Puerto Rico. The popularity of Hispanic theater supported Mexican American playwrights in Los Angeles, including Eduardo Carrillo, Adalberto Elías González, Esteban V. Escalante, and Gabriel Navarro. In New York, the Puerto Rican playwright Gonzalo O'Neill was successful.

May 21, 1920 ◆ Mexico's President Carranza assassinated.

Mexican president Venustiano Carranza was assassinated in Taxcalantongo, in the mountains of Mexico.

1921 ◆ Immigration quotas set.

For the first time in U.S. history, the country passed laws to limit the number of immigrants allowed to enter during a single year. This law was designed to reduce immigration from eastern and southern Europe as well as Asia. It did not affect immigrants from the Americas. As a result, Mexico and Puerto Rico become major sources for workers.

1922 ◆ The *Partido Nacionalista Puertorriqueño* was founded.

The *Partido Nacionalista Puertorriqueño* (Nationalist Party of Puerto Rico) was founded with José Coll y Cuchí as president. The party has struggled for Puerto Rican independence from 1922 to the present.

December 1922 ◆ A Central American conference in Washington.

The U.S. government grew concerned that political unrest in Central America would spill over into Panama and affect the canal. For this reason, it called for a Central American conference in Washington, D.C. The conference ended in 1923. The attendees agreed on a definition of a revolutionary government that would not be eligible for recognition, established a new Central American Court, and forced arms limitations. (*Also see entry dated 1916: The U.S. continued to pursue a Nicaraguan canal.*) Despite these accords (agreements), the United States soon found reason to intervene in the internal affairs of Honduras, Nicaragua, El Salvador, and Guatemala.

1923–25 ◆ Cuban José Méndez led the Kansas City Monarchs to three championships.

Because of his African ancestry and dark skin, José Méndez was never allowed to play in the U.S. major leagues. Instead, he played in the Negro National League in the United States and in Cuban professional baseball. Few statistics are available from these leagues, but people who saw him play recognized Méndez's talents. Baseball Hall of Famer John Henry Lloyd said that he never saw a better pitcher than Méndez. New York Giants Manager John McGraw said that Méndez would have been worth $50,000 in the U.S. major leagues. ($50,000 was a high salary for the 1920s.) Méndez came to the United States in 1908 with the Cuban Stars. In 1909, he posted a record of 44 wins and 2 losses as a pitcher for the Stars. During the winters he played in Cuba. Before 1914, he was 62–17 in the Cuban winter leagues. From 1912 to 1916, Méndez played for the All-Nations of Kansas City, a racially mixed barnstorming (traveling) club. From 1920 to 1926, he served as a player-manager for the Kansas City Monarchs. From 1923 to 1926, he managed and pitched the Monarchs to three straight Negro National League pennants (championships). During his long career, he also played for the Los Angeles White Sox, the Chicago American Giants, and the Detroit Stars, all Negro League teams.

1924 ◆ A new effort to unite Spanish America.

In Peru, the *Alianza Popular Revolucionaria Americana* ("American Popular Revolutionary Alliance") was formed by Víctor Raúl Haya de la Torre (1895–1979). The alliance led a widespread movement that became known as Aprism. Aprism sought to improve conditions for Native Americans, create a universal system of social security, redistribute lands, and raise taxes on mining, oil, and agricultural industries. Aprism's ultimate goal was to create one economy for all of Spanish America and then a politically unified Spanish America.

1924 ◆ The pioneers of Hispanic radio.

Pedro J. González was among the pioneers of Spanish-language radio in California. In 1924, together with his musical group *Las Madrugadores* (The Early Birds), González hosted a show broadcast from station KMPC in Los Angeles. The show aired from 4:00 to 6:00 A.M., reaching thousands of Mexican and Mexican American workers throughout the Southwest as they began their day. González's radio program featured Hispanic music and culture, as well as his progressive political views. His career in the United States ended when he was convicted of rape in 1934, although some question the legitimacy of the conviction.

1924 ◆ The U.S. Border Patrol was created.

The United States Border Patrol was created this year to supervise and control migration, especially from Mexico.

1926–29 ◆ The war between the Mexican government and the Catholic Church.

In the 1920s, the Mexican government took many steps to reduce the power of the Catholic Church. The steps extended the goals of the Constitution of 1917 to separate church and state. Because of laws passed in 1926, the church could no longer celebrate Mass or perform the holy sacraments (including weddings and baptisms). President Plutarco Elías Calles (1877–1945) ordered the closing of several convents and churches. He also expelled 200 foreign priests from Mexico and had the bishop of Huejutla arrested. Calles also pushed for laws to imprison priests and clerics who criticized the new restrictions or conducted religious acts outside of church. (This included wearing religious clothes in public.) On July 31, 1926, the government outlawed Catholicism in Mexico. The next day, 40,000 workers rallied in front of the National Palace to support the decision.

The Catholic bishops tried in September to get the Mexican Congress to repeal the laws, but failed. Dozens of radical priests and their followers responded by preparing for war. The Cristero War (1926–29) followed. More than 50,000 Mexicans took to the streets to fight the new laws. Almost 90,000 lives were lost and another wave of refugees entered the United States. Neither

Coronation church in Mexico City, Mexico.

side was strong enough to win the bloody war. It finally came to an end through the negotiations of the church leaders and the government of President Emilio Portes Gil. The two parties signed an agreement on June 21, 1929, stating that the government would limit itself to civil and legal matters and the church would limit itself to spiritual and moral issues.

1926 ◆ Anger toward Puerto Ricans in New York City.

During the 1920s, the number of Puerto Ricans in New York City neighborhoods continued to grow. By 1930, there were 53,000 Puerto Ricans in the city. In a 1926 riot in Harlem, Puerto Ricans were attacked by non-Hispanics resentful of their presence.

1926 ◆ Mexican American music grew in popularity.

During the early 1920s, Mexican American vocal music became very popular in the American Southwest. The Mexican *corrido* (ballad) and the *canción-corrido*, a mixture of the ballad and the *canción* (song), were especially important. As these musical forms grew in popularity, American record companies began to seek out performers. In 1926, RCA, Columbia, Decca, and Brunswick began setting up studios in hotel rooms in cities such as Dallas, San Antonio, and Los Angeles.

September 16, 1926 ◆ *La Opinión* began publishing in Los Angeles.

In the 1920s, Ignacio E. Lozano, Sr., a Mexican citizen, saw the need for a Spanish-language daily newspaper in Los Angeles to serve the growing Mexican and Mexican American population in that area. He founded *La Opinión,* a daily paper that is still published in Los Angeles. By the early 1990s, the paper had a circulation of almost 110,000 during the week and over 80,000 on Sunday.

1928 ◆ *Las adventuras de Don Chipote* was published.

Journalist and novelist Daniel Venegas influenced modern Chicano (Mexican American) literature through novels such as *Las aventuras de Don Chipote* ("The Adventures of Don Chipote"). *Don Chipote* tells the story of a Mexican immigrant to the United States. He travels through the Southwest looking for the streets of gold promised to all immigrants. Instead, he suffers at the hands of criminals, officials, and his bosses. The book offered a darkly humorous look at immigration.

July 17, 1928 ◆ Mexican president Obregón assassinated.

General Alvaro Obregón had served under President Venustiano Carranza in the late 1910s. He helped put down the civil war led by Pancho Villa and Emiliano Zapata. In 1920, he opposed Carranza and became president, serving until 1924. He was elected president again in 1928. However, before he could take office, he was assassinated by a Catholic who opposed the president's actions against the church. (*Also see entry dated May 21, 1920: Mexico's President Carranza assassinated.*)

December 1, 1928 ◆ Mexico's *Partido Nacional Revolucionario* was founded.

The *Partido Nacional Revolucionario* (National Revolutionary Party) was formed in Mexico by President Plutarco Elías Calles. Calles moved to put an end to the years of rule in Mexico by *caudillos* (grassroots leaders). The new party would give the supporters of the Mexican Revolution a place to resolve their differences and choose the president. Between 1928 and 1934, Calles and the other presidents chosen by the party peacefully built the Revolution's reforms into the Mexican government. They also peacefully transferred power from one president to the next. The Partido Nacional Revolucionario later became the *Partido Revolucionario Institucional* (Institutional Revolutionary Party), which still rules Mexico today.

1929 ◆ Hispanic immigration during the Great Depression.

During the 1920s, the demand for labor in the United States had lured many Mexicans and Puerto Ricans to come to the United States to work and live. After the stock market crash of 1929, the country slipped into economic depression.

Hispanic men waiting in line at the relief office during the Depression.

At times over the next decade, over 30 percent of the population was unemployed, and many Americans began to see Mexican and Puerto Rican workers as unwanted competition. Throughout the United States, communities and their leaders called for Mexicans and Puerto Ricans to leave.

Immigration from Mexico came to a complete stop and reversed, with many Mexicans going south over the border to avoid abuse. The Mexicans who stayed had put down roots and saw their future in the Anglo culture of the United States. Between 1930 and 1934, about 20 percent of the Puerto Ricans living in the United States returned to the island. Hispanic migrant farm workers were soon replaced by southern whites and blacks. (*Also see entry dated 1931–38: The U.S. government repatriated Mexicans by force.*)

1929 ◆ The League of United Latin American Citizens (LULAC).

LULAC was founded in Texas to promote the interests of Mexican Americans. Many Mexican Americans in Texas were frustrated by the barriers they faced in the United States because of their ethnic origin.

1930–43 ◆ Lefty Gómez pitched his way into baseball's Hall of Fame.

One of baseball's greatest pitchers, Vernon Louis "Lefty" Gómez was born on November 26, 1907, in Rodeo, California. In his 13 seasons with the New York Yankees and 1 season with the Washington Senators, Gómez won 189 games and lost 102 games. This record put him among major league baseball's leaders for regular-season wins and winning percentage. He pitched 2,503 innings in his career and had an earned-run average (ERA) of 3.34. He posted 20 wins or more in 1931, 1932, 1934, and 1937. He led all American League pitchers in wins in 1934 (26 wins) and 1941 (15 wins), and he led the American League in strikeouts in 1933, 1934, and 1937.

Gómez also set records for his pitching in the World Series and all-star game. In five World Series for the Yankees, he pitched in seven games. He holds the record for most wins without a loss (6–0, with 1 no-decision). Gómez made all-star teams every year from 1933 to 1939. He had a record of three wins against one loss in all-star play. During winter seasons, Gómez played in Cuba, where he served as manager of the Cienfuegos team. He once taught a class on pitching at the University of Havana. Gómez died on February 2, 1989, in San Rafael, California.

An elementary school classroom in San Angelo, Texas, 1949.

1930 ✦ Mexican Americans fought school segregation in U.S. courts.

After the Mexican War ended in 1848, Mexican Americans faced discrimination and segregation (separation) in all aspects of their life. For many years in the late nineteenth and early twentieth centuries, Mexican American communities built their own schools to try to overcome this situation. But during the 1930s, these communities began using the courts to attack school segregation. In the 1930 case of *Independent School District (Texas) v. Salvatierra*, the court found that Mexican Americans had indeed been segregated, without regard for individual ability. The court stated that the only legitimate use of segregation should be for special education. Many other court victories followed.

1930 ✦ A revolution in El Salvador.

In 1930, the price of coffee crashed on the world market. This caused much social unrest and led to a revolution in El Salvador. When it ended, Maximiliano

Hernández Martínez had became dictator. He ruled for 14 years until he was unseated by a military coup in 1944.

1930 ◆ Tariffs raised barriers to Cuban imports.

As the United States economy descended into depression, Congress and President Herbert Hoover took steps to protect American jobs and farms. Congress passed the Hawley-Smoot Tariff in 1930. The tariff raised the tax on imports 7 percent. The new tariffs were a serious blow to the Cuban sugar industry. Cuba's entire economy, but especially its sugar industry, was dependent on trade with the United States. Higher costs for imported goods meant that Americans bought fewer Cuban products and less Cuban sugar. By 1934, however, negotiations reduced the tariff from 2.5 cents per pound of sugar to less than $.01 per pound.

1930 ◆ Trujillo Molina seized power in the Dominican Republic.

General Rafael L. Trujillo Molina (1891–1961), head of the national police force, came to power in the Dominican Republic. He set up a dictatorship that lasted until his assassination in 1961. In 1930, Trujillo Molina took over a nation that was in chaos, bankrupt and poverty stricken, with a foreign debt of $20 million. His first act as leader of the Dominican Republic was to rebuild the capital, Santo Domingo, which had been destroyed by a hurricane. (In 1936, he named the city after himself—Ciudad Trujillo.) By 1957, Trujillo Molina had eliminated both the foreign and domestic debts. The national income was 40 times higher than when he took power. In that same year, the national budget reached a high point of $131 million. (He had already balanced the annual budget for 20 years.) Trujillo Molina launched many programs that improved the country's economy and the lives of its people. Improvements came in land use, communications, industry, transportation, hydro-electric power, farming programs, and social laws. Even so, the vast majority of the economic growth went into the private coffers of the Trujillo Molina family, and Trujillo Molina himself ruled as a ruthless dictator assisted by a brutal secret police force.

1930 ◆ U.S. control of Puerto Rico.

By 1930, the United States controlled 44 percent of the cultivated land in Puerto Rico. U.S. businesses controlled 60 percent of the banks and public services, and all of the shipping lines.

1931–38 ◆ The U.S. government repatriated Mexicans by force.

As the Depression deepened, officials in the United States became more and more hostile toward Mex-

---

HISPANIC "RAGS-TO-RICHES" SPORTS FIGURES

- Cuban boxer Eligio "Kid Chocolate" Sardinas
- Cuban batter Alejandro Oms
- Argentine race car driver Manuel Fangio
- Tennis player Pancho González
- Outfielder Roberto Clemente
- Golfer Chi Chi Rodríguez
- Football coach Thomas Flores
- Golfer Lee Treviño

---

ican immigrants. Federal officials, including the U.S. Secretary of Labor, expressed the opinion that removing Mexicans from the United States would help bring an end to the Depression by freeing up jobs and welfare money for American citizens. The federal government began anti-alien drives across the country. In southern California, about 75,000 Mexicans were forced to leave by 1932. Between 1931 and 1934, local police, sheriffs, and welfare authorities joined forces with the federal officials to repatriate trainloads of Mexicans. In these deportation drives, thousands of American citizens—many of them Mexican American children—were driven from their own country.

This wholesale repatriation of Mexicans spread from the Southwest to the Midwest during the early years of the Depression. In some Midwestern cities, such as Gary and East Chicago, Indiana, and Detroit, Michigan, many families were forcefully deported. By 1938, most of the repatriation drives had ended. By World War II, Mexican immigration was once again welcome and encouraged in the United States. (*Also see entry dated 1929: Hispanic immigration during the Great Depression.*)

July 15, 1931 ◆ Sardiñas won the junior lightweight title.

Cuba's Eligio "Kid Chocolate" Sardiñas became the first Hispanic boxer to win a world title, in the junior lightweight class. Born in Havana on October 28, 1910, Sardiñas lived the rags-to-riches-to-rags story common among boxers. After winning 86 amateur fights and 21 professional fights in Cuba, he made his New York debut in 1928. Over the next 10 years, he fought over 100 bouts in the United States. He became a true champion, supported his community, and was memorialized on stage and screen. However, he was exploited by his managers and owners and ultimately fell victim to poverty and alcoholism.

Eligio "Kid Chocolate" Sardiñas.

1932 ✦ **Hispanics competed for the United States in the L.A. Olympics.**
Two Hispanics from the United States were part of the U.S. Olympic team:
Roland Lee Romero was a triple jumper and fencer Miguel de Capriles won a
bronze medal.

1933–40 ✦ **The Cuban military took control of the government.**
On September 4, 1933, a revolt led by sergeants in the Cuban army, including
Fulgencio Batista (1901–73), led to the downfall of dictator Gerardo Machado.
The revolt marked a turning-point in modern Cuban politics. The army became
one of the two political forces battling for control of Cuba. The other force was
the *Auténtico* (Authentic) Party, founded by the faculty and students at the University of Havana. Eventually, Batista and the army had complete control of
Cuba. From 1933 to 1940, Batista ruled from behind the scenes through various
puppet leaders, including Carlos Mendieta, Miguel Mariano Gómez, and Federico Laredo Brú.

During the 1930s, the United States followed its Good Neighbor Policy and
stayed out of Cuba. It accepted military rule in Cuba in order to maintain stability and favorable treatment for U.S. government and business interests. For the
U.S. government, Batista was a symbol of this order and stability, and it treated
him as a head of state even though he did not officially hold that position.

1933–38 ✦ **The Chaco War.**
War broke out between Bolivia and Paraguay over the part of their shared border that ran through the inhospitable Chaco jungle (an area rich in oil deposits).
The bloody conflict threatened to drive both countries into bankruptcy. In 1935,
Paraguay succeeded in taking control of most of the land it wanted. At this point,
friendly countries intervened to call a halt to the war. Carlos Saavedra Lamas
(1878–1959), an Argentine statesman and international jurist, worked to end the
Chaco War between Bolivia and Paraguay. For his efforts, Saavedra Lamas was
awarded the Nobel Prize for Peace in 1936. The final peace treaty was signed
in Buenos Aires, Argentina, in 1938.

1933 ✦ **The Good Neighbor Policy.**
In his inaugural address, President Franklin D. Roosevelt announced the "Good
Neighbor Policy." This policy would greatly change the relationship between the
United States and Latin America. It suggested that the United States should not
intervene in the internal affairs of Latin America countries. Later in the year, at
the Inter-American Conference in Montevideo, Uruguay, the United States del-
egates repeated the pledge not to intervene. As part of the new policy, the U.S.
Marines withdrew from Haiti, the Dominican Republic, and Nicaragua. The
United States signed a new, more agreeable canal treaty with Panama. Roo-

sevelt's government recognized the revolutionary governments of Jorge Ubico in Guatemala, Maximiliano Hernández Martínez in El Salvador, Tiburcio Carías in Honduras, Anastasio Somoza in Nicaragua, Rafael Trujillo Molina in the Dominican Republic, and François Duvalier in Haiti.

1933 ◆ Roosevelt changed the official language policy for Puerto Rico.

The Jones Act of 1917 had established English as the official language in Puerto Rico. In 1933, the Roosevelt administration ended the policy.

May 1933 ◆ The El Monte Berry Strike.

Farm workers in Los Angeles County began the El Monte Berry Strike to seek better conditions. In June, members of the Mexican Farm Labor Union, an affiliate of the Confederation of Mexican Farm Workers Union (founded in 1927 by the Los Angeles Federation of Mexican Societies), officially sanctioned the strike and called for a 25-cent-per-hour minimum wage. The strike spread from Los Angeles County to Orange County and the union grew rapidly. The strike ended later in the month, with the strikers winning a small increase in wages and recognition of the confederation. That same year, the confederation became the largest and most active agricultural union in California. In 1935, the confederation was responsible for 6 of the 18 strikes in California agriculture. It was also successful at winning changes without striking. In 1936, the confederation was a leader in establishing the Federation of Agricultural Workers Union of America. By the end of the 1930s, however, the confederation's power had decreased, growers and legislators offered greater resistance, a surplus of workers decreased their leverage, and disputes between unions further reduced their power.

A cotton picker in 1933. Photograph by Dorothea Lange.

October 1933 ◆ The San Joaquin Cotton Strike.

Mexican farm workers in the cotton industry launched a strike in the counties of the Central Valley in California. The San Joaquin Cotton Strike was the largest and best-organized of labor actions started by the radical Cannery and Agricultural Workers Industrial Union in the 1930s. Some 12,000 to 18,000 cotton pickers walked out, demanding a raise from $.60 to $1 a pound for picked cotton. Growers and armed groups attempted to put down the strike with violence, killing two strikers and wounding various others. California Governor James Rolf called in the National Guard and established a fact-finding board. The board eventually worked out a compromise in which the cotton pickers would receive $.75 per pound and the growers would be condemned for violation of the strikers' civil rights.

1934–40 ✦ Mexican land reforms.

As president of Mexico, Lázaro Cárdenas (1895–1970) distributed about 8.2 million acres per year to peasant families. By the time he left office, more than half of all Mexicans belonged to these *ejido* (land parcel) communities with lands of their own. Almost half of all of Mexico's crop land was owned and worked in this manner. Even with Cárdenas's efforts, however, more than 200 million acres still remained in private hands, much of it as large *haciendas* (ranches). Also, almost 35 percent of all Mexicans still worked for meager wages on the land of others.

May 29, 1934 ✦ Roosevelt revoked the Platt Amendment.

Following through on his promise to make the United States a "good neighbor," President Franklin Delano Roosevelt annulled the Platt Amendment. This document had given the United States the right to intervene in Cuban affairs and had long been hated by the Cubans. Roosevelt's action confirmed the United States' blessing of Fulgencio Batista's rule. (*Also see entries dated 1901: Cuba was promised limited independence; 1906–09: American occupation of Cuba; 1912: The U.S. Marines were sent to Cuba; and 1916–22: The U.S. military occupied Cuba.*)

1935 ✦ *Conjunto* music took shape.

Música norteña or *conjunto* grew out of many folk music traditions that came together in Texas and northern Mexico. In the mid-1930s, this instrumental music (and the ensembles that play it) took the form that it still holds today. At this time, the characteristic instruments of conjunto came together to stay. At the heart of conjunto is the accordion. With it are the *tambora de rancho* (ranch drum) and the *bajo sexto* (a twelve-string guitar). With these and other instruments, *Tejanos* (Mexican Texans) created a music to go with their distinct culture. At first, conjunto was popular only along the U.S.-Mexican border. In the 1970s, it spread to urban centers in the United States and Mexico.

1936 ✦ A new Panama Canal Zone treaty.

Panama and the United States worked out a new Canal Zone treaty, canceling Panama's "protectorate" status and guaranteeing the nation's independence. The United States also promised not to intervene in Panamanian affairs. The treaty was not ratified by the U.S. Senate until 1939, when Panama agreed that the United States could shoot first and consult later in case of a threat to the canal.

August 31, 1936 ◆ Sixto Escobar became the bantam weight champion.

Sixto Escobar became the first Puerto Rican boxer to win a world championship in boxing when he knocked out Tony Marino in the thirteenth round of their fight. *"El Gallito de Barceloneta"* ("The Barceloneta Fighting Cock"), as he was known, later lost the title. However, Escobar regained the crown (twice, in fact), becoming one of very few boxers to do so.

1937–56 ◆ Anastasio Somoza ruled Nicaragua.

From 1933 to 1937, Anastasio Somoza (1896–1956) directed Nicaragua through President Juan B. Sacasa. Somoza was the head of the U.S. Marine-trained national guard in Nicaragua. In 1937, Somoza took control of the country and established himself as dictator. Under Somoza, Nicaragua enjoyed many years of economic and political stability. It also enjoyed a very close relationship with the United States, its chief trading partner. Somoza became wealthy at the expense of his nation. He also arranged for power to pass to his son, Luis Anastasio Somoza Debayle (president of the national congress). When Somoza was assassinated in 1956, the Nicaraguan Congress quickly affirmed Luis as president. Somoza Debayle was president until 1963, at which time his brother, Anastasio Somoza, Jr., continued the family dynasty. (*Also see entries dated 1956: Somoza Debayle took over Nicaragua; 1974: Somoza reelected; and 1980: Somoza assassinated.*)

1937 ◆ The Ponce Massacre.

Over 2,000 people gathered in Ponce, Puerto Rico, to demonstrate for independence on the anniversary of the abolition of slavery. Police attacked and broke up the demonstration, killing 22 protesters and wounding 200 others.

1938 ◆ The *Congreso de Pueblos de Habla Hispana* was founded.

A national congress of Spanish-speaking people, the *Congreso de Pueblos de Habla Hispana,* was founded in Los Angeles by Bert Corona, Luisa Moreno, and others to protect the civil rights of Hispanics in the United States. The organization was investigated by the FBI, which considered it subversive. Its membership declined during World War II.

1938 ◆ The Texas pecan shellers' strike.

In January 1938, young Mexican and Mexican American pecan shellers went on strike in San Antonio. Since the late nineteenth century, the Texas pecan industry had been centered in San Antonio. The industry had traditionally used mostly Mexican American labor. It paid only two or three cents a pound for shelling pecans, and it rejected efforts by the U.S. National Recovery Administration to raise wages. By 1937, a number of unions had started to organize the pecan

Pecan shellers in San Antonio, Texas, during the 1930s.

industry. A January 1938 announcement by the industry gave the unions a cause for action. Employers announced a 15 percent wage cut. In response, workers throughout the industry went on strike. A Mexican American pecan sheller, Emma Tenayuca, emerged as a leader. She joined the Communist Party, because she believed that it was the only group willing to help the shellers. The strike became more and more violent. More than 1,000 of the 6,000 strikers were arrested. In March the strike was settled through arbitration. The union received recognition but had to accept a 7.5 percent decrease in wages. In October, the Fair Labor Standards Act replaced the agreement with a nationwide $.25 per hour minimum wage. Management turned to machine shelling as a way to get around the labor requirements and, eventually, many jobs were lost.

1939–44 ◆ World War II united Spanish America with the Allies.
During World War II, all of the Spanish American countries eventually declared war against the Axis (Germany, Italy, and Japan) and joined the Allies.

1939–43 ◆ Eduardo Chávez's murals.
Eduardo Chávez painted murals for post offices and other government buildings during this period. In his murals, Chávez portrayed the life and industry of the communities in which he painted. He painted murals for buildings in Denver, Colorado; Geneva, Nebraska; Center, Texas; and Fort Warren, Wyoming. Other

Chicano (Mexican American) painters who came after Chávez also chose murals as their art form. These murals can be found in urban settings throughout the Southwest and the Great Lakes region. They often portray the issues that Hispanics face every day.

1939 ◆ The Rio Grande Conference was founded.

As Hispanic Americans in Texas and New Mexico joined Protestant churches, they began to recognize that the traditional Anglo leadership could not help them protect their Hispanic culture and language. For this reason, Hispanic Methodist churches in these states banded together. In the early 1930s, the churches formed the Texas American Conference. In 1939, they created the Rio Grande Conference. To this day, this powerful group of churches has remained independent of the larger Methodist Church.

1940s ◆ Rita Hayworth, Hollywood star.

During the 1940s, Rita Hayworth (1918–87) became one of the hottest stars at Columbia Studios. She acted in films such as *Angels over Broadway* (1940), *Cover Girl* (1944), *Gilda* (1946), *The Lady from Shanghai* and *The Loves of Carmen* (both 1948), and *Pal Joey* (1957). Hayworth was born Margarita Carmen Cansino, the daughter of a Spanish-born dancer and his Ziegfeld Follies partner. Hayworth danced professionally as a teenager and was discovered while performing in Mexican nightspots near the U.S. border.

1940–44 ◆ Batista served as president of Cuba.

Fulgencio Batista had been leading Cuba from behind the scenes since his successful 1933 military revolt against Gerardo Machado. (*Also see entry dated 1933–40: The Cuban military took control of the government.*) In 1940, he made his leadership official when he was elected president under a new Cuban constitution. Batista encouraged the growth of democracy through elections. However, government corruption under Batista eroded public confidence in him. In 1944, he retired from Cuban politics and moved to Florida, where he lived comfortably on the millions of dollars he had made during his rule.

1940 ◆ Industrialization for Mexico.

With social and land reform a part of the past, President Manuel Avila Camacho (1897–1955) set the policy for Mexico's future. The government's focus now shifted to industry and the country's urban centers, home to the urban working class and the new middle class. Foreign investment and technology started to flow back into Mexico's "mixed" economy, in which the government invested one third and the private sector two thirds. Between 1940 and 1960, economic production more than tripled. Between 1960 and 1978, it increased 2.7 times. Average annual growth was 6 percent. In 1940, agriculture was 10 percent of the

Luis Muñoz-Marín.

economy; in 1977, only 5 percent. Manufacturing grew from less than 19 percent to 23 percent. In 1940, only 20 percent of the population lived in urban centers; in 1977, more than 50 percent did. Overall, population increased from 19.6 million in 1940 to 67 million in 1977.

1940 ◆ The *Partido Popular Democrático* was formed in Puerto Rico.

A new Puerto Rican political party, the *Partido Popular Democrático* (Popular Democratic Party), was organized with Luis Muñoz-Marín (1898–1980) as its leader. It was the country's ruling party from 1940 to 1964. Since 1972 it has alternated power with the *Partido Republicano* (Republican Party). Under Muñoz-Marín's leadership, the party became a pro-autonomy (for self-government) party. The Partido Popular Democrático fulfilled its mission when the U.S. Congress made Puerto Rico a commonwealth of the United States in 1952.

1940 ◆ Puerto Rico's major labor union was founded.

The independent union *Confederación de Trabajadores Generales* (Confederation of General Workers) was organized and soon became the major labor organization in Puerto Rico.

1941 ◆ The Fair Employment Practices Act.

The Fair Employment Practices Act was passed in the United States to eliminate discrimination in employment. The law led to the formation of the Fair Employment Practices Committee (FEPC). The FEPC investigated companies with government contracts to be sure that they did not discriminate in any way. In the Southwest, over one-third of the cases investigated by the FEPC involved discrimination against Mexicans. The FEPC was disbanded at the end of World War II.

1941 ◆ Hispanics joined the U.S. war effort.

After the U.S. declaration of war in 1941, Hispanics throughout the country joined the war effort with enthusiasm. Thousands of Hispanic American men joined the armed forces and were sent overseas. Most Hispanic American women stayed behind, but like other American women, they worked hard to support the war effort at home, on farms, on railroads, and in factories. Also, Mexico was one of the first countries to pledge help to the United States.

Migrant farm workers under the *Bracero* Program.

July 30, 1941 ◆ **The Office of Inter-American Affairs was established.**
With the spread of World War II, the threat of Axis (German, Italian, and Japanese) influence in Latin America spread. To head off this threat, President Franklin Delano Roosevelt set up the Office of Inter-American Affairs to improve relations with Latin America. In April 1942, author-journalist Carey McWilliams started a Spanish-Speaking Division of the office to help reduce discrimination against Mexican Americans and to help integrate them into American society. In April 1946, President Harry S Truman terminated the office.

1942–64 ◆ **The *Bracero* Program.**
As the United States became more involved in the war overseas, the labor shortage at home increased. In order to increase the labor supply, the United States turned to Mexico. In 1942, the U.S. and Mexican governments reached an agreement called the Mexican Farm Labor Supply Program. The U.S. Congress passed Public Law 45 on April 29, 1943, to finance and regulate the program. The agreement between the two governments was informally known as the

113

Defendants in the
"Sleepy Lagoon"
murder trial.

Bracero Program (from the Spanish word for "arm," *brazo*, referring to strong-armed workers). The program permitted Mexicans to enter the Southwest and work as farm and railroad laborers. Mexican labor proved a great help to the American war effort. Even after the war the program continued and extended to the fields in the Midwest.

The Bracero Program became the subject of much controversy over the years. From time to time various interest groups, such as farmers and organized labor, argued for or against it. Congress extended the program in 1947 and again in 1951. In December 1964, under President Lyndon B. Johnson, the United States ended the program. During the 22 years of its existence, over 4.8 million Mexican workers had come to the United States.

January 13, 1943 ◆ The "Sleepy Lagoon" murder trial.

On this date, a jury in Los Angeles, California, returned verdicts in a murder trial involving 22 Mexican American youths. Three were found guilty of first-degree murder, nine of second-degree murder, five of assault, and five others acquitted (the charges against them were released). The trial has become famous as an example of the anti-Mexican feelings in California at the time. During court-room proceedings, the Los Angeles Police and the press that covered the trial

Two Mexican American youths, both beaten and one stripped of his clothing during the
Zoot Suit Riots, June 7, 1943.

inflamed public opinion against Mexicans in general and Pachucos in particular. (Pachucos were young Mexican Americans who had their own culture, clothing, and slang.)

The trial concerned the murder of José Díaz, a Mexican American youth. Díaz was found dead on August 2, 1942, near a popular swimming hole, which the press called "Sleepy Lagoon." The death was the result of a fight among gangs. Twenty-two members of the 38th Street Gang were tried together on a total of sixty charges. After the youths were found guilty, a Sleepy Lagoon Defense Committee appealed the case. The committee was headed by Carey McWilliams, a former federal official responsible for reducing discrimination against Mexican Americans. (*Also see entry dated July 30, 1941: The Office of Inter-American Affairs was established.*) On October 4, 1944, the District Court of Appeals reversed the case, dismissing it for lack of evidence.

June 3, 1943 ◆ The Zoot Suit Riots.

The Zoot Suit Riots began in southern California. The riots represented a campaign by some elements of the California press to portray Mexican Americans as unwelcome foreigners. Bands of hundreds of sailors, marines, and soldiers in southern California would go through *barrio* (Hispanic neighborhood) streets looking for Mexican youths wearing zoot suits. (Zoot suits were the special style of clothing worn by the Mexican American youth culture of that time.) The servicemen would beat the young men and tear their zoot suits from their bodies. In response, the police often arrested the victims of these assaults.

The public view of Mexican Americans as criminals and social problems did not reflect the reality of the time, but the positive side of the story was not told. In fact, there were proportionately more Mexican Americans in the armed services than whites. These servicemen were so courageous in battle that they were awarded proportionately more medals of honor than whites. In World War II, they were more decorated than any other ethnic group in the United States.

1944 ◆ Operation Bootstrap began.

The Puerto Rican government launched Operation Bootstrap to help meet U.S. labor demands caused by World War II and to encourage American industry to build on the island. Under the program, which lasted until 1960, U.S. factories that relocated to Puerto Rico would receive a ten-year tax exemption. Operation Bootstrap succeeded in bringing industry to the island. It also increased migration from the Puerto Rican countryside to urban centers and emigration to the U.S. mainland. On the negative side, the program hurt the island's farms.

1945 ◆ A social revolution in Guatemala.

Guatemala suffered for many years under dictators supported by the military, the Creoles (Spanish Americans), and the landlords. Finally in 1945, a social revolution overthrew the government, and Juan José Arévalo took control of the country with the support the middle class and workers. That same year, the nation adopted a new constitution based on the Mexican model authorizing land reform and guaranteeing the rights of labor and free institutions. Arévalo, who served from 1945 to 1950, and Jacobo Arbenz Guzmán, who followed him from 1950 to 1954, set out to make other reforms. They took actions to democratize the country, further education, and limit foreign interests. (*Also see entry dated 1952: Land reform in Guatemala.*)

1945 ✦ The United Nations was founded.

As World War II was drawing to a close, many countries saw the need to form an organization that would keep the peace. The United Nations brought together 51 countries to create a body that could solve international problems through negotiation and sometimes military cooperation. All of the Spanish American countries have been members of the United Nations from its beginning.

March 21, 1945 ✦ *Méndez et al. v. Westminster School District et al.*

Mexican American parents in California won a suit against four Orange County elementary school districts. The parents argued that the segregation practiced by the schools deprived more than 5,000 Mexican American students of the constitutional guarantees of due process and equal protection under the law. The school districts appealed to the Ninth Circuit Court in 1947, but the appeals court upheld the lower court ruling.

1946 ✦ A governor for Puerto Rico.

The first Puerto Rican governor, Jesús T. Piñero, was appointed by President Harry S Truman.

1946 ✦ A new name for Mexico's ruling party.

The dominant political party in Mexico changed its name to *Partido Revolucionario Institucional* (Institutional Revolutionary Party), the name it bears today. The party was founded in 1928 as the *Partido Nacional Revolucionario* (National Revolutionary Party). In 1938, it changed its name briefly to the *Partido de la Revolución Mexicana* (Party of the Mexican Revolution).

1946 ✦ The *Partido Independentista Puertorriqueño* was founded.

The *Partido Independentista Puertorriqueño* (The Puerto Rican Independence Party) was created under the leadership of Gilberto Concepción de Gracia. Unlike the Nationalist Party, it proposed to move towards independence through peaceful means, including elections. It held its first elections in 1948. Since its beginning, the party has promoted a socialist ideology.

1947 ◆ **The American G.I. Forum was organized.**
Mexican American veterans founded a new organization to fight for civil rights. The group formed when the owners of a funeral home in Three Rivers, Texas, refused to bury a Mexican American killed in the Pacific. The G.I. Forum movement spread throughout the Southwest and even to Puerto Ricans in the Northeast. It became one of the largest organized efforts by Hispanics to protect their civil rights.

1947 ◆ **Puerto Ricans began coming to the mainland by airplane.**
More than 20 airlines began providing service between San Juan, Puerto Rico, and Miami, Florida, or New York City. The flights made it easy for Puerto Ricans to go back and forth between the island and mainland. They also made possible history's first large migration by air.

1948 ◆ *El Diario* **was published in New York City.**
Porfirio Domenicci, who came to the United States from the Dominican Republic, began publishing the newspaper *El Diario de Nueva York* to serve the Spanish-speaking public in New York City. (*Also see entry dated 1963:* El Diario de Nueva York *and* La Prensa *merged.*)

1948 ◆ **Pancho González won the U.S. Open.**
Richard Alonzo "Pancho" González, a native of Los Angeles, won the U.S. men's singles tennis championship at Forest Lawn, New York. In 1949, he won the U.S. championship again, as well as the men's doubles championship at Wimbledon in England. González went on to become a top-ranked professional player from 1954 to 1961.

July 4, 1948 ◆ **A new Puerto Rican political party.**
The pro-statehood Republican Party was founded in Puerto Rico.

1950–65 ◆ **Segregation came to an end in Texas and Arizona.**
From the 1950s through the early 1960s, segregation was abolished in Texas, Arizona, and many other communities. The change came about largely through the efforts of the League of United Latin American Citizens (LULAC) and the *Alianza Hispano Americana* (Alliance of Hispanic Americans). (*Also see entries dated 1894: The* Alianza Hispano Americana; *and 1929: The League of United Latin American Citizens.*)

1950–59 ◆ **Mexican immigration increased.**
During the 1950s, immigration from Mexico doubled from 5.9 percent to 11.9 percent of the total number of immigrants to the United States.

1950 ✦ **José Ferrer named best actor.**

José Ferrer was one of the most distinguished actors of Hispanic background to make a career in films and on stage in the United States. He was born in Santurce, Puerto Rico, on January 8, 1912. Raised and educated in Puerto Rico, he graduated from Princeton University in 1933. In 1950, he won the Academy Award as best actor for his role in *Cyrano de Bergerac*. He was awarded a Gold Medal by the American Academy of Arts and Sciences in 1949 and was inducted into the Theater Hall of Fame in 1981. Ferrer died in 1992.

1950 ✦ **Mexican and Mexican Americans as migrant workers.**

Black workers continued to be the largest group of migrant workers along the east coast. But beginning in the 1950s, Mexican and Mexican American workers became the dominant group among migrant workers in the Midwest and West: from Texas to the Great Lakes, in the Rocky Mountain region, and from California to the Pacific Northwest.

Pedro Albizu Campos, leader of the *Partido Nacionalista Puertorriqueño*, at a press conference in Puerto Rico, December 16, 1947.

July 3, 1950 ✦ **Congress cleared the way to make Puerto Rico a U.S. Commonwealth.**

The U.S. Congress started the process of upgrading Puerto Rico's political status from protectorate to commonwealth. Puerto Rico was also authorized to write its own constitution. Angry that the United States was granting a change to commonwealth status and not independence, nationalist groups demonstrated and attacked officials all over the island during this year. Blanca Canales Torresola and her followers declared the independent Republic of Jayuya, a small mountain town. She was arrested and eventually spent more than ten years in prison. Other nationalist groups attacked the fortifications at San Juan and other targets in Arecibo and Mayaguez. Pedro Albizu Campos, the leader of the *Partido Nacionalista Puertorriqueño* (Nationalist Party of Puerto Rico), was arrested. In all, there were more than 2,000 arrests of nationalists on the island during the year. (*Also see entries dated 1922: The* Partido Nacionalista Puertorriqueño *was founded; and November 1, 1950: Puerto Rican nationalists made an attempt on President Truman.*)

November 1950 ✦ *Temas* **was first published.**

A group of Spaniards and Hispanic Americans came together in New York City

A migrant
work camp.

to launch a monthly Spanish-language magazine. *Temas* featured articles on culture, current events, fashion, and home decoration, as well as interviews with people of interest to Spanish speakers in the United States. By the early 1990s, the magazine had a circulation of over 110,000 copies per month.

November 1, 1950 ◆ Puerto Rican nationalists made an attempt on President Truman.

Puerto Rican nationalists took their violent protest for independence to the mainland. In an attempt to assassinate President Harry S Truman, two Puerto Ricans attacked Blair House in Washington, D.C. (The Trumans were living there during a renovation of the White House.) One of the Puerto Ricans and a White House guard died, but Truman was not harmed.

1951–64 ◆ The Migratory Labor Agreement.

On July 12, 1951, the U.S. Congress passed Public Law 78, formalizing the *Bracero* Program as the Migratory Labor Agreement. (*Also see entry dated 1942–64: The* Bracero *Program.*) The new agreement brought an average of 350,000 Mexican workers to the United States per year until its end in 1964. The law was passed to address labor shortages during the Korean War and the needs of Southwestern agribusinesses. P.L. 78 gave the Secretary of Labor the power to recruit, transport, process, negotiate contracts for, and regulate the use of Mexican laborers. It also permitted contracts for undocumented workers who had lived in the United States for five years or more. Employers were supposed to repay the government for transportation costs and agree to minimum wage and working conditions. After years of complaints about the program and abuses by agribusinesses, the program was allowed to expire in 1964.

1951 ◆ Cuban stars in *I Love Lucy.*

Comedienne Lucille Ball and her husband Desi Arnaz, a Cuban-born singer and band leader, began their very popular television program, *I Love Lucy.* The program became a part of American culture during the 1950s and reruns are still popular today. But, it did nothing to counter the stereotypes of Hispanics. Arnaz, born in Santiago, Cuba, on March 2, 1917, had starred in Hollywood films during the 1940s. After his divorce from Ball in 1960, he stayed involved in the entertainment business through his production company. Arnaz died from lung cancer in 1986 in California.

1951 ◆ Minnie Miñoso led the major leagues in stolen bases.

Cuban-born Orestes "Minnie" Miñoso became the first Hispanic ballplayer to lead the U.S. major leagues in stolen bases (31). Miñoso made his professional debut with the New York Cubans of the Negro Leagues in 1948. He moved to the major league Cleveland Indians in 1949 when the color line was broken. Miñoso had a long career playing for various teams. In 1976, when he was a designated hitter for the Chicago White Sox, he became one of only six players to have been active in baseball for four decades.

1952 ✦ Anthony Quinn named best supporting actor.

Born on April 21, 1915, in Chihuahua, Mexico, of Irish-Mexican ancestry, Anthony Quinn has lived in the United States since childhood. In 1952, he won the best supporting actor Academy Award for his role in *Viva Zapata!* He won the Academy Award for best supporting actor again in 1956 for his role in *Lust for Life*.

1952 ✦ Land reform in Guatemala.

The government of Jacobo Arbenz Guzmán in Guatemala passed a decree that gave the government the power to redistribute land. (*Also see entry dated 1945: A social revolution in Guatemala.*) The government could seize abandoned and uncultivated lands and turn them over to peasants. This land reform proceeded rapidly. It even included the seizure of almost 420,000 acres from the powerful United Fruit Company. (*Also see entry dated 1890: The king of the Banana Republics.*) This land reform came to a halt in 1954, when Arbenz Guzmán was overthrown in a U.S.-supported coup. The program was then replaced with one designed to open up undeveloped lands for cultivation. (*Also see entry dated 1954: American intervention in Guatemala.*)

DESILU PRODUCTIONS

Desi Arnaz and Lucille Ball formed their own production company in 1950 called Desilu Productions (they combined their first names to come up with it.) *I Love Lucy* was their idea, but no television network would take on the show, believing that the 1950s American audience wouldn't accept Ball's marriage to a Cuban. CBS finally agreed to air the show if the couple paid for the making of the pilot ($5,000) with their own money. The show was an immediate success, and ran until 1959.

1952 ✦ The McCarran-Walter Act.

The United States Congress passed the Immigration and Nationality Act of 1952, also known as the McCarran-Walter Act. The act reaffirmed the basic features of the 1924 quota law, keeping limits on immigration from particular countries. There were no limits on immigration from the Western Hemisphere, however. The only exceptions were that applicants had to clear a long list of barriers devised to exclude homosexuals, Communists, and other "undesirables."

March 10, 1952 ✦ Batista returned to power in Cuba.

From his self-imposed exile in Florida, Fulgencio Batista sought to return to power in Cuba. When he realized he would lose the 1952 election, he seized power. As an arrogant dictator, Batista took Cuba to new heights of repression

Border patrol
agent finger-
printing an
undocumented
worker before
deporting him.

and corruption. A 26-year-old lawyer, Fidel Castro, pursued court action against Batista for violating six articles of the constitution. Castro demanded action from the judges or their resignations. Unsuccessful in court, Castro founded a small newspaper, *El Acusador* ("The Accusor"), to continue his attack on Batista. Castro eventually led a revolt against the dictator. (*Also see entries dated 1933–40: The Cuban military took control of the government; 1940–44: Batista served as president of Cuba; and July 26, 1953: Castro led an armed revolt against Batista.*)

July 25, 1952 ✦ Puerto Rico became the first U.S. Commonwealth.

The Commonwealth of Puerto Rico, in Spanish called the *Estado Libre Asociado* (Free Associated State), came into existence on this date. The relationship between the United States and Puerto Rico outlined in the island's new constitution remains in effect today. Under the commonwealth form of colonial government, Puerto Ricans remained U.S. citizens with all the rights of citizens, except the right to elect representatives and senators from the island to the U.S. Congress. Instead, Puerto Ricans could elect their own legislature. Under this arrangement, Puerto Rico could not conduct foreign policy, foreign commerce, or act in any other ways as an independent nation. However, its citizens were subject to federal taxes, military service, and other duties of citizens in the states. If Puerto Ricans take up residency in any of the U.S. states, they would have the full rights of citizenship, including the right to vote in all federal elections.

July 26, 1953 ✦ Castro led an armed revolt against Batista.

Fidel Castro (1926–) and his young revolutionaries began their armed struggle against dictator Fulgencio Batista with an assault on the Moncada military post near Santiago de Cuba. Castro's guerrillas were inexperienced and outnumbered 15 to 1. They suffered numerous casualties and took refuge in the mountains. Castro was later captured and sentenced to 15 years in prison. (*Also see entry dated March 10, 1952: Batista returned to power in Cuba.*)

1954–58 ✦ Operation Wetback forced Mexicans and Mexican Americans to return to Mexico.

During the mid-1950s, there was increased competition for jobs in the United

States. Under President Dwight D. Eisenhower, Attorney General Herbert Boswell, Jr., created a special mobile force to locate undocumented workers and encourage or force them to return to Mexico. These efforts became known as "Operation Wetback." In 1954 alone, Operation Wetback deported more than 1 million people of Mexican descent from the United States. By 1958, the United States had deported almost 3.8 million Mexicans and Mexican Americans. Very few of those forced to leave the United States were allowed deportation hearings before being deported. The vast majority of deportees went to Mexican border cities, causing many social problems. In addition to the deportees, thousands more U.S. citizens of Mexican descent were arrested and jailed.

1954 ◆ American intervention in Guatemala.

In 1950, the Communist Party gained influence in Guatemala and began to attack American-owned businesses. Among these companies was the United Fruit Company, a producer of bananas. A 1952 land reform law took unused lands from foreign owners and turned them over to small farmers. The United Fruit Company lost hundreds of thousands of acres of land. In May 1954, Washington protested the arms shipments that the Guatemalan government was receiving from the Soviet Union. Fearing the socialist programs of Guatemalan President Jacobo Arbenz Guzmán and the influence of the Soviet Union, the Central Intelligence Agency (CIA) of the United States supported a plan to overthrow Arbenz Guzmán with Guatemalan opposition forces. The CIA trained an army of about 300 men in Honduras and Nicaragua in early 1954. On June 18, the agency used its base at the U.S. embassy in Guatemala City to direct these forces. They entered the capital and attacked Arbenz Guzmán and his supporters. U.S. Ambassador John Puerifoy directed the air assault himself. Arbenz Guzmán finally fled the country on June 27. An interim government served until the September presidential election. At that time, Colonel Carlos Castillo Armas, who had led the coup d'etat, was elected to lead the country. Castillo Armas served as Guatemala's dictator until he was assassinated in July 1957. (*Also see entries dated 1890: The king of the Banana Republics; 1945: A social revolution in Guatemala; and 1952: Land reform in Guatemala.*)

1954 ◆ Avila won a major league batting title.

Mexican second baseman Roberto (Beto) Avila became the first Hispanic to win a batting championship in the U.S. major leagues. That year, for Cleveland, Avila batted .341, hit 15 home runs, drove in 67 runs, and scored 112 runs.

1954 ◆ Hispanic Americans were recognized as a separate minority.

In the landmark case of *Hernández v. Texas,* the Supreme Court of the United States recognized Hispanic Americans as a separate class of people, who suffered profound discrimination because of their national origin. Up to this time,

Hispanics had officially been recognized as "white." Because they were, therefore, not a separate minority class, they had not received the protections from discrimination offered other minorities. This case was the first Mexican American discrimination case to reach the Supreme Court. The court ruled that Pete Hernández, who had been convicted of murder, had been denied equal protection under the law because the jury selection process had excluded Mexican Americans. (In Jackson County, Texas, where the suit originated, no Mexican Americans had ever been selected for jury duty in the previous 25 years, despite the county's 14 percent Mexican American population.) The 1954 decision paved the way for Hispanic Americans to use legal means to attack all types of discrimination throughout the United States. It was also the first U.S. Supreme Court case to be argued by Mexican American attorneys.

1954 ◆ A new Panama Canal Zone treaty.
The United States and Panama signed a new Canal Zone treaty. The treaty raised the annual payment by the United States to Panama from $430,000 to $1,930,000, it provided the same wage scale for both American and Panamanian workers, it ceded property in Panama City to the Panamanian government, and it gave Panama the right to tax Canal Zone employees living in the zone.

1954 ◆ A Paraguayan dictator began his long reign.
General Alfredo Stroessner took power in Paraguay when he was elected to serve for four years as Paraguay's president. He later refused to give up power. Stroessner eventually became the longest-ruling dictator in Latin America, holding on to power in Paraguay until 1989.

1954 ◆ Puerto Rican nationalists attacked the U.S. Congress.
A group of nationalists led by Lolita Lebrón attacked the U.S. House of Representatives, hoping to bring national attention to the colonial status of Puerto Rico. The nationalists shot five congressmen. Lebrón and her followers, including Ramón Cancel Miranda, Irving Flores, and Oscar Collazo, were quickly arrested. Lebrón spent 25 years in federal prison without recanting. She has become a heroine for the Puerto Rican independence movement.

1955 ◆ The first Hispanic television station.
In the early 1950s, Hispanic Americans began to buy time on local television stations for Spanish-language programs. Cities with extensive Hispanic programming included New York City and San Antonio, Corpus Christi, and Harlingen, Texas. The first Spanish-language television station in the United States was San Antonio's KCOR-TV in San Antonio. It broadcast from 5:00 P.M. to midnight, offering live variety shows and prerecorded programs from Mexico.

1956 ◆ Aparicio named the American League Rookie of the Year.

Venezuelan short stop Luis Aparicio became the first Hispanic to be named Rookie of the Year for one of the U.S. major leagues. During this season for Baltimore, Aparicio drove in 56 runs, scored 69 runs, and led the leagues in stolen bases. (*Also see entry dated 1984: Aparicio inducted into baseball's Hall of Fame.*)

1956 ◆ Hispanic Americans at the Olympic Games.

The U.S. Winter Olympic team that traveled to Cortina d'Ampezzo, Italy, included the first Hispanic American to compete for the United States in the winter games. She was Catherine Machado, the U.S. Senior Women's Figure Skating champion. The U.S. Summer Olympic team that competed in Melbourne, Australia, included a record 11 Hispanic Americans. Among them was José Torres, who won a silver medal for boxing in the middleweight division. Torres later became a world professional boxing champion.

Memorial plaque honoring baseball great Luis Aparicio.

1956 ◆ Somoza Debayle took over Nicaragua.

Luis Anastasio Somoza Debayle became president of Nicaragua when his father, Anastasio Somoza, was assassinated. (*Also see entries dated 1937–56: Anastasio Somoza ruled Nicaragua; 1974: Somoza reelected; and 1980: Somoza assassinated.*)

December 2, 1956 ◆ Castro led a second attempt to overthrow Batista.

After he was released from prison as a part of a general pardon, Fidel Castro raised money from supporters in Miami, Tampa, and New York. With these funds, Castro went to Veracruz, Mexico, where he trained a small guerrilla force. On December 2, Castro landed in Cuba with 82 men. The rebels had been discovered from the air by a military plane, so the Cuban army was waiting for them when they arrived. On December 5, all but 12 of Castro's men were killed. Castro and the survivors took refuge in the mountains, where he built up his forces and led a propaganda campaign against Batista and the Cuban government. (*Also see entries dated March 10, 1952: Batista returned to power in Cuba; and July 26, 1953: Castro led an armed revolt against Batista.*)

1957 ✦ Land reform in Venezuela.

The government of Rómulo Betancourt in Venezuela began a well-organized program to redistribute land. First, the government bought land for prices as high as $30,000, paid part in cash and part in bonds. Then, a commission of representatives of all the interested parties redistributed the land. The government provided support and training to all those who received land. Not only did the government redistribute large quantities of land, it also raised the productivity of its farms.

1957 ✦ The 1957 Civil Rights Act.

The U.S. Congress passed its first civil rights legislation since the end of the Civil War, creating the Civil Rights Commission to investigate and report on violations of the law. Violations included denying voting rights for reasons of color, race, religion, or national origin. The commission was also charged with advising Congress on civil rights policies and laws.

1958 ✦ Vice President Nixon threatened in Venezuela.

Vice President Richard M. Nixon led a goodwill tour through eight countries in Latin America. Along the way, he met many protesters of U.S. economic imperialism and U.S. support for Latin American dictators. In Caracas, the capital of Venezuela, the protesters became violent and threatened Nixon's life. President Eisenhower put U.S. Marines and paratroopers on alert. Nixon sought refuge in the U.S. embassy in Caracas until the Venezuelan army gained control of the civilian disorder. Eisenhower's quick military response reminded many Latin American countries of the U.S. gunboat diplomacy (the nation's military supremacy backing the foreign relations of a weaker nation) of the late 1800s.

1959 ✦ Latin American free trade.

The Latin American Association for Free Commerce was founded by Argentina, Brazil, Chile, Mexico, Paraguay, Peru, and Uruguay. The goal of this group was to set up a free trade zone among the member nations that would become a common market. Ecuador and Colombia joined later. Despite the efforts of the association, trade barriers were slow to come down because several of the countries continued to protect their industries. Political unrest in several of the member countries also hurt the organization.

January 1, 1959 ✦ Castro replaced Batista.

After five years and five months of struggle, Fidel Castro's rebellion against the dictatorship of Fulgencio Batista succeeded. In the last days of 1958, Batista abandoned Cuba and went into exile in the Dominican Republic. The Cuban Revolution officially triumphed on New Year's Day. Castro, the leader of the revolution, had spent two years in jail, a year and a half in exile, and twenty-five

Richard Nixon and his wife, Pat, greet the crowd on one of his many foreign diplomatic trips during the late 1950s.

months in battle. On January 8, he marched into Havana at the head of his revolutionary army. At the capital, Castro announced the end of Batista's government, the army, the political parties, and the congress. (Many Cubans from these groups went into immediate exile, most in the United States.)

Nicholasa Mohr.

During the course of the year, Castro set up a revolutionary government. He also introduced numerous reforms. He nationalized industries, redistributed lands, and constructed schools and hospitals. Most of these reforms and new laws were dictated by Castro without debate or vote. Castro's dictatorial rule and his revolutionary ideals frightened the middle and upper classes of Cuba. Between 1959 and 1962, over 215,000 Cubans came to the United States, encouraged by U.S. government policies. The Eisenhower administration hoped that the Cubans coming to the U.S. would bring their money and skills, depriving Castro of the resources he needed to keep Cuba's economy going. The U.S. also believed that the Cuban exiles would show that people preferred democracy to communism. (*Also see entries dated March 10, 1952: Batista returned to power in Cuba; July 26, 1953: Castro led an armed revolt against Batista; and December 2, 1956: Castro led a second attempt to overthrow Batista.*)

May 17, 1959 ✦ Castro's Agrarian Reform Law.

This land reform law gave peasants the right to take over the lands on which they had worked or sharecropped. It limited each family to approximately 1,000 acres of farmland.

1960s ✦ The Chicano Movement began among Mexican Americans.

The 1960s and early 1970s were a time of social and political unrest in the United States. Caught up in this mood, young Mexican Americans throughout the country renewed the struggle for civil rights. They also sought to create a new identity for themselves. These efforts became known as the Chicano Movement. The term "Chicano" was originally used in the 1920s to label lower-class Mexican immigrants. In the 1940s and 1950s, it was used as a slang substitute for Mexicano. In the 1960s, Mexican Americans began to wear the name Chicano with pride. It offered them a way to recognize the separate culture and historical experience of Americans of Mexican descent.

The Chicano Movement sparked a renaissance in the arts among Mexican Americans. In literature, the theater, and art Mexican Americans questioned commonly accepted ideas and values. Through their works, they drew attention to the inequality faced by Mexican Americans throughout the country, but especially in the Southwest. They joined the political, economic, and educational struggle and used their works to inspire action. Eventually, these writers, playwrights, and artists made a place for themselves and their art in universities and in the mainstream literary and art scene.

1960s ◆ The rise of Nuyorican literature.

In the late 1960s, a group of poet-playwrights began meeting at the Nuyorican Poets' Café on the Lower East Side of New York. Together, they set out to define a new literature, by, for, and about Nuyoricans (Puerto Ricans born or raised in New York). They drew inspiration from Spanish and African oral traditions. Many who had started writing while in prison also drew on prison life for their writings. As their influence spread, so did Nuyorican literature. The best-known Nuyorican novelist of the 1970s and 1980s was Nicholasa Mohr. Her award-winning books reached beyond New York to a wide audience of mainstream American readers.

1960 ◆ Minnie Miñoso led the major leagues in hits.

Cuban Orestes "Minnie" Miñoso became the first Hispanic ballplayer to lead the U.S. major leagues in hits, with 184 hits for the Chicago White Sox. (*Also see entry dated 1951: Minnie Miñoso led the major leagues in stolen bases.*)

January 1960 ◆ Eisenhower aimed economic sanctions at Castro's Cuba.

President Dwight D. Eisenhower began to apply economic pressure against Cuba's increasingly radical government. The president requested that the U.S. Congress give him the power to reduce imports of Cuban sugar. Eisenhower continued to increase pressure throughout the spring. In May, he suspended all U.S. technical assistance to Cuba.

May 8, 1960 ◆ Cuba established ties with the U.S.S.R.

In response to American economic pressure, Castro and Cuba turned to the Soviet Union. The two countries established diplomatic and economic relations. Soon, Cuban sugar made its way to the Soviet Union in return for Soviet oil.

July 6, 1960 ◆ Cuba seized U.S. assets on the island.

Cuba passed Law 851 to seize and nationalize all property and businesses owned by U.S. citizens and interests. At this point, the United States recognized the Cuban government as a communist dictatorship.

1961 ◆ Aspira of America was founded.

Aspira, meaning "hope," was founded in the United States to promote the education of Hispanic youth by raising public and private sector funds. Aspira soon gathered a national following, serving Puerto Ricans wherever they lived in large numbers.

1961 ◆ Cepeda won the National League home run and RBI titles.

Puerto Rican Orlando Cepeda became the first Hispanic American home run champion in the U.S. major leagues. He hit 46 home runs for the San Francisco Giants. He also became the first Hispanic American to be the champion in runs batted in (RBIs) with 142. Cepeda had a good year overall, batting .311 with 182 hits and 105 runs scored.

1961 ◆ Rita Moreno named best supporting actress.

Born Rosita Dolores Alverio on December 11, 1931, in Humacao, Puerto Rico, Rita Moreno danced and sang her way to Broadway at age 13 and Hollywood at age 14. In 1961, she won the Academy Award as best supporting actress for her role in *West Side Story.* Moreno has appeared in several other films and television programs. She has won Emmy Awards for her performances on television.

1961 ◆ Trujillo Molina's dictatorship ended in the Dominican Republic.

Thirty years of dictatorship in the Dominican Republic came to an end when President Rafael Trujillo Molina, the nation's iron-fisted dictator, was assassinated. Juan Bosch was elected to lead the country in the 1962 elections. (*Also see entry dated 1930: Trujillo Molina seized power in the Dominican Republic.*)

March 13, 1961 ◆ The Alliance for Progress.

President John F. Kennedy announced the creation of the Alliance for Progress, an ambitious, $100 billion, ten-year program to bring political reform and social and economic progress to the Southern Hemisphere. The alliance's goals were expressed in the Charter of Punta del Este. It called for democracy, industrialization, land reforms, housing, education, and health care. The alliance failed to reach its goals because the leaders of the Latin American governments resisted social, political, and economic change. It also failed because the United States became more involved in Vietnam. By 1971, there was little to show for the effort. Many Latin Americans still lived under military control in countries with little social and economic opportunities.

April 1961 ◆ The Bay of Pigs invasion.

President Eisenhower had encouraged Cuban exiles to plan an invasion to overthrow Castro's government. President Kennedy inherited the plan and decided not to stop it. The Cuban exiles were trained and armed by the United States. However, when they launched their invasion, they received no direct military support from the United States, dooming the invasion from the beginning. The

Bay of Pigs failure angered thousands of Cubans living in exile. It also strengthened Castro's position at home. To many observers throughout the world (especially in the Third World), the invasion clearly showed U.S. intervention against a popular government. Two weeks after the Bay of Pigs failure, Castro officially announced that he was a Marxist-Leninist and would remain so until his death. The United States officially broke off diplomatic relations with Cuba.

1962 ✦ César Chávez led the United Farmworkers Organizing Committee.

César Chávez (1927–93) was born near Yuma, Arizona, to a family of migrant farm workers. As a boy, he attended almost 30 schools. He left school after receiving a seventh-grade education. After serving in the U.S. Navy during World War II, Chávez worked as a migrant farm worker. He settled down in 1948 in the *barrio* (Hispanic neigh-

César Chávez encouraging people to start a new grape boycott.

borhood) of *Sal Si Puedes* (Get Out If You Can) in San Jose, California. There, he began working as a community organizer for the Community Service Organization (CSO). By 1958, he had become general director of the CSO in California and Arizona. In 1962, he decided to turn his efforts toward organizing farm workers, so he moved to Delano, California, where he became head of the United Farmworkers Organizing Committee (UFWOC). This union would have a great impact on the working conditions of migrant farm workers in California. (*Also see entry dated September 16, 1965: The Delano grape strike.*)

1962 ✦ A dictator for El Salvador.

Colonel Julio Adalberto Rivera was elected president of El Salvador. He became a dictator, the first in a string of military dictators that controlled El Salvador until 1984.

April 21, 1962 ✦ Lightweight boxing champion, Carlos Ortiz.

Puerto Rico's Carlos Ortiz won the lightweight boxing championship from Joe Brown. He successfully defended his crown several times, but on April 10, 1965, he lost to Panama's Ismael Laguna. Ortiz recovered the title on November 13, 1965, in San Juan, Puerto Rico. Again he defended his crown until June 29, 1968, when he lost it to Dominican Carlos "Teo" Cruz. Ortiz was the second Puerto Rican boxer to win a world championship—Sixto Escobar had been the first. (*Also see entry dated August 31, 1936: Sixto Escobar became the bantam weight champion.*)

October 22, 1962 ◆ The Cuban Missile Crisis.

The relationship between Cuba and the United States had long been a rocky one. Cubans had struggled for over a century to be free from outside control. During the same time, Americans had tried to take advantage of the Cuban economy. The U.S. government had also tried to keep Cuba from falling into foreign hands and becoming a threat to American security. The Bay of Pigs invasion had caused the situation to worsen. Cuba feared another invasion and the United States and President John F. Kennedy still stung from the foreign policy failure.

Such was the situation when Cuba invited the Soviet Union to secretly build nuclear missile bases on the island. The United States discovered the plan and Kennedy ordered a blockade against Cuba, hoping to keep out additional missiles. For a short time, the United States and the Soviet Union seemed on the verge of nuclear war. Finally, however, Soviet premier Nikita Khrushchev agreed to remove the missiles from Cuba. On October 28, Kennedy promised Khrushchev in return that the United States would not invade Cuba. Moreover, it would not cooperate with any other nation in such an invasion. There would be no more Cuban missile crises and no more Bay of Pigs invasions. The only weapon the United States would have against Fidel Castro would be to encourage Cubans to leave the island and come to the United States.

The crisis angered Fidel Castro, who criticized Kennedy for violating Cuba's self-determination and sovereignty. In front of the United Nations, the Cuban leader stated that his country had a right to arm itself. (*Also see entry dated April 1961: The Bay of Pigs invasion.*)

1963 ◆ *El Diario de Nueva York* and *La Prensa* merged.

In 1961, O. Roy Chalk bought *El Diario de Nueva York* from Porfirio Domenicci, the Dominican who had founded the paper in 1948. Two years later, Chalk purchased *La Prensa* from Fortune Pope, its owner since 1957. Chalk merged the two newspapers into *El Diario-La Prensa,* creating New York City's most important Spanish-language daily. By the early 1990s, the newspaper had a circulation of over 50,000 on weekdays and over 35,000 for its weekend edition. (*Also see entries dated 1913:* La Prensa *was published in New York City; and 1948:* El Diario *was published in New York City.)*

1963 ◆ Mexican Americans asserted their political power in Texas.

In many cities in Texas, Mexican Americans were a majority of the population. Even so, they had rarely used their numbers to bring about political change. One city with a Hispanic majority was Crystal City, Texas. Here Mexican Americans made up 85 percent of the population. In 1963, the Hispanic community voted out the five Anglo city council members and elected five Mexican Americans. This election was the first big success for Hispanic political action in the United States. The new city government received support from the Teamsters Union at the local Del Monte cannery and the Political Association of Spanish-Speaking Organizations. With this help, it made important reforms, despite Anglo opposition.

A second Hispanic political surge took place in 1969. The second wave of Mexican American leaders made greater, more successful reforms. The success of political action and protest against discrimination in Crystal City schools led some local Hispanics to create their own political party in 1971. The *Raza Unida* Party (United Hispanic People's Party) expanded very quickly throughout Texas under the leadership of José Angel Gutiérrez. Crystal City soon became the first city in the United States to have a Chicano party controlling the local government. Later, the Raza Unida won a majority of the seats in the Zavala County government and representation in other areas. By 1981, however, the party had lost much of its support. The Democratic Party had won over many Mexican Americans by including issues of interest to Hispanics. The Crystal City experience and the Raza Unida Party were key factors in forcing the Democrats and Republicans to take Hispanics into account. (*Also see entry dated January 17, 1971: The* Raza Unida *Party was founded.*)

Cover of *Réplica* magazine.

1963 ◆ *Réplica* was founded.

Alex Lesnik, a Cuban immigrant to Miami, started a monthly magazine to reach bilingual/bicultural policy makers in the United States. *Réplica* featured articles on travel, fashion, sports, entertainment, and news from the Caribbean and Latin America. By the early 1990s, the magazine reached over 110,000 readers monthly.

July 15, 1963 ◆ Juan Marichal pitched a no-hitter.

Dominican pitcher Juan Marichal became the first Hispanic to throw a no-hitter in the U.S. major leagues. Pitching for the San Francisco Giants, he beat Houston 1–0 on this date. (*Also see entry dated 1983: Marichal joined baseball's Hall of Fame.*)

September, 1963 ◆ The *Alianza Federal de los Pueblos Libres.*

After the Anglo settlement of the American Southwest in the mid-1800s, many of the Hispanics living in New Mexico and Arizona lost their lands. In 1963, Reies López Tijerina started an organization in Albuquerque, New Mexico, to help Hispanic Americans reclaim the lands taken away from their ancestors. The *Alianza Federal de los Pueblos Libres* (Federal Alliance of Free Towns) worked through the courts to recover these lands. By 1965, the Alianza reported 20,000 members (mostly small farmers and ranchers who were losing the right to graze their livestock on federal land). When the public actions of some of the members turned to vandalism and arson, police began to clamp down. The Alianza disbanded early in 1967, but was reformed later in June of the same year. However, the police and court officials still tried to break it up. After an Alianza meeting was broken up by the district attorney, the organization raided the courthouse in Tierra Amarilla, New Mexico, on June 5, 1967. The raid was celebrated by Chicano militants throughout the Southwest. Tijerina was arrested and convicted for his role as leader of the militants, and he was sent to prison in 1970. He was released in 1971 and finished his five-year probation in 1976. At that time, he returned to the presidency of the Alianza.

1964 ◆ The Civil Rights Act of 1964.

This legislation, passed by Congress and signed by the president, was the first major civil rights law since the post-Civil War Reconstruction (1865–77). The act established affirmative action programs to protect and improve minority opportunities. Title VII of the Civil Rights Act of 1964 addressed job discrimination. It prohibited discrimination on the basis of gender, creed, race, or ethnic background, "to achieve equality of employment opportunities and remove barriers that have operated in the past." Discrimination was prohibited in advertising, recruitment, hiring, job classification, promotion, discharge, wages and salaries, and other terms and conditions of employment. Title VII also established the Equal Employment Opportunity Commission (EEOC) as a monitor to find and prevent job discrimination.

1964 ◆ The end of the *Bracero* Program.

The *Bracero* Program, which had brought Mexican workers to the United States starting in 1942, ended in 1964. There followed a brief decline in Mexican immigration. However, workers from Mexico soon began to come to the United States under the guidelines of the Immigration and Nationality Act of 1952. Many other Mexicans immigrated under family unification guidelines or as undocumented workers. During the 1960s, immigration from Mexico rose to 13.3 percent of the total number of immigrants to the United States. (*Also see entries dated 1942–64: The* Bracero *Program; and 1952: The McCarran-Walter Act.*)

1964 ✦ Oliva became a major league leader in his first season.

Cuban-born baseball player Tony Oliva earned the American League Rookie of the Year award for his outstanding year with the Minnesota Twins. He became the first Hispanic to win the U.S. major league scoring title, with 109 runs. He was also the leader in hits (217), doubles (43), and batting average (.323). When he led the league in batting average the following year, he became the first player to win the batting crown in his first two major league seasons. He went on to win it again in 1971.

Tony Oliva.

1964 ✦ The War on Poverty.

For decades, poverty, and discrimination had limited the opportunities of many in American society. In 1964, President Lyndon B. Johnson launched his War on Poverty. The U.S. Congress and the president passed programs to give social, economic, and educational opportunities to all segments of the society. The Economic Opportunity Act (EOA) of 1964 was the centerpiece of the War on Poverty. The EOA also created the Office of Economic Opportunity (OEO) to head up several programs for the nation's poor. These programs included the Job Corps, the Community Action Program (CAP), and the Volunteers in Service to America (VISTA).

July 1964 ✦ The OAS cut ties with Cuba.

The Organization of American States (OAS) met in Washington, D.C., voting to cut diplomatic and commercial relations with Cuba and to impose restrictions on travel there. The OAS made exceptions for food and medical supplies. The Latin American members agreed to this U.S. policy because many of their governments feared a revolution similar to Cuba's.

1965 ✦ The first limits on immigration from the Americas.

The United States revised the Immigration and Nationality Act of 1952. In doing so, it abolished the quota system and placed a limit on immigration from the Western Hemisphere for the first time. The new law became effective in 1968.

1965 ✦ Hispanic theater of and for the workers.

Luis Valdez (1940–) founded the most important and long-standing Hispanic theater, *El Teatro Campesino* (The Farm Theater), among the farm workers of California. Valdez was born into a family of migrant workers in Delano, Cali-

Luis Valdez.

fornia. Even though his education was regularly interrupted by the demands of migrant farm work, he graduated from high school and from San Jose State University in 1964. He then spent some time learning agit-prop (agitation and propaganda) theater with the San Francisco Mime Troupe. In 1965, he took his skills and placed them at the service of César Chávez and the farm workers union.

In the fields of California, Valdez brought together college students, farm workers, and drama to publicize the working conditions of migrant workers. Valdez's Teatro inspired a theatrical movement in fields and *barrios* (Hispanic neighborhoods) across the country. For this reason, many call Valdez the father of Chicano theater. For nearly three decades, El Teatro Campesino and Luis Valdez have dramatized the political and cultural concerns of Hispanics. At first, he directed productions among workers and their supporters. Later, Valdez took his theater to students in universities and to the general public through mainstream theater, television, and film.

1965 ◆ President Johnson sent the marines to the Dominican Republic.
Fidel Castro's revolution in Cuba had given the United States a communist neighbor. It also raised fears in the U.S. government that other Caribbean nations might follow the same course and turn to communism. Juan Bosch, who had been elected president of the Dominican Republic in 1962, seemed to be moving his country closer and closer toward communism. The Dominican military took action in 1963 and overthrew Bosch's government. The generals picked three men to run the country, of which Donald Reid Cabral held the most power. However, the public protested against Cabral and created political unrest throughout the country.

In 1965, a group of younger military officers who supported Bosch overthrew Cabral's government. Still fearful that Bosch would turn toward communism, older military officers resisted. U.S. president Lyndon B. Johnson responded to the Dominican civil war by sending in the U.S. Marines. He stated that he hoped to prevent another Cuba—another communist revolution. The U.S. action was sharply criticized by many of the Latin American countries. Eventually, the United States arranged an election for the Dominican Republic. Joaquín Balaguer was elected to guide the U.S.-controlled democratic

A *maquiladora* plant at the Texas-Juarez border.

experiment. (*Also see entry dated 1961: Trujillo Molina's dictatorship ended in the Dominican Republic.*)

1965 ◆ The rise of *maquiladoras*.

Between 1942 and 1964, the *Bracero* Program brought hundreds of thousands of Mexican manual laborers and farm workers to the United States to work each year. When the program ended in 1964, many Mexicans were forced to return to Mexico. Many settled in northern Mexico near the U.S. border. Because there were few jobs in this area, the influx of unemployed braceros threatened to cause economic and political problems for the border region. As a result, the Mexican and U.S. governments looked for ways to create more jobs in the border area. In 1965, Mexico launched the *Programa Nacional Fronterizo* (National Border Program). Five years later, Mexico started the Border Industrialization Program. These programs allowed foreign corporations to build and operate assembly plants on the border. These plants, known as *maquiladoras,* multiplied rapidly and transformed the border region in Mexico and the United States.

The maquiladoras attracted U.S. and multinational companies because they provided cheap labor close to American markets. These companies could also take advantage of weak labor unions, weak environmental laws, and cooperative Mexican officials. As they grew in size and number, these maquiladoras employed hundreds of thousands of Mexicans, mostly women, in assembly work. By the late 1980s, they had become Mexico's second most important generator of foreign exchange. This meant that the maquiladoras helped Mexico reduce its foreign debt, especially to the United States.

On the negative side, maquiladoras did not adequately improve the border towns and cities in Mexico. These cities did not create the sanitation and social services, schools, and hospitals necessary for their growing populations. As a result, many of these cities saw an increase in health risks and disease. Many in the United States believed that maquiladoras led to the loss of American jobs and the weakening of labor unions. (*Also see entries dated 1942–64: The* Bracero *Program; and 1964: The end of the* Bracero *Program.*)

1965 ✦ The Voting Rights Act of 1965.

The U.S. Congress passed the Voting Rights Act of 1965 primarily to protect and assist African Americans in the South in participating in the political process. It also helped other minorities to vote. Therefore, the act offered great promise for Hispanic American voting rights.

1965 ✦ A wave of Cuban immigration began.

Fidel Castro announced in 1965 that Cubans with relatives in the United States could emigrate there. However, he required Cubans already in Florida to come and get their relatives at Camarioca Bay. Boats of all types sailed from Miami to Camarioca and back, filled with Cubans eager to rejoin their families. Many of the boats were in poor condition, making the trip dangerous. When a number of boats sank, an airlift was organized to offer a safer journey. These flights continued until 1973. (*Also see entry dated 1966–73: The Cuban airlift.*)

September 16, 1965 ✦ The Delano Grape Strike.

César Chávez directed the United Farm Workers Organizing Committee (UFWOC) to join a labor strike started by Filipino grape pickers in Delano, California. Chávez and his organization successfully turned the strike into a movement for social justice for farm workers. This movement especially benefitted Mexican and Mexican American farm workers who were the majority of pickers.

For the next decade, Chávez's union organized strikes and national boycotts as well as court cases and legislative action in California. These efforts made it the largest farm worker union in the country. It soon turned its attention from table grapes to lettuce to other crops. The UFWOC eventually won from growers better wages and working conditions, safer use of pesticides, and the right to unionize and strike. Because of its nonviolent approach, including hunger strikes and crusades, the UFWOC was also able to win the support of national leaders, such as Robert F. Kennedy, the Catholic Conference of Bishops, and organized labor. When César Chávez died in 1993, he was mourned in the United States as a national hero. (*Also see entry dated 1962: César Chávez led the United Farmworkers Organizing Committee.*)

1966–73 ◆ The Cuban airlift.

After a number of boats carrying Cuban exiles to Miami sank, a program was started to transport Cubans to the United States by airplane. The airlift was stopped by Fidel Castro in 1973 after having brought over 250,000 Cubans to the United States (about 10 percent of the island's population). (*Also see entry dated 1965: A wave of Cuban immigration began.*)

1966 ◆ The Crusade for Justice was founded.

One of the most successful Mexican American civil rights organizations, the Crusade for Justice, was founded in Denver, Colorado, by Rodolfo "Corky" Gonzales, a former boxer. The organization worked for better housing, education, and jobs for Hispanics in and around Colorado's capital city. As part of its efforts, the Crusade bought a building and converted it into a multipurpose community center, including classrooms, a gym, a nursery, and a library. During the late 1960s, the Crusade led protest marches and walkouts against the Denver public schools to bring about better educational opportunities.

Chicano protest march for better employment and fair housing in El Paso, Texas.

From March 27 to 31, 1969, the Crusade sponsored the first national Chicano Youth Liberation Conference. The conference explored the political, economic, and educational concerns of Chicanos. It also drafted a document which represented the nationalistic sentiments of Chicanos: *El Plan Espiritual de Aztlán* (The Spiritual Plan of Aztlán). The plan called for economic, political, social, and educational independence for Chicanos in their homeland, Aztlán (the states of the American Southwest, believed to be the birthplace of Aztec civilization).

During the late 1960s and early 1970s, the Crusade for Justice outlined the demands, philosophy, and policies that were essential to the Chicano Movement. Corky Gonzales wrote a widely distributed epic poem, *Yo soy Joaquín* ("I Am Joaquín"), which eloquently expressed the history and hopes of Chicanos.

1966 ◆ Puerto Ricans rioted in Chicago.

Hundreds of Chicago Puerto Rican youths went on a rampage, breaking windows and burning down many businesses in their neighborhoods. The immediate cause for the riot was an incident of police brutality. However, many other factors, including the poverty, unemployment, and poor housing, also contributed.

1966 ◆ **The Supreme Court struck down Texas barriers to voting.**
The Texas poll tax, which had prevented many minorities from voting, was declared unconstitutional.

1967–69 ◆ **Important Hispanic theater companies were founded in New York.**
In the late 1960s, New York City's three most important Hispanic theater companies were set up to serve Hispanic playwrights and audiences. The Puerto Rican Traveling Theater began performing in the streets of Puerto Rican neighborhoods in 1967. Over the years, it has staged plays in both Spanish and English by prominent Puerto Rican, Spanish, and Latin American playwrights. It opened a permanent theater house in the Broadway area on 47th Street in 1974. INTAR was founded in 1967 (then known as ADAL). In its West 42nd Street theater near Broadway, INTAR built a following for its new approaches to classical plays. It also supported Hispanic playwrights through readings and workshops. The *Teatro Repertorio Español* was founded in 1969. It set out to offer both classical Spanish and contemporary Latin American plays from its location at the Gramercy Arts Theater and through touring companies.

1967 ◆ *El grito* **was launched.**
The influential Chicano literary magazine *El grito* was founded to promote Chicano writers and shape Chicano literature. Together with its publishing house, Editorial Quinto Sol, the magazine tried to publish the best examples of Chicano culture, language, themes, and styles. The 1968 anthology *El espejo* ("The Mirror"), which featured the writing of Tomás Rivera, Miguel Méndez, and Rolando Hinojosa, reflected the literature of the magazine.

1967 ◆ **Language education required.**
The U.S. Congress passed legislation that required schools to provide programs for children with limited English-speaking ability. These programs included bilingual classrooms (classes taught in both Spanish and English) and English as a second language instruction. By 1971, there were 450 full- or part-time teachers of bilingual education and/or English as a second language in New York City. They worked with 122,000 Hispanic children.

1967 ◆ **Rosie Casals, champion tennis player.**
The daughter of Salvadoran immigrants to the United States, Rosemary Casals joined Billie Jean King in winning the doubles tennis championship at Wimbledon, England. The pair went on to win the Wimbledon doubles crown another four times. King and Casals also won the U.S. Open doubles championship twice at Forest Hills, New York.

1968 ✦ The Civil Rights Act of 1968.

The U.S. Congress passed the Civil Rights Act of 1968, which, among other things, prohibited discrimination in housing and made promoting riots a federal crime.

1968 ✦ A new dictator for Panama.

General Omar Torrijos overthrew the civil government in Panama and began a dictatorship. Torrijos's rule lasted until 1981, when he died in a plane crash.

1968 ✦ The Mexican American Legal Defense and Education Fund.

The Ford Foundation established the Mexican American Legal Defense and Education Fund to protect the civil rights of Mexican Americans. The fund used its resources to inform Mexican Americans about their legal rights and to help them prepare court cases.

1968 ✦ The Summer Olympic Games were held in Mexico City.

For the first time in history, the Olympics were held in Latin America. Almost every country in Latin America sent a team to Mexico City, and the Latin American athletes from Mexico and Argentina performed well, winning medals in the swimming, diving, and kayak competitions.

1969 ✦ A border war between Honduras and El Salvador.

The establishment of the Central American Common Market in the 1960s led to economic growth and improved social conditions in the region. However, a border war between Honduras and El Salvador led to the collapse of the common market. Economic conditions in Central America soon declined rapidly. The war also forced many Salvadorans living in Honduras to give up their lands. The war lasted until 1980.

February 18, 1969 ✦ Armando Ramos became the world lightweight boxing champion.

Mexican American boxer Armando Ramos won the world lightweight championship from Carlos Cruz in Los Angeles. On February 19, 1972, Ramos defeated Pedro Carrasco to claim the World Boxing Congress lightweight championship.

October 2, 1969 ✦ Violence preceded the Olympics in Mexico City.

Just before the Olympic Games, demonstrators began protesting the lack of democracy in Mexico, especially in the workings of the dominant *Partido Revolucionario Institucional* (Institutional Revolutionary Party). The protesters, mostly students, gathered at the Plaza of the Three Cultures in Tlaltelolco, Mexico City. There the Mexican army and the police opened fire on the protesters, killing several dozen people.

141

Salvador Allende waves to cheering crowds on the way to a military parade in his honor, November 4, 1970.

1970s–80s ◆ Latin American economic and political problems fueled immigration to the United States.

During the 1970s and 1980s, brutal dictators and military governments took power in Argentina, Brazil, Chile, Peru, El Salvador, and Guatemala. Most of these governments feared the spread of communism among their people. Political and civil rights were trampled, and the militaries acted on the slightest suspicion to arrest, torture, exile, or kill thousands of their countrymen. In other Latin American countries, economic turmoil pushed people to leave their homelands for opportunities in the United States.

Many of these new Latin American immigrants lacked the documents needed to give them legal status in the United States. With the increase in immigration, Immigration and Naturalization Service (INS) commissioner Leonard Chapman called for more money and power for his agency. He claimed that there were as many as 12 million undocumented workers in the country. Other observers placed the number in the range of 3.5 million to 5 million people.

One problem for undocumented immigrants was a U.S. foreign policy that supported the dictatorships in Latin America. Immigrants from these countries could not be considered political refugees under INS policy. This policy especially affected the many Salvadorans and Guatemalans who sought asylum in the United States. Because the U.S. government policy refused to help these people, many American churches acted to smuggle, support, and give asylum to refugees from El Salvador and Guatemala.

1970 ✦ The Congress protected minority voting rights.
The U.S. Congress approved an amendment to the landmark Voting Rights Act of 1970 designed to overcome new and inventive barriers to voting. It required federal approval of all changes to voting procedures in certain areas, most of which were in the South. This act prevented states from diluting the votes of blacks, Hispanics, or other minorities by rearranging voting districts.

1970 ✦ Hispanic Americans in the census.
The 1970 U.S. Census showed that 82 percent of Hispanic Americans lived in just nine states. (By 1990, the proportion would rise to 86 percent.) The states were California, Arizona, New Mexico, Colorado, Texas, New York, New Jersey, Florida, and Illinois. Most new Hispanic immigrants were going to California, Texas, and New York.

1970 ✦ Reverse discrimination challenged affirmative action.
Opponents of affirmative action in the United States coined the term "reverse discrimination" to argue against government programs to help women and minorities. They suggested that white males were being denied opportunities because of programs that offered jobs, education, and special treatment to women, blacks, Hispanics, and other under-represented groups.

August 1970 ✦ The Salinas Lettuce Strike.
Strikes by César Chávez and the United Farmworkers Organizing Committee (UFWOC) against table grape growers succeeded. The union signed contracts with most of California's Central Valley table grape growers. Next, the union chose to take on the Salinas Valley lettuce growers. In an effort to get around the strike, about 70 growers signed special "sweetheart" contracts with another union, the International Brotherhood of Teamsters. Even with the Teamster contracts, however, over 7,000 farm workers went on strike in August. In September, the UFWOC launched a national boycott of lettuce.

This labor struggle continued through 1974. The UFWOC continued its strikes and boycotts. It also continued its power struggle with the Teamsters Union. Finally in 1974, newly elected governor Jerry Brown directed the passage of the California Agriculture Labor Relations Act. Under this law, union elections could be held by workers. In these elections, the UFWOC, which had been renamed the United Farm Workers (UFW), won 65 percent of the vote and regained many lost contracts. In 1977, the UFW and Teamsters resolved

Chicano antiwar protest turns violent, August 29, 1970.

their dispute. However, the lettuce boycott did not end until February 1978. Success in unionizing the lettuce fields came in September 1979. At that time, the UFW signed contracts with California's major lettuce growers.

August 29, 1970 ✦ Chicanos protested the Vietnam War.

In Los Angeles, more than 20,000 Chicanos and their supporters protested against the Vietnam War. The demonstrators announced a Chicano Moratorium to draw attention to the disproportionately high number of Chicano casualties in that war. Then they led a march from Belvedere to Laguna Park. Along the way, police moved to break up the rally in response to rock and bottle throwing. At Laguna Park, where leaders were giving speeches, the police broke up the proceedings with tear gas. For the next two hours the police and demonstrators battled for control of the situation. Rubén Salazar, a journalist who was not involved in the struggle, was accidentally killed by police. Salazar's death became a symbol of police brutality and the suppression of Hispanic civil rights.

November 3, 1970 ✦ Allende sworn in as president of Chile.

When Salvador Allende (1903–73) was elected president of Chile, he became the first freely elected Marxist head of state in Latin America. His goal was to socialize the economy. He began with a government takeover of the copper industries, which were controlled by U.S. businesses—a symbolic act against the United States. Soon afterward, Allende took action in other segments of the foreign-dominated economy. In an effort to win the support of workers, he froze prices and ordered large wage increases. He started a land reform program. He also tried to change the national legislature so that it would better represent the common people rather than the elite.

Allende's programs were quickly opposed by foreign-owned companies, Chilean landowners, and the middle class. Many workers criticized Allende because they could not keep up with rising costs and shortages of goods. The U.S. policy toward Chile made the situation worse. President Richard M. Nixon cut U.S. trade relations, forbade private bank loans, and prevented loans from the Inter-American and World Banks. Soon the country was racked by political protest, labor discord, and a general strike. This unrest led to a CIA-organized military coup d'etat (government overthrow) and the assassination of Allende in September 1973. (*Also see entry dated September 11, 1973: Allende assassinated.*)

1971 ✦ Bañuelos named treasurer of the United States.

President Richard Nixon chose Romana Acosta Bañuelos to be the treasurer of the United States. She was the first Mexican American and the sixth woman to hold that post. Bañuelos served as treasurer from December 1971 to February 1974. After her government service, she returned to her business activities.

Bañuelos was born in Miami, Arizona, to parents who were undocumented workers there. During the Great Depression of the 1930s, U.S. officials forced many Mexican workers to return to Mexico. Bañuelos and her parents were among those repatriated in 1931. She grew up in Mexico, but moved back to the United States at age 19 and settled in Los Angeles. In 1949, she started a small tortilla factory with $400. Twenty years later, Romana's Mexican Food Products produced dozens of food items, employed hundreds of workers, and earned $12 million per year. She helped found the Pan American Bank in Los Angeles and served as a director and chairwoman.

1971 ✦ Davidovsky won the Pulitzer Prize for his music.

Composer Mario Davidovsky won the Pulitzer Prize for his "Sincronism No. 6." Born in Buenos Aires, Argentina, in 1934, Davidovsky was teaching at Princeton University in New Jersey when he won the award.

1971 ✦ Treviño dominated men's professional golf.

Lee Treviño (1939–) won his second U.S. Open Golf Tournament in 1971. He won six other tournaments that year, including the British Open, which he won again a year later. For his year-round performance in 1971, Treviño was named

Lee Treviño bites his golf club in frustration after just missing a birdie putt, May 31, 1980.

the Professional Golfer's Association (PGA) Player of the Year, the Associated Press Athlete of the Year, and the *Sports Illustrated* Sportsman of the Year. Treviño retired from the PGA tour in 1985, with 34 victories and total career earnings of over $3 million. He was elected to the Texas Sports Hall of Fame, the American Golf Hall of Fame, and the World Golf Hall of Fame.

January 17, 1971 ◆ The *Raza Unida* Party was founded.

A Chicano political party, the *Raza Unida* Party (United Hispanic People's Party) was founded by 300 Chicanos in Crystal City, Texas. The party's first major victory was winning the city elections in Crystal City in 1971. By 1972, the Raza Unida Party had chapters in 17 states and the District of Columbia. On Labor Day of that same year, it held its first national convention in El Paso, Texas. The delegates elected José Angel Gutiérrez as their first president.

The Raza Unida Party was successful in some local and county elections during the 1970s (principally in Texas). However, the real, long-lasting success of the party was its influence on the Democratic Party. Because of the efforts of the

Raza Unida Party, Democrats began to pay attention to Mexican American issues and to run Mexican American candidates. (*Also see entry dated 1963: Mexican Americans asserted their political power in Texas.*)

August 1971 ◆ Court action forced California to reform school financing.

John Serrano, a father in predominantly Hispanic East Los Angeles, filed a lawsuit against the California State Treasurer. Serrano charged that his son was receiving an inferior education because East Los Angeles was a poor area and its schools were financed by local property taxes. In *Serrano v. Priest,* the California courts found that financing schools through local property taxes did not provide equal protection under the law. Therefore, the court ordered, the financing system had to be changed. The court's decision was upheld in April 1974 and December 1977 (California Supreme Court). As a result of the decision, the California state legislature mandated that income taxes be used for financing education.

Roberto Clemente.

1972 ◆ Baseball's Roberto Clemente died taking aid to Nicaraguan earthquake victims.

One of the greatest baseball players of all time, Roberto Clemente, was born on August 18, 1934, in Carolina, Puerto Rico. He rose from poverty to become a star outfielder for the Pittsburgh Pirates from 1955 to 1972. He helped the Pirates win two World Series, in 1960 and 1971. As a player, Clemente won the National League batting championship four times, in 1961, 1964, 1965, and 1967. He was voted the league's Most Valuable Player in 1966. He won twelve Golden Gloves and set a major league record in leading the National League in assists five times. He played on fourteen all-star teams. By 1972, he had accumulated 240 home runs and a lifetime batting average of .317. He had also joined the exclusive club of players who had 3,000 or more hits during their careers.

Clemente looked ahead to more years in baseball. But he died in a plane crash while taking relief supplies to victims of an earthquake in Nicaragua. When he died, the Baseball Hall of Fame immediately elected him to membership. (To do so, it waived its usual five-year waiting period after a player's retirement.) Puerto Ricans consider Roberto Clemente a national hero for his generosity, leadership, outstanding athletic achievements, and heroism.

1972 ✦ *Bless Me, Ultima.*

Rudolfo Anaya's novel about a boy's coming of age was first published by a Chicano publishing house in 1972. Since that time, it has reached more non-Chicano readers than any other Chicano literary work. In 1994, Anaya finally received recognition from mainstream publishers when Warner Books agreed to publish six of the author's books, including *Bless Me, Ultima.*

1972 ✦ Land reform in the Dominican Republic.

In 1960, there were some 450,000 farmers in the Dominican Republic. Even so, the richest 1 percent owned over 50 percent of the land. In 1962, land reform laws were passed and the *Instituto Agrario Dominicano* (Dominican Agrarian Institute) was founded to carry out reform. However, throughout the 1960s, the land remained concentrated in a few hands. By 1972, economic, political, and social pressures had grown strong enough to force reform. The country badly needed more agricultural output. Peasant groups came together to create political pressure. The Catholic Church supported reform from the pulpit through teachings called liberation theology. Under this pressure, the Dominican government passed a reform law in which the government seized much private land, most of it used for growing rice. Over the next ten years, more than 32,000 individuals received an average of 5.3 hectares (approximately 13 acres) of farm land. Another 16,000 shared land in 118 collectives, with an average of 4 hectares (approximately 10 acres) per individual. During this period, the government carried out two-thirds of its redistribution project. Today, farms created through land reform produce about one-third of the Dominican Republic's rice.

1972 ✦ Molina became dictator of El Salvador.

Despite growing opposition to military dictatorships and demands from the poor for land and jobs, El Salvador elected another dictator, Colonel Arturo Armando Molina.

May 3, 1972 ✦ Hispanic workers joined the strike against Farah.

Hispanic and other workers launched a strike against the Farah Manufacturing Company in El Paso, Texas. They also organized a national boycott of the company's products. The strikers were represented by the Amalgamated Clothing Workers of America, but the union was not recognized by the owner, William Farah. After numerous unfair labor practices and anti-boycott lawsuits, the strike came to an end in February 1974. At that time two-thirds of the workers voted to have the union represent them.

1973 ✦ Job discrimination against non-citizens.

Mexican workers often faced discrimination in U.S. factories. Their lack of citizenship rights was used against them. In 1973, an employee of the Farah Manufacturing Company charged the clothing maker with discrimination of this type, claiming that the Civil Rights Act of 1964 protected him from job discrimination. In *Espinoza v. Farah Manufacturing Company*, however, the Supreme Court ruled in favor of the company. It held that Title VII, the equal employment opportunity provision of the Civil Rights Act of 1964, did not offer protection against discrimination on the basis of citizenship or alienage (foreign nationality).

1973 ✦ A new union to protect Hispanic workers.
The Labor Council of Latin American Advancement (LCLAA) was formed to promote the interests of Hispanics within organized labor.

1973 ✦ *Revista Chicano-Riqueña* appeared.
The Hispanic literary magazine *Revista Chicano-Riqueña* ("Chicano-Rican Review") was founded and soon developed a following in American universities. It was edited by Nicolás Kanellos and Luis Dávila.

1973 ✦ School funding was challenged in the courts.
Poor schools in poor neighborhoods continued to deprive schoolchildren, most of whom were from minority groups, of educational opportunities. Many charged that this problem was caused by the school funding system. In most states, schools raised most of their money from local property taxes. In poor neighborhoods, there was not as much money to collect. A lawsuit brought on behalf of poor schoolchildren in San Antonio, Texas, sought to change the situation. It charged that the school funding system was unconstitutional because it denied children equal protection under the law guaranteed in the Fourteenth Amendment to the U.S. Constitution. In *San Antonio Independent School District v. Rodríguez*, the U.S. Supreme Court of the United States ruled in favor of the school district. It held that the system did not violate the Fourteenth Amendment. In a 5–4 decision, the court ruled that education is not a fundamental right and poverty is not a reason to hold otherwise. (*Also see entry dated August 1971: Court action forced California to reform school financing.*)

1973 ✦ U.N. support for Puerto Rican independence.
The United Nations approved a resolution that officially recognized Puerto Rico as a colony of the United States. It also resolved that the Puerto Rican people had the right to decide their own future as a nation. The act was of great support to the independence movement on the island and in the United States.

September 11, 1973 ✦ Allende assassinated.
The Chilean military (army, navy, air force, and national police) staged a bloody coup d'etat (overthrow of the government) during which Socialist President Salvador Allende was killed. The military acted with support from the U.S. Central

A rally in support of Puerto Rican independence in East Lower Harlem (El Barrio) in Manhattan.

Intelligence Agency (CIA). A military dictatorship led by General Augusto Pinochet took Allende's place. Pinochet began exiling, imprisoning, and executing his opponents, many of whom were students. (*Also see entry dated 1970: Allende was elected president of Chile.*)

1974 ✦ *Chico and the Man.*
Comic Freddie Prinze brought a Hispanic character to network television. Prinze's streetwise Chico played on stereotypes of Hispanics and relationships with prejudiced Anglos. The show was on the air until Prinze committed suicide in 1977.

1974 ✦ **Cordero rode to victory in the Kentucky Derby.**
Puerto Rican jockey Angel Cordero reached the winner's circle at the 1974 Kentucky Derby. Cordero went on to win the Derby again in 1976 and 1985. He also

won the Preakness Stakes in 1980 and 1985, and the Belmont Stakes in 1976. In 1982, he was named Jockey of the Year.

1974 ✦ Educational reforms for non-native speakers of English.

The fight to improve the education of schoolchildren in the United States who did not speak English as a native language continued in the courts and in Congress. Supporters of Kenny Lau, a student who did not speak English, brought a lawsuit against the San Francisco Unified School District. In January 1974 in the case *Lau v. Nichols*, the U.S. Supreme Court held that the school district discriminated against Lau. It discriminated by not providing a program to deal with Lau's inability to speak English. The school district thereby deprived Lau of the opportunity to participate in school. This Supreme Court decision gave a push to bilingual education programs across the country.

The U.S. Congress also passed the Equal Educational Opportunity Act of 1974 to create equality in public schools. Its most important goal was to make bilingual education available to Hispanic youth. The lawmakers who framed the act argued that equal education meant more than equal facilities and equal access to teachers. Students having trouble with the English language had to be given programs to help them overcome their language difficulties. (*Also see entry dated 1967: Language education required.*)

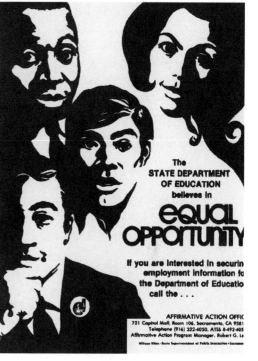

The
STATE DEPARTMENT
OF EDUCATION
believes in

equal opportunity

If you are interested in securing employment information for the Department of Education call the . . .

AFFIRMATIVE ACTION OFFICE
721 Capitol Mall, Room 106, Sacramento, CA 95814
Telephone (916) 322-6050. ATSS 8-492-4050
Affirmative Action Program Manager, Robert G. Lu

Wilson Riles - State Superintendent of Public Instruction - Sacramento

A poster encouraging affirmative action and equal opportunity education in California

1974 ✦ Somoza reelected.

Nicaraguan dictator Anastasio Somoza (son of the senior Anastasio Somoza, who served as the Nicaraguan dictator from 1937–56) was reelected to another six-year term. (*Also see entries dated 1937–56: Anastasio Somoza ruled Nicaragua; 1956: Somoza Debayle took over Nicaragua; and 1980: Somoza assassinated.*)

1975 ✦ Barriers to Hispanic voting toppled.

The Voting Rights Act Amendments of 1975 extended the provisions of the Voting Rights Acts of 1965 and 1970. They made permanent the national ban on literacy tests. These tests had been used in some states to keep those who could not read or who could not read English from voting. The amendments also required specific actions to make voting by Hispanic Americans easier, including making bilingual ballots a requirement in certain areas.

May 1975 ◆ The California Labor Relations Act.

Newly elected California governor Jerry Brown proposed laws to protect both farm laborers and the growers. In May 1975, the California Labor Relations Act was passed by the California legislature. It gave agricultural workers the same benefits that the National Labor Relations Act (1935) had guaranteed all industrial workers. The law authorized secret elections among the workers. In so doing, it removed barriers to organizing farmworker unions.

1976 ◆ Spanish Information Systems was founded.

Many of the Spanish-language radio stations throughout the United States depend on mainstream news services for their news programs. The first Spanish-language news service was Spanish Information Services (SIS) of Dallas, Texas. SIS set out to provide five-minute news programs in Spanish each hour during the day and a 15-minute program at noon. It also provided special sports programs.

1977 ◆ The Antonio Maceo Brigade.

A group of young Cuban exiles called the Antonio Maceo Brigade (named after the general in José Marti's movement for Cuban independence from Spain in 1891) traveled to Cuba from the United States. The goal of the group was to participate in service work and to build a better relationship with the Cuban government.

1977 ◆ The Congressional Hispanic Caucus was founded.

In an attempt to raise and address issues of concern to Hispanic Americans, 12 Hispanic members of the House and Senate organized the Congressional Hispanic Caucus. The caucus also set out to monitor the policies and actions of the president and the federal courts. Hispanic legislators and non-Hispanic associate legislators from both major parties joined the group. The caucus grew to represent 20 states, Puerto Rico, Guam, and the U.S. Virgin Islands. It raised the money for its efforts from dues and other private sources.

1977 ◆ A new Panama Canal Treaty.

President Jimmy Carter led an effort to revise the Panama Canal Treaty. The U.S. Congress approved a new Panama Canal Treaty in 1977, stating that the United States would turn over control of the canal to Panama in the year 2000. (*Also see entries dated 1850: Plans for a Central American canal; 1869: Proposals for a Nicaraguan canal; 1901–03: Treaties and laws cleared the way for a Central American canal; November 1903: A canal for an independent Panama; August 3, 1914: The Panama Canal opened; 1916: The United States continued to pursue a Nicaraguan canal; 1933: The Good Neighbor Policy; 1936: A new Panama Canal Zone treaty; and 1954: A new Panama Canal Zone treaty.*)

1977 ✦ **Romero elected president of El Salvador.**
General Carlos Humberto Romero became the latest military dictator to be
elected to the presidency of El Salvador.

1977 ✦ **Undocumented workers on the rise.**
The number of undocumented workers coming to the United States continued
to increase. In response, the Immigration and Naturalization Service (INS)
renewed its efforts to catch these workers and return them to their homelands.
Beginning in 1977, the INS was catching more than 1 million undocumented
workers each year.

1978–89 ✦ **Poverty increased among Hispanic families.**
The median income of Hispanic families below the poverty level in the United
States fell from $7,238 to $6,557 in 1987. From 1978 to 1988, the proportion
of Hispanic children living in poverty rose more than 45 percent. By 1989, 38
percent of Hispanic children were living in poverty.

1978–88 ✦ **Hispanic women in the U.S. work force.**
From 1978 to 1988, Hispanic women joined the U.S. work force in increasing
numbers. During this decade, the number of Hispanic working women more than
doubled, from 1.7 million to 3.6 million. In 1988, 56.6 percent of Hispanic
women were in the work force. This compared with 66.2 percent of white
women and 63.8 percent of blacks.

1978 ✦ **Civil war in Nicaragua.**
A violent civil war broke out in Nicaragua when the Sandinista Front for
National Liberation (FSNL), known as the Sandinistas, attempted to overthrow
dictator Anastasio Somoza. Because of this civil war, many Nicaraguan refugees
eventually came to the United States.

On July 19, 1979, Somoza abandoned Nicaragua. He had come under great
pressure not only from the Sandinistas but also from the United States, Mexico, and other Central American governments. On July 20, the *Junta* of the Government of National Reconstruction was sworn into office. On September 24,
President Jimmy Carter met with the Junta in the White House. Under the Carter
administration, the United States had supported Somoza's overthrow. It had also
funneled considerable aid to Nicaragua.

The Sandinistas immediately took over Somoza's land holdings and those of
his close associates, made up of about one-fifth of Nicaragua's farmland. These
lands were organized as state farms under the direction of the Nicaraguan Agrarian Reform Institute established in July. To continue land reform, the Agrarian
Reform Act of 1981 was passed, giving the government the power to take over
land in the Pacific region and in the central region. Many of these new lands were

organized into cooperative farms. In 1984, the government began to grant property titles to squatters. About 30,000 families received land titles within the next two years. After 1984, the government turned over control of the land reforms to regional authorities. The Atlantic coast region decided to focus on giving land titles to Native American communities. To date, over 55 percent of the rural poor have received land under these reforms. The Nicaraguan government's efforts were one of the most far-reaching land reform programs in Latin America. (*Also see entries dated 1937–56: Anastasio Somoza ruled Nicaragua; 1956: Somoza Debayle took over Nicaragua; 1974: Somoza reelected; and 1980: Somoza assassinated.*)

1978 ✦ López dominated women's golf.

In her first full season as a professional golfer, Nancy López (1957–) won 9 tournaments, including the Ladies Professional Golf Association Tournament (LPGA). She was named Rookie of the Year, Player of the Year, Golfer of the Year, and Female Athlete of the Year. She won the Vare Trophy, and won more money than had any other rookie in women's golf: $189,813. López had another excellent season in 1985, winning 5 tournaments, including the LPGA. She finished in the top 10 in 21 other tournaments.

1979 ✦ Arte Público Press was founded.

Nicolás Kanellos founded a publishing house to promote the prose and poetry of the United States' Hispanic writers. Arte Público Press quickly took a leading role in publishing the works of Hispanic women. During the 1980s, it published the San Antonio poets Evangelina Vigil and Angela de Hoyos and the Chicago writers Ana Castillo and Sandra Cisneros. It also published short story writer Helena María Viramontes, from Los Angeles, and novelist and playwright Denise Chávez, from New Mexico. (*Also see entry dated 1973:* Revista Chicano-Riqueña *appeared.*)

1979 ✦ Civil war began in El Salvador.

On October 15, 1979, a military *junta* (committee) overthrew President Carlos Humberto Romero and took power in El Salvador. The military hoped to prevent a civil war between the leftists and the Salvadoran ruling class. The Farabundo Martí National Liberation Front (FMLN), a leftist guerrilla movement, had gained enough support to challenge the power of the "fourteen families." These wealthy families had long dominated the nation's economic, political, and social structures.

Instead of heading off a civil war, the coup commenced years of bloodshed. The Salvadoran military jailed and killed many of its opponents, including Catholic nuns and priests who supported reforms for the poor. Archbishop Oscar Romero was one of the victims of the military death squads. He was killed

March 24, 1980, while in the pulpit. The Salvadoran civil war as well as political unrest and wars in Nicaragua and Guatemala contributed to large migrations of refugees to the United States. Salvadorans, in particular, soon became a substantial immigrant community in the United States.

1979 ◆ *El Super.*

León Ichaso directed this film, which was billed as the first Cuban-American comedy. It was an American production filmed on location in New York City in Spanish. *El Super* ("The Super") is the story of a homesick Cuban exile who works as the superintendent in a Manhattan apartment building.

1979 ◆ Flores assumed leadership of the Oakland Raiders.

Thomas Flores became the first Hispanic American to be named a coach of a professional football team in the United States. After long-time Oakland Raiders coach John Madden stepped down in 1978, Flores became interim coach. He was officially named head coach in 1979. Flores was born on March 21, 1937, in Fresno, California, into a family of Mexican American farm workers. He went on to become one of the most successful coaches in the history of the National Football League (NFL). Flores led the Raiders to two Super Bowl championships. (*Also see entry dated 1989: Flores named to head the Seattle Seahawks.*)

Archbishop Oscar Romero.

1979 ◆ Hernández named the National League Most Valuable Player.

Keith Hernández, a first baseman for the St. Louis Cardinals, helped lead his team to victory in the 1979 World Series. His performance during the season and the playoffs also earned him the National League's Most Valuable Player honor. Hernández was born October 20, 1953, in San Francisco and later attended nearby San Mateo College. He broke into the major leagues with the Cardinals in 1974 and played with that club until 1983. He played for the New York Mets until 1989 and then played briefly for the Cleveland Indians of the American League. During his career, Hernández was a strong hitter and one of the best first basemen ever. He played in five all-star games in 1979, 1980, 1984, 1986, and 1987. Despite his success, Hernández battled a drug problem for much of his early career.

Mass citizenship swearing-in ceremony at Hoffberg Pavilion in Houston, Texas, February 1987.

1979 ◆ Puerto Rican nationalists released from prison.

The Puerto Rican nationalists who had shot up the House of Representatives in 1954 were released from prison. Lolita Lebrón, Ramón Cancel Miranda, Irving Flores, and Oscar Collazo had served 25 years in prison. (*Also see entry dated 1954: Puerto Rican nationalists attacked the U.S. Congress.*)

1980s ◆ Cuban exiles became citizens in great numbers.

Throughout the 1960s, the majority of Cubans in the United States maintained their Cuban citizenship, as they hoped to return to a free Cuba someday. During the 1970s, however, many Cuban exiles finally became American citizens. Their rate of naturalization became the highest of any ethnic group. The rapid growth in the number of Cuban Americans soon led to their greater involvement in the political process. (*Also see entry dated 1982: The rise of Cuban American political power.*)

1980s ✦ Immigration increased.

During the 1980s, the number of immigrants that came to the United States approached the levels of the early 1900s. Legal immigration during the first decade of the century was 8.8 million. During the 1980s, 6.3 million immigrants were granted permanent residence. The majority of these new immigrants were young and in search of a job. Hispanic immigrants accounted for more than 40 percent of the total. From 1980 to 1988, the number of Hispanics in the work force increased by 48 percent, and is growing faster than any other major group.

1980 ✦ Duarte rose to power in El Salvador.

The military *junta* (committee) ruling El Salvador appointed José Napoleón Duarte to lead the country. Duarte initiated reform programs that included the redistribution of land. First, the government took estates larger than 500 hectares (approximately 1,235 acres) and converted most of them to cooperatives. Then sharecroppers were allowed to claim up to 7 hectares (approximately 17 acres) of land that they worked. About 22 percent of the rural poor benefitted from this land redistribution in El Salvador. Even with these reforms, however, Duarte's government continued to face protests and widespread discontent. Civil war between government forces and the leftist Farabundo Martí National Liberation Front (FMLN) continued during Duarte's reign. (*Also see entry dated 1979: Civil war began in El Salvador.*)

1980 ✦ Nava named ambassador to Mexico.

President Jimmy Carter named Julián Nava ambassador to Mexico. Nava was the first Mexican American to hold that post, serving until 1981. Julián Nava was born on June 19, 1927, in Los Angeles, into a family that had fled Mexico during its revolution. He grew up in East Los Angeles and then served in the Navy Air Corps during World War II. When he returned from the war, Nava went to college with the help of the G.I. Bill. After receiving a Ph.D. from Harvard University in 1955, Nava held positions as lecturer and professor of history at universities in Colombia, Venezuela, Puerto Rico, Spain, and California. In 1967 he was elected to the Los Angeles school board, for which he later served as president.

1980 ✦ Peace between El Salvador and Honduras.

These two nations signed a peace treaty, ending their decade-old dispute. (*Also see entry dated 1969: A border war between Honduras and El Salvador.*)

Prospective U.S. citizens wait outside of the Immigration and Naturalization Service office to get their papers approved, April 29, 1988.

1980 ✦ Plunkett led the Oakland Raiders to a Super Bowl victory.

James William "Jim" Plunkett (1947–) was born in Santa Clara, California, to William and Carmen Blea Plunkett. Plunkett excelled in football and played for Stanford University in Palo Alto, California. In his senior year, he was awarded the Heisman Trophy, recognizing him as the nation's best college football player. He was the first draft pick for the New England Patriots in 1971 and was named the NFL Rookie of the Year that season. After injuries interrupted his career, Plunkett joined the Oakland Raiders in 1978. Two years later, he led his team to victory in the Super Bowl, where he was named Most Valuable Player and the NFL Comeback Player of the Year. In 1983, Plunkett again led the Raiders to a Super Bowl victory.

1980 ✦ The Refugee Act of 1980.

For many years, a refugee had been defined by the U.S. government as someone fleeing a Communist country. The Refugee Act of 1980 changed that definition.

Cuban refugees board a vessel during the Mariel Boat Lift.

It dropped the requirement that the person had to come from a Communist country. The new law allowed thousands to enter the United States as refugees. However, at the same time, the Immigration and Naturalization Service (INS) was also cracking down on undocumented immigrants. In catching and returning undocumented immigrants to their native countries, the authorities also generated thousands of reports of civil rights violations.

1980 ◆ Somoza assassinated.

After being overthrown by the Sandinista National Liberation Front in 1979, Nicaraguan dictator Anastasio Somoza fled from Nicaragua to South America. In 1980, Somoza was assassinated in Paraguay. (*Also see entries dated 1937–56:*

A protest march against President Ronald Reagan's policies toward Nicaragua.

Anastasio Somoza ruled Nicaragua; 1956: Somoza Debayle took over Nicaragua; and 1974: Somoza reelected.)

April–September 1980 ✦ The Mariel Boat Lift.

One of the most dramatic waves of immigration to the United States began when a bus carrying a load of discontented Cubans crashed through the gates of the Peruvian embassy in Havana. Peru granted the Cubans political asylum. The event attracted worldwide attention to the fact that many Cubans wanted out of Castro's Cuba. Faced with this negative press, Castro tried to turn the situation around, changing his policy of allowing Cubans to leave gradually. He announced that whoever wanted to leave Cuba should go to the Peruvian embassy. The bus riders were soon joined by over 10,000 others on the embassy grounds. There the Cuban government gave exit visas to these people. They could leave through Mariel Harbor if they could find transportation. Cuban Americans in Florida organized a *flotilla* (fleet) of boats to pick up the refugees. The Mariel Boat Lift continued until September. By the time Castro ended the exodus, more than 125,000 *Marielitos* had migrated to the United States.

April 22, 1980 ✦ *Noticias del Mundo* was launched.

The daily Spanish-language newspaper *Noticias del Mundo* was founded to fight communism in Latin America and to promote Hispanic concerns at home. It set out to serve the Hispanic populations of New York City, New Jersey, Los Angeles, and San Francisco, but it spread through secondary distribution to 18 other American cities. By the early 1990s, *Noticias del Mundo* had a circulation of 32,000 in the New York metro area, 7,300 in New Jersey, and 2,450 in Boston.

1981–88 ✦ The Reagan administration fought affirmative action.

From 1981 to 1988, the Reagan administration maintained that affirmative action programs required quotas. These quotas prevented qualified white men from getting jobs and educational opportunities. In this way, the administration charged, the programs caused a form of reverse discrimination.

1981 ✦ Reagan's Latin American policy.

The administration of the new U.S. president, Ronald Reagan, saw Latin American affairs as a struggle between democracy and communism. The Reagan administration argued that the Soviet Union, through its Cuban proxies (those acting on the authorization of others), were using issues such as the distribution of wealth and property to push local Marxists into power. These groups, it was felt, would destroy the economies, offer no hope for political reform, and create communist outposts through which Moscow could threaten U.S. interests.

Given this view, the Reagan administration took action to maintain Central America's existing order, except in Nicaragua. There the administration sought to overthrow the leftist Sandinista government. To carry out this Central American policy, the United States increased its military presence in Honduras. It gave over $300 million in military aid to the government in El Salvador for its battle against the Farabundo Martí National Liberation Front (FMLN), and offered money and other support to the Nicaraguan Contras for their counter-revolution against the Sandinistas.

1981 ✦ *Zoot Suit.*

In this filmed version of his hit stage play, Luis Valdez, known as the father of Chicano theater, turned a critical eye on the California justice system's treatment of Hispanics. He also took on Hollywood's stereotyped views of Hispanics. (*Also see entry dated 1965: Hispanic theater of and for the workers.*)

1982 ✦ *The Ballad of Gregorio Cortez.*

This film produced by Moctezuma Esparza is based in part on Américo Paredes's nonfiction account of a man who eluded the Texas Rangers around the turn of the century. The film depicts the life of an outlaw in the context of the widespread prejudice in Texas at the time. The film tries to erase the stereotyped version of the "bandido" common in early Hollywood films.

1982 ✦ Latin America became a nuclear-free zone.

Mexican diplomat Alfonso García Robles won the Nobel Prize for peace with Alva Myrdal for developing and promoting the Treaty of Tlaltelolco. This treaty declared Latin America to be a nuclear-free zone.

HISPANIC NOBEL PRIZE WINNERS

- Argentine statesman Carlos de Savdera Lamas—Peace, 1936
- Chilean poet Gabriela Mistral—Literature, 1945
- Argentine doctor and biologist Bernardo A. Houssay—Physiology and medicine, 1947
- Guatemalan novelist Miguel Angel Asturias—Literature, 1967
- Argentine chemist Luis F. Leloir—Chemistry, 1970
- Chilean poet Pablo Neruda—Literature, 1971
- Argentine architect and sculptor Adolfo Pérez Esquivel—Peace, 1980
- Colombian novelist Gabriel García Márquez—Literature, 1982
- Mexican diplomat Alfonso García Robles (co-winner)—Peace, 1982
- Argentine doctor César Milstein (co-winner)—Medicine, 1984
- Luis Walter Alvarez—Physics, 1986
- Costa Rican president Oscar Arias—Peace, 1987
- Mexican poet and essayist Octavio Paz—Literature, 1990
- Guatemalan Indian leader Rigoberta Menchu—Peace, 1992
- Mexican American scientist Mario Molina—Chemistry, 1995

Members of the anti-Sandinista Contra rebels stand guard in Matagalpa, Nicaragua, September 2, 1985.

1982 ✦ The rise of Cuban American political power.

In the late 1970s and early 1980s, more and more Cuban Americans were elected to city councils throughout Dade County, Florida. During this period, the people of Miami elected their first Cuban American mayor. In 1982, they elected three Cubans to the state legislature, and the number has grown in the years that have followed. Finally, in 1989, a Cuban American was elected for the first time to the U.S. Congress when Ileana Ross Lehtinen was chosen to represent Florida's 18th Congressional District. Similar trends emerged in Union City and West New York, both centers of Cuban American population in New Jersey.

February 1982 ✦ Mexico in economic crisis.

Mexico announced that it was devaluing its currency more than 70 percent. The country faced a huge foreign debt and was not able to service its loans. It was running a deficit in its balance of payments, partly because the price of oil had been depressed for some time.

August 1982 ✦ U.S. aid to Mexico.

Mexico announced that it would not be able to pay its foreign debt on time. The United States Federal Reserve, the United States Treasury, and 11 large international banks lent Mexico almost $2 billion. A large part of the loan would have to be paid back by selling oil at a low price to the United States Strategic Oil Reserve. Mexico's economic independence was in danger.

1983–86 ✦ The Contadora peace process.

In order to pursue peace in the troubled nations of Central America, four of the region's neighbors—Mexico, Venezuela, Colombia, and Panama—met on the Panamanian island of Contadora on January 8 and 9, 1983. In July, the Contadora Group issued its first proposals. These included the withdrawal of all foreign military advisors from Central America, the end of all aid to irregular forces, and an end to military maneuvers in the border regions. In September, the group produced a draft of a 21-point peace treaty. These peace proposals were accompanied by intense diplomatic activity. The Contadora Group met eleven times in 1983. Central American ministers participated on six of those occasions. In January 1984, the Contadora Group and the Central American nations attempted to strengthen the peace process. They created three joint committees to cover security, political, social, and economic issues.

The United States was slow to respond to this peace process. Instead, it continued to focus on military solutions to Central American conflicts. The United States invaded the island of Grenada on October 25, 1983. It also held troop maneuvers in Honduras in 1983, funded the Contras, and mined Nicaraguan ports. Eventually, however, the Contadora Group was successful in urging the

U.S. government to hold talks with the Nicaraguan government. The talks at Manzanillo, Cuba, started in June 1984 and ended in January 1985. The United States abandoned the negotiations. On September 21, 1984, the Nicaraguan government was the first Central American nation to sign the Contadora Group's "Draft Act on Peace and Cooperation."

The next group to endorse the Central American peace process was the Lima Group in 1985, which included Argentina, Brazil, Peru, and Uruguay. The next important step was the Caraballeda Declaration in January 1986, in which the Contadora and Lima Groups called on the United States to resume talks with Nicaragua, to suspend aid to the Contras, and to withdraw its troops from the region. The declaration was supported by the Central American presidents and representatives from all the major political parties in Western Europe. The United States refused to follow the declaration. It stated that the Nicaraguan government had to negotiate with the Contras.

On June 27, 1986, the International Court of Justice in The Hague, Netherlands, found that the United States had broken international law by intervening economically and politically in Nicaragua. In November 1986, the secretary generals of the United Nations and the Organization of American States launched a joint initiative to further peace in Central America. Both of these events strengthened the Contadora process.

1983 ◆ The Contras invaded Nicaragua.

Several thousand Nicaraguan counter-revolutionaries (Contras) invaded northeastern Nicaragua. Their goal was to topple the leftist Sandinista regime. The Contras were supported militarily by the U.S. government.

1983 ◆ Marichal joined baseball's Hall of Fame.

Juan Marichal joined the San Francisco Giants as a starting pitcher in 1962. From 1962 to 1971, he averaged 20 wins per year. He led the National League in wins in 1963 with a record of 25 wins to 8 losses and in 1968 with 26 wins to 9 losses. He lead the league in shutouts in 1965 with 10 and in 1969 with an ERA of 2.10. He pitched in 8 all-star games, earning a record of 2–0 and a 0.50 ERA over 18 innings. Marichal's pitched a total of 3,509 innings. He had a record of 243 wins and 142 losses and an ERA of 2.89. He was inducted into the Hall of Fame in 1983. (*Also see entry dated July 15, 1963: Juan Marichal pitched a no-hitter.*)

1984 ◆ Aparicio inducted into baseball's Hall of Fame.

Venezuelan-born Luis Aparicio was selected for the baseball Hall of Fame because he was one of the greatest shortstops of all time in the U.S. major leagues. He held the records among shortstops for games played, assists, and double plays, and the American League record for putouts. His 506 stolen bases ranked among baseball's highest. Aparicio played most of his career for the Chicago White Sox. He broke into the major leagues in 1956 and was the American League's Rookie of the Year. He continued to play inspired baseball until his retirement in 1973. Aparicio played on all-star teams from 1958 to 1964 and again from 1970 to 1972. He won the Golden Glove for his play in the field eleven times. (*Also see entry dated 1956: Aparicio named the American League Rookie of the year.*)

1984 ◆ *The Ballad of an Unsung Hero.*

Paul Espinosa and Isaac Artenstein released their extraordinary documentary film about Pedro J. González, one of the pioneers of Spanish-language radio in the United States. The film examined the social and political pressures faced by Hispanics during the Great Depression. González spread his progressive political ideas throughout the Southwest by radio. However, his career ended when he was convicted of rape in Los Angeles in 1934. Many believe the charges were created to stop his message. (*Also see entry dated 1924: The pioneers of Hispanic radio.*)

Pedro J. González, pioneer of Spanish-language radio in California.

1984 ◆ Duarte elected president of El Salvador.

José Napoleón Duarte had been appointed to lead El Salvador by a military *junta* (committee) in 1980. In 1984, he was elected president, defeating Roberto D'Aubuisson, a far right-wing candidate linked to the country's death squads.

1984 ◆ *El Norte.*

Gregory Nava directed this film which retells the familiar coming-to-America story. A Guatemalan brother and sister flee from oppression in their homeland and seek the opportunity of *El Norte* ("The North"). The tragic tale of hope and loss won critical acclaim when it was released.

1984 ◆ The Los Angeles Olympic games.

The United States had boycotted the 1980 Olympic games in Moscow because of Soviet military action in Afghanistan. In retaliation, the U.S.S.R. and many of its satellite nations boycotted the 1984 Olympics in Los Angeles. Latin America's greatest sports power, Cuba, was among the teams boycotting. The U.S.

team had the largest Hispanic representation ever. Hispanic American Paul Gonzales won a gold medal in flyweight boxing.

1984 ✦ Ortega elected president of Nicaragua.

Daniel Ortega, head of the Sandinista revolutionary government, was elected president of Nicaragua.

May 10, 1984 ✦ The World Court ruled against the United States.

In a unanimous decision, the World Court in The Hague, Netherlands, ordered the United States to stop mining Nicaraguan ports. The CIA had been mining Nicaragua's ports in an attempt to keep out arms shipments to the country. The Reagan administration refused to abide by the ruling.

October 1, 1984 ✦ Congress halted aid to the Contras.

The U.S. Congress voted to end the policy of aiding the Nicaraguan Contras, over objections from the Reagan administration. The National Security Council, nevertheless, launched a secret scheme to launder money, pay a ransom to Iran for hostages, and indirectly supply the Contras with military aid. The scheme, headed by Oliver North, was eventually uncovered, and it came to be known as the "Iran-Contra Affair." It damaged the careers of a number of politicians and military leaders in the United States. It even cast suspicions on President Reagan and Vice President George Bush.

1985 ✦ Radio Martí.

The United States created Radio Martí, a 24-hour Spanish-language news/propaganda service based in Florida. The station was named after the Cuban poet and exiled rebel José Martí (1853–95) who led the movement for Cuban independence from Spain. (*Also see entry dated 1891: Unity in the Cuban independence movement.*) The goal of the service was to broadcast news to Cuba from an American viewpoint. In response, the Cuban government suspended its immigration agreement with the United States.

September 1985 ✦ Two bilingual magazines were founded.

Both *Vista* and *Saludos Hispanos* began distributing regular inserts to selected American newspapers in 1985. *Vista,* an English-language magazine with articles of interest to Hispanics and a Spanish-language supplement, was inserted in newspapers in Arizona, California, Colorado, Florida, Illinois, New Mexico, New York, and Texas. By the early 1990s, it had a circulation of over 900,000 for its monthly publications. *Saludos Hispanos* set out to offer side-by-side Spanish and English versions of its stories through inserts in American newspapers. Later it switched to direct distribution to paid subscribers. By the early 1990s, it had a circulation of over 300,000 for its bimonthly (published every two months) magazine.

1986 ✦ Alvarez won the Nobel Prize for Physics.

Luis Walter Alvarez, a Nobel Prize-winning physicist, was born on June 13, 1911, in San Francisco, California. Alvarez studied at the University of Chicago and earned a B.S. in 1932 and a Ph.D. in 1936. After graduating, he went on to become one of the United States' most distinguished and respected physicists. Alvarez was a pioneer in particle physics, astrophysics, ophthalmic and television optics, geophysics, and air navigation. He did most of his work at the University of California-Berkeley from 1936 to 1988. From 1954 to 1959 and from 1976 to 1978, he served as Associate Director of the prestigious Lawrence Berkeley Lab. In 1986, Alvarez was awarded the Nobel Prize for Physics. He received the Collier Trophy (1946), the Scott Medal (1953), the Einstein Medal (1961), the National Medal of Science (1964), and many other awards. Alvarez was also awarded a number of honorary degrees from universities in the United States and abroad. Alvarez died in 1988.

1986 ✦ The Immigration Reform and Control Act of 1986.

After more than a decade of debate, the U.S. Congress enacted the Immigration Reform and Control Act (IRCA). The act created an alien legalization program, a process through which illegal aliens could become legal immigrants. The act gave legal status to applicants who had been in the United States illegally since January 1, 1982. The program offered relief to many Hispanics who had long feared being caught. It also helped to decrease abuses by employers who took advantage of undocumented workers by calling for penalties against employers of undocumented aliens.

June 27, 1986 ✦ The International Court of Justice ruled against the United States.

The International Court of Justice found the United States in breach of international law for supporting the Contras and for intervening militarily and economically in Nicaragua. (*Also see entry dated 1981: Reagan's Latin American policy*).

November 25, 1986 ✦ The Iran-Contra scandal went public.

News of the Iran-Contra scandal reached the United States from sources in the Middle East. According to the investigations that followed, members of the U.S. National Security Council (NSC) had organized an illegal scheme to win the release of American hostages in the Middle East and fund Nicaraguan Contras at the same time. The NSC, it was reported, secretly sold arms to Iran in order to help win the release of American hostages. The NSC then diverted the money from the arms sales to the Nicaraguan Contras. This action violated the Boland

Senator Daniel Inouye, chairman of the Senate Iran-Contra Committee, swears in Lieutenant-Colonel Oliver North as he prepares to testify, July 7, 1987.

Edward James
Olmos (left) and
Jaime Escalante
during the filming
of *Stand and
Deliver.*

Amendment, a law passed by Congress to forbid funding of the overthrow of the Nicaraguan government.

Shortly after the U.S. Congress launched an investigation into the matter, Colonel Oliver North and Admiral John Poindexter resigned from the NSC. Throughout 1987, the Senate and the House of Representatives held joint hearings on the Iran-Contra Affair. These hearings detailed the elaborate private operation run by North and the NSC. (*Also see entry dated October 1, 1984: Congress halted aid to the Contras.*)

1987–88 ◆ The Chicano experience came to Hollywood.

Between the summer of 1987 and the spring of 1988, Hollywood released four feature films that focused on Chicanos: *La Bamba, Born in East L.A., The Milagro Beanfield War,* and *Stand and Deliver.* Of these, *Stand and Deliver* had the greatest Hispanic involvement. Its financiers, producers, writers, directors, and lead actors were all Hispanic. This film tells the story of Jaime Escalante, a Bolivian-born math teacher in East Los Angeles. Escalante earned national recognition for his success in inspiring poor Hispanic children in the *barrio* (neighborhood) to excel in math and to go on to the nation's most important colleges. Actor Edward James Olmos was nominated for an Academy Award for his role as Escalante.

1987 ✦ The growth of Hispanic-owned businesses.

Between 1977 and 1987, the number of Hispanic-owned businesses in the United States increased from 219,000 to 422,000, according to the U.S. Census Bureau. This growth was much faster than the growth for non-minority owned businesses during the same period. Together, Hispanic-owned businesses had gross sales of more than $24.7 billion.

1987 ✦ Univisión was born.

Univisión, the largest Spanish-language television network in the United States, was the grandchild of KCOR-TV, the first Hispanic television station in the country. The owners of KCOR-TV used their success in San Antonio, Texas, to expand their television holdings. In the early 1960s, they founded the Spanish International Communications Corporation (SICC), a group of Hispanic stations from Texas to California. They also founded the Spanish International Network (SIN) to purchase and provide Spanish-language programming. On January 1, 1987, SICC and SIN were renamed Univisión. In 1987 and 1988, a group of investors, including Hallmark Cards Inc. and First Capital Corporation of Chicago, bought Univisión.

Univisión moved its headquarters and studios to the Miami, Florida, area in 1991. In the early 1990s, it offered a wide range of Spanish-language programs through its broadcast stations and through cable companies. (*Also see entry dated 1955: The first Hispanic television station.*)

August 7, 1987 ✦ A Central American peace plan.

Despite opposition from President Reagan, the Central American governments ratified their own peace plan on August 7, 1987. The plan, called "Procedure for the Establishment of a Strong and Lasting Peace in Central America," was based on the work of Costa Rican president Oscar Arias Sánchez. It called for withdrawal of all foreign military advisors from the area, a complete ceasefire, and free elections in all of the countries of Central America. The Group of 8 (the Contadora and Lima Groups), the foreign ministers of the Central American countries, and the secretary generals of the United Nations and the Organization of American States would monitor each of these provisions.

Even though Nicaragua had accepted the peace plan and was beginning a ceasefire in three of the northern war zones, President Reagan continued to pursue a military solution. He asked for and received from Congress another $3.2 million for the Nicaraguan Contras on September 23, 1987. Later in the year, when Reagan called for even more Contra funding, there was a public outcry in the United States. Even some of the president's allies in Congress refused to go along. The outgoing Reagan administration and the newly elected Bush administration continued to support military solutions.

The Nicaraguan government went ahead and started negotiations with the Contras. The efforts were supported regionally and internationally. Eventually, the two sides in the Nicaraguan civil war were able to establish a ceasefire in 1988. In 1990, Nicaragua held free elections, including political parties from both the Sandinista and Contra camps. Violeta Chamorro and her moderate supporters won the elections and shifted the country's political power to the center. The Sandinistas turned over the government to Chamorro nonviolently. For his efforts to bring about an end to the civil war in Nicaragua through a Central American peace plan, President Oscar Arias Sánchez of Costa Rica was awarded the Nobel Peace Prize. (*Also see entries dated 1983–86: The Contadora peace process; 1988: A ceasefire in the Nicaraguan civil war; and February 1990: Chamorro was elected president in Nicaragua.*)

Dr. Lauro F. Cavazos.

November 21, 1987 ✦ *El Nuevo Herald* was founded.

In 1976, the *Miami Herald* had begun publishing a Spanish-language insert called *El Miami Herald* in its daily English edition. In 1987, the newspaper's parent company recognized the need for a separate Spanish-language daily to serve the Hispanic population of south Florida, so it launched *El Nuevo Herald*. By the early 1990s, the newspaper had a circulation of over 100,000 for weekdays and Saturdays, and over 118,000 for its Sunday edition.

1988 ✦ Cavazos named Secretary of Education.

President Ronald Reagan chose Dr. Lauro F. Cavazos, the president of Texas Tech University, to be Secretary of Education. He was the first Hispanic American to hold that post. Cavazos was born on January 4, 1927, on the King Ranch in Texas. He was an excellent student who eventually earned a B.S. (1949) and M.S. (1952) in zoology from Texas Tech, and a Ph.D (1954) in physiology from Iowa State University. Cavazos became a professor of anatomy and a college administrator at the Medical College of Virginia, Tufts, and Texas Tech. Shortly before joining the Reagan administration, Cavazos became president of Texas

Tech, the first Hispanic American to head a major research university. He served as Secretary of Education from 1988 to 1990.

1988 ◆ A ceasefire in the Nicaraguan civil war.
The Sandinistas and the Contras negotiated a ceasefire and planned for free and open elections.

April 1988 ◆ *Hispanic* published its first issue.
In 1988, Fred Estrada, a native of Cuba, founded a monthly magazine in English about Hispanic Americans, their achievements, and their contributions to American society. By the early 1990s, the magazine had a circulation of about 150,000 per month.

1989 ◆ Calls for Puerto Rican statehood.
On January 20, 1989, President George Bush announced in his State of the Union address that he supported Puerto Rican statehood. Later in the year, the U.S. Senate Energy and Resources Committee prepared three bills that offered Puerto Ricans a vote on their status. A final bill was killed later that year, and another similar bill was killed in 1991. The feeling in Congress was that the United States was not ready to grant statehood to Puerto Rico. (*Also see entry dated 1991: Puerto Ricans endorsed statehood.*)

1989 ◆ Cristiani elected president of El Salvador.
Alfredo Cristiani was elected to the presidency of El Salvador while the civil war was worsening. (*Also see entry dated February 1992: Peace in El Salvador.*)

1989 ◆ Flores named to head Seattle Seahawks.
In 1989, Thomas Flores became president and general manager of the Seattle Seahawks. This was the highest rank ever reached by a Hispanic American in professional sports in the United States. (*Also see entry dated 1979: Flores assumed leadership of the Oakland Raiders.*)

1989 ◆ Hispanic American income.
Median family income in the United States for white families was $35,210; for blacks, $20,210; and for Hispanics, $23,450. Per capita (per person) income was $14,060 for whites, $8,750 for blacks, and $8,390 for Hispanics. Seventy percent of Hispanic female-headed households lived below the poverty level.

1989 ◆ Immigration from the Americas.
Immigration from the Americas rose from 44.3 percent of the total in 1964 to 61.4 percent. Of the leading sources for immigration, Mexico accounted for 37.1 percent of the total documented immigration to the United States. El Salvador supplied the next highest number of immigrants, with 5.3 percent.

Oscar Hijuelos.

December 1989 ◆ The U.S. invasion of Panama.

The United States invaded Panama as part of the U.S. war against drugs. The United States had evidence that drug traffickers were using Panama as a communications and banking post. These drug runners had the help and support of the Panamanian president, General Manuel Noriega. During the invasion, American troops captured Noriega and took him to the United States for trial and (upon being found guilty) imprisonment.

December 28, 1989 ◆ An open letter to Castro.

More than 400 public figures, intellectuals, and artists from Europe and Latin America published an open letter to Fidel Castro, requesting that he allow the Cuban people to vote on whether he should remain in power.

1990 ◆ Hispanic immigration.

U.S. government sources reported that from 1981 to 1990 the countries that sent the most documented Hispanic immigrants and refugees to the United States were Mexico, Cuba, the Dominican Republic, El Salvador, Colombia, and Guatemala.

1990 ✦ *The Mambo Kings Play Songs of Love.*

Cuban American Oscar Hijuelos became the first Hispanic American author to win the Pulitzer Prize. His novel *The Mambo Kings Play Songs of Love* was published by Simon and Schuster, a major mainstream publisher, and marketed to a wide audience.

February 1990 ✦ **Chamorro was elected president in Nicaragua.**

The revolutionary Sandinista government in Nicaragua was removed from power peacefully when President Daniel Ortega lost the national elections to Violeta Chamorro and her moderate supporters. (*Also see entry dated August 7, 1987: A Central American peace plan.*)

March 20–23, 1990 ✦ **Cuban attitudes.**

The Mexican newspaper *El Norte* published the results of a random survey taken of 400 Cubans living in Havana. The respondents thought that the greatest achievement of the Cuban government was guaranteed education (60 percent) and free medical care (30 percent). The greatest problems were that Castro had become a dictator (66 percent) and that there was no freedom of the press (87 percent). Many of the respondents said they were unhappy in Cuba (63 percent), did not like what they did (74 percent), and had relatives abroad (83 percent).

December 1990 ✦ **The Soviet breakup affected Cuba.**

In the early 1990s, the Soviet Union and Eastern Europe found themselves in the middle of great political, social, and economic changes. These changes put an end to Cuba's position as Moscow's most important Third World client. Russia—the Soviet Union was dissolving into independent republics—no longer had the resources nor the desire to pump economic and political support into Cuba. In 1990, the two countries signed a one-year treaty of cooperation, instead of the usual five-year treaty.

During the 1970s and early 1980s, Cuba had received annually an estimated $4 billion to $6 billion worth of economic aid from the Soviet Union. It had also received approximately $1.5 billion worth of military equipment between 1960 and 1970, and twice that amount from 1970 to 1975. In addition, throughout the 1970s, approximately 70 percent of Cuba's trade was with the Soviet Union. Cuba had received all of its oil and development loans from the Soviet Union. By the late 1980s, trade with the Soviet Union had risen to 85 percent of Cuba's total. But in 1990, the beginning of the end of the Cuba-Soviet Union commercial and political relationship was in sight.

1991 ✦ **The Civil Rights Act of 1991.**

Civil rights laws passed in the 1960s and 1970s were successfully challenged in the U.S. Supreme Court during the Reagan and Bush administrations. In

Cuban president Fidel Castro delivers a speech on the 20th anniversary of the failure of the Bay of Pigs invasion.

response, black and Hispanic organizations as well as other civil rights supporters began to push for new civil rights laws in 1990. The groups hoped to raise civil rights in the United States to previous standards. After a series of compromises, the U.S. Congress produced the Civil Rights Act of 1991.

1991 ◆ *Maquiladoras* and NAFTA.

The proposed North American Free Trade Agreement (NAFTA) between Mexico, the United States, and Canada expanded the opportunity for *maquiladoras,* foreign-owned assembly plants located in Mexico along the U.S.-Mexican border. NAFTA promised to make it easier for U.S. businesses to put factories in Mexico.

1991 ◆ Puerto Ricans endorsed statehood.

Despite the U.S. Congress's refusal to consider the statehood of Puerto Rico, Puerto Ricans voted in a referendum that they were in favor of statehood. (*Also see entry dated 1989: Calls for Puerto Rican statehood.*)

March 1991 ◆ Unemployment among Hispanics

The unemployment rate for Hispanic Americans reached 10.3 percent, roughly double the rate for whites.

Guerillas of the Farabundo Martí National Liberation Front in El Salvador.

July 17–12, 1991 ✦ New calls for Cuban democracy.

At the Guadalajara Summit of Ibero-American leaders, Prime Minister Felipe González of Spain and President Carlos Salinas de Gortari of Mexico urged Fidel Castro to democratize Cuba. Castro had heard similar calls to democratize from other Latin American heads of state in the past. (*Also see entry dated December 28, 1989: An open letter to Castro.*)

September 11, 1991 ✦ The Soviet military began to pull out of Cuba.

Mikhail Gorbachev announced the withdrawal of Soviet troops from Cuba. The withdrawal was to be completed by July 1993.

February 1992 ✦ Peace in El Salvador.

The Farabundo Martí National Liberation Front (FMLN) ended its guerrilla movement by signing a peace treaty with the government of El Salvador. The bloody civil war, which had killed almost 75,000 people, had finally come to an end. In exchange for peace, the FMLN became a legal political party. The government, for its part, agreed to sweeping changes in the military. This included forced retirement for more than 100 officers believed to be responsible for widespread human rights abuses.

El Salvador had been a key battleground in the cold war during the 1980s. The United States poured in more than $6 billion in economic and military aid in an attempt to defeat the FMLN. The fall of the communist states in Europe had brought an end to the cold war and had brought considerable peace benefits to Central America. (*Also see entry dated April 24, 1994: El Salvador held free elections.*)

October 23, 1992 ✦ The Cuban Democracy Act.

President George Bush signed the Cuban Democracy Act, also known as the Torricelli Bill. This act banned trade with Cuba by U.S. subsidiary companies in other countries and prohibited ships docking in U.S. ports if they had visited Cuba. The Torricelli Bill was heavily backed by Cuban Americans, and President Bush made a point of signing it in Miami. The bill showed the power of U.S. ethnic groups in creating legislation and affecting foreign policy.

The Cuban Democracy Act was quickly criticized by the United Nations General Assembly. The U.N. condemned the United States for maintaining its 30-

year embargo of Cuba. The vote was 59 to 3, with 71 countries abstaining. Even most of the United States' allies either voted to end the embargo or abstained.

1993 ✦ Clinton named Hispanics to his cabinet.

President Bill Clinton appointed the first Hispanic Secretary of Housing and Urban Development, Henry Cisneros, the former mayor of San Antonio, Texas. Clinton also named Federico Peña, former mayor of Denver, Colorado, to be his Secretary of Transportation.

1993 ✦ Political unrest in Guatemala fueled immigration.

On May 25, a coup d'etat (violent overthrow of the government) forced Guatemalan president Jorge Serrano out of power. Serrano had taken on near-dictatorial powers in an attempt to silence his critics' charges of corruption and human rights abuses. On June 5, the Guatemalan Congress picked Ramiro de León Carpio, a former human rights ombudsman (a public official appointed to investigate complaints by private citizens against government officials or agencies), from a slate of three candidates to fill Serrano's term through 1995. De León Carpio was forced to work with the military and a corrupt congress. As a result, human rights abuses actually have increased under de León Carpio. According to the Catholic Church's human rights office, January 1994 was the bloodiest month in three years, with 46 murders and executions.

March 31, 1993 ✦ The end of Soviet aid for Cuba.

The breakup of the Soviet Union under Mikhail Gorbachev created political, social, and economic problems in that country. These problems finally led Russia to withdraw economic support from Cuba. Cuba was left foundering with a faltering economy. The economic blockade enforced by the United States hurt Cuba even more now.

1994 ✦ Hispanics and religion.

Surveys of American religions recorded that almost 30 percent of U.S. Roman Catholics were Hispanic. Even so, Protestant sects were working hard to attract Hispanics. Methodist, Southern Baptist, and Pentecostal churches increased their outreach to Hispanic communities.

January 1, 1994 ✦ The North American Free Trade Agreement (NAFTA).

The North American Free Trade Agreement went into effect. In this treaty trading partners Canada, Mexico, and the United States agreed to eliminate all tariffs between them 15 years from this date. The measure was a first step toward integrating the economies of the three countries. It was also a possible first step

Subcomandante Marcos of the Zapatista National Liberation Army talks to reporters about the peasant uprising in Chiapas, February 1994.

toward the future creation of an American common market which would include all the Americas.

On this date, 53.8 percent of U.S. imports from Mexico became duty free, while 31 percent of imports from the United States became duty free. The most immediately affected industries were energy, automobiles, textiles, agriculture, electricity, banks and insurance, bus and trucking services, ports, railroads, and telecommunications. U.S. labor unions had opposed NAFTA, fearing the loss of more U.S. jobs to Mexico. U.S. industries protected by tariffs, such as textiles, had also opposed the measure. In Mexico, farmers feared imports of American agricultural products.

January 1, 1994 ◆ The Zapatista uprising in southern Mexico.

In Mexico, well-planned and well-executed revolutionary outbreaks by Mayan peasant farmers in Chiapas were timed to coincide with the beginning of NAFTA. As many as 2,000 Mayan guerrillas, baptizing themselves the Zapatista National Liberation Army (in honor of the revolutionary general Emiliano Zapata), took over the important southern city of San Cristobal de las Casas, as well as the towns of Ocosingo, Las Margaritas, Altamirano, and others. The takeovers led to bloody confrontations with the Mexican Army. Both parties agreed to a ceasefire on January 12. They also agreed to discuss the problems of the Mayas in Chiapas, a state in southeastern Mexico.

The Mayas of southern Mexico had lost their lands and suffered from poverty for years. Under NAFTA, they faced the prospect of imported corn displacing their main farm product and dietary staple. This together with other economic and environmental pressures pushed the Mayas to take strong actions in the form of an uprising.

After a ceasefire was established, the government and Mayan rebels signed a tentative 32-point accord on March 2. This agreement called for a new local government designed to serve Indian communities and a redrawn Chiapas state legislature to increase Indian representation. It also called for the government to build roads, improve schools, upgrade health services, and extend electricity and water to remote areas in Chiapas, the poorest state in the Mexican republic. The government agreed to grant rebels amnesty, to outlaw discrimination against Indians, and begin land reforms. The land reforms would allow officials to take large landholdings in Chiapas and divide them among the peasants. The government also promised to help retrain farmers harmed by NAFTA.

In the months following the ceasefire, Mayan farmers seized almost 75,000 acres of ranch lands. They claimed that the lands had been stolen from them as far back as 1819. An agrarian court in 1989 had ruled in favor of the Mayas, but the government had done nothing to enforce the ruling. President Carlos Salinas de Gortari announced, however, that redistribution of farmland was no longer an option in Mexico. Thus, the issue of land remained on the table in the continuing negotiations with the Mayas. (*Also see entries dated 1870–1934: Guatemalan laws caused Mayas to suffer; and August 1995: Zapatista ceasefire.*)

February 24–25, 1994 ♦ Northern Mexican farmers protested NAFTA.

Farmers protested in marches and sit-ins in banks in Chihuahua, Guadalajara, and other northern cities. They claimed that they could not pay off their loans because of the North American Free Trade Agreement (NAFTA). By abolishing guaranteed prices for agricultural products and allowing increased U.S. imports, they argued, the Mexican government had created a farm crisis. The changes left many farmers unable to repay millions owed to private and government banks. Many of the farmers threatened a Chiapas-style armed revolt. As a result of the protests, leaders of several banks promised that no more property would be seized for the time being. El Barzón, a national independent organization representing farmers in 17 of Mexico's 32 states, threatened to take action. It announced it would blockade Mexico's seaports on the Gulf and Pacific coasts if the government did not quickly resolve the agricultural crisis.

March 24, 1994 ♦ Increased U.S. aid to Mexico.

One day after Luis Donaldo Colosio, presidential candidate for Mexico's Institutional Revolutionary Party (PRI), was assassinated in Tijuana, Mexico, the United States extended a $6 billion line of credit to Mexico. Later, both of Mexico's partners in NAFTA, Canada and the United States, created a multibillion-dollar fund to stabilize Mexico's currency. The centerpiece of this fund was a $6.7 billion line of credit for the Central Bank of Mexico. Canada and the United States offered the monetary support to Mexico because their economies were intertwined and interdependent.

Critics of the loans charged that the United States had repeatedly supported the PRI with loans during elections to keep the party in power. They charged that the party of the Democratic Revolution candidate, Cuauhtémoc Cárdenas, would have defeated Carlos Salinas de Gortari in the previous election if not for American money.

April 24, 1994 ♦ El Salvador held free elections.

El Salvador held its first free elections in 64 years. The right-wing Republican National Alliance (ARENA) candidate, Armando Calderón Sol, won 70 percent of the vote. Calderón and ARENA had been associated with dictator Roberto d'Aubuisson, death squads, and the murder of Archbishop Oscar Romero. The opposition left-wing alliance of three parties included the Farabundo Martí National Liberation Front (FMLN), which had waged a guerrilla war for years. The left-wing alliance won 21 out of 84 legislative seats. Calderón took office peacefully on June 1. (*Also see entry dated February 1992: Peace in El Salvador.*)

Names of illegal immigrants who died trying to avoid the Operation Gatekeeper blockade at the U.S.-Mexican border are inscribed on crosses on the Mexican side of the wall.

May 8, 1994 ✦ Presidential elections in Panama.

In Panama's first elections since the United States had overthrown dictator Manuel Noriega, Ernesto Pérez Balladares won the presidency. Pérez Balladares won despite the fact that he was from Noriega's Democratic Revolutionary Party. He also won despite a strong challenge from international recording and film star, Rubén Blades. Blades had founded an independent party to break the cycle of dictatorial regimes and corruption in Panama. This was the first time in 26 years that the country did not vote under the shadow of a military dictatorship.

October 1994 ✦ Operation Gatekeeper was launched.

As the Mexican economy fell, the number of immigrants trying to pass illegally into the United States in search of work soared; anti-immigrant feelings in the United States soared with them. Operation Gatekeeper, a comprehensive border patrol system, was put in place in California to stop illegal immigrants crossing the border from Mexico into the United States. The plan was put into effect at Imperial Beach, which begins at the Pacific Ocean at the border between California and Mexico and extends inland for 14 miles. The area had traditionally accounted for 25 percent of all illegal border crossings into the United States.

Under Operation Gatekeeper, the number of border agents was significantly increased and agents were placed in highly visible positions along the border. Modern military-style strategies were used to track down immigrants. Better equipment was provided, such as four-wheel drive vehicles, infrared night scopes, and electronic sensors.

With the new militarized border patrol at Imperial Beach, migrants tried to cross the border at points farther inland where the terrain (the features of the land) was far more rough. Within the first year a significant number of migrants died making the trip. In the following years, billions of dollars went into the project, which extended westward with miles of fences along the border. Hundreds of immigrant deaths due to crossing in harsher terrain were attributed to the initiative.

November 1994 ✦ California's Proposition 187.

In state elections, Californians passed a measure designed to keep undocumented immigrants from receiving state-funded social services, including welfare and non-emergency medical treatment. It would also force hundreds of thousands of undocumented schoolchildren out of California schools. A federal court order kept the law from taking effect. Even so, Hispanics across the state, who were citizens, reported a rise in discrimination against them.

1995 ✦ Mexican American scientist received Nobel Prize.

Mario Molina, a professor at the Massachusetts Institute of Technology, won the Nobel Prize in chemistry for his vital part in discovering the behavior of chlorofluorocarbons (CFCs), chemicals often used in spray cans and air conditioners. With two other scientists, Molina discovered that these gases release chlorine atoms when they enter the atmosphere. The chlorine atoms destroy the ozone layer, a layer that filters out most of the sun's harmful ultraviolet rays.

January 1995 ✦ Díaz-Balart appointed to House Rules Committee.

Incoming House Speaker Newt Gingrich announced that the Republican majority would make Lincoln Díaz-Balart the first Hispanic member of the House Rules Committee.

February 1995 ✦ U.S. support for the Mexican peso.

Economic problems in Mexico caused the peso to lose value against other currencies. The loss threatened to send Mexico into an economic crisis and to hurt American investors severely. In response, the Clinton administration offered a $20 billion line of credit to help stabilize the Mexican currency.

May 1995 ✦ More immigrants sought citizenship.

The Immigration and Naturalization Service (INS) reported a 75 percent surge in the number of immigrants electing to become naturalized (with the rights of a citizen) U.S. citizens. The Los Angeles, California, INS district received 1,500 or more naturalization applications every day in the first months of 1995, twice as many as the previous year. The INS also reported that there were between 4 and 5 million illegal immigrants living in the United States at that time.

June 12, 1995 ✦ *Adarand Constructors, Inc. v. Peña.*

Affirmative action programs (programs designed to improve employment and educational opportunities of minority groups and women) within the federal government were considered by the U.S. Supreme Court when Adarand Constructors, Inc., a Colorado highway guardrail subcontracting company owned and managed by a white male, brought suit to challenge the constitutionality of a federal program designed to provide contract awards for minority business enterprises. The Court called for "strict scrutiny" (a very careful examination) in determining whether discrimination (behavior influenced by racial or other prejudice) existed before using a federal affirmative action program.

Two Supreme Court justices, Antonin Scalia and Clarence Thomas, were in favor of eliminating affirmative action altogether, but the majority framed their opinion that "the unhappy persistence of both the practice and the lingering effects of racial discrimination against minority groups in this country" justified the use of affirmative action programs in some circumstances. President Bill Clinton observed that *Adarand* reaffirmed the need for affirmative action while reforming the way it was carried out. Clinton called for the elimination of any program that "(a) creates a quota [a proportional number of people—the set number of people or percentage allowed]; (b) creates preferences for unqualified individuals; (c) creates reverse discrimination; or (d) continues even after its equal opportunity purposes have been achieved." *(Also see entries dated 1964: The Civil Rights Act of 1964; 1970: Reverse discrimination challenged affirmative action; 1981–88: The Reagan administration fought affirmative action.)*

August 1995 ✦ Zapatista ceasefire.

Subcomandante Marcos of the Zapatista National Liberation Army called for a temporary ceasefire in the southern Mexican state of Chiapas. He warned that fighting would begin again unless the Mexican government agreed to acknowledge the concerns of the Mayas in Chiapas. *(Also see entries dated 1870–1934: Guatemalan laws caused the Mayas to suffer; and January 1, 1994: The Zapatista uprising in southern Mexico.)*

HISPANIC NEWSPAPER STATISTICS, MARCH 1995

El Diario-La Prensa was New York City's fastest-growing newspaper in any language over a two-year period from 1993 to 1995. The *Dallas Morning News* began publishing a weekly advertising and marketing newspaper in Spanish: *La Fuente* ("The Source"). It included information on food, culture, entertainment, and special events of interest to Hispanics in the Dallas area. The circulation was expected to be around 100,000.

1996 ✦ **Number of Hispanic children increased.**

The U.S. Census Bureau reported that Hispanic children had become the largest group of children in the country after non-Hispanic white children.

February 24, 1996 ✦ Cuban exiles flying over Cuban airspace were shot down.

Two planes flown by Brothers to the Rescue were shot down by the Cuban Air Force. For several years Brothers to the Rescue, a Cuban exile group based in Florida that helped Cubans flee the island for the United States, had been flying in Cuban airspace, violating its territorial boundaries and dropping leaflets in Havana that expressed profound opposition to Cuban dictator Fidel Castro. On February 24, 1996, three Brothers to the Rescue planes were repeatedly warned to leave Cuban airspace, but the pilots continued their flight. Cuban fighter planes then downed two of the three planes, killing all on board. The planes were unarmed.

March 1996 ✦ Clinton signed the Helms-Burton Act.

The United States passed the Helms-Burton Act, officially known as the Cuban Liberty and Democratic Solidarity Act, stepping up the embargo (prohibition on trade and commerce) on Cuba in retaliation for shooting down the Brothers to the Rescue planes. The act was created by conservative members of Congress and championed by the Cuban exile community in Florida. (Conservatives are those who prefer to keep things as they are, particularly by opposing communism and anything remotely connected with it.) Under this law Americans would have the right to sue foreign businesses that dealt with Cuba. In question was the use of property once owned by U.S. businesses that had been seized after Castro took power in 1959. The act sought to punish those foreign corporations that the United States said trafficked in such confiscated property in the course of their business with Cuba. The Helms-Burton Act drew tremendous criticism from U.S. allies worldwide, and the provision about foreign business dealings was repeatedly suspended (not put into effect) by U.S. presidents.

March 18, 1996 ✦ *Hopwood v. University of Texas Law School.*

The University of Texas Law School's affirmative action program was challenged when four white law school applicants claimed they were rejected because of unfair preferences granted to minority applicants. The 5th U.S. Court of Appeals suspended the university's affirmative action admissions program and, in doing so, overturned the 1978 *Regents of the University of California v. Bakke* decision, which had supported race as a determining factor in school admissions. One of the strong arguments in favor of affirmative action in school admission policies was the beneficial effect of having a diverse student population. In *Hopwood* the Court asserted that "educational diversity is not recognized as a compelling state interest." When the Supreme Court allowed the ruling to stand, Texas public universities were required to change their admissions process to conform to race-neutral criteria." *(Also see entries dated 1964: The Civil Rights Act of 1964; 1970: Reverse discrimination challenged affirmative action; and 1981–88: The Reagan administration fought affirmative action).*

September 30, 1996 ◆ The Illegal Immigration Reform and Immigrant Responsibility Act.

In an attempt to make it harder for illegal immigrants to enter at various U.S. borders, the United States passed the Illegal Immigration Reform and Immigrant Responsibility Act (IIRIRA), providing for a huge increase in border patrol personnel and equipment. The act aimed to adopt stronger penalties against illegal immigration; streamline the deportation (sending illegal aliens out of the country) process; make it harder for terrorists from other countries to enter and operate in the United States; and restrict the use of public welfare benefits by new immigrants. The bill was criticized because it did not allow for the nation's court systems to have any input on decisions regarding legal and undocumented immigrants.

November 1996 ◆ Proposition 209 in California.

The ballot initiative Proposition 209 was passed by the California voters. The initiative prohibited preferential treatment based on race or gender, virtually eliminating affirmative action in state hiring, public contracts, and education. The U.S. Supreme Court refused to hear the appeal, and Proposition 209 took effect in California the following year. *(Also see entries dated 1964: The Civil Rights Act of 1964; 1970: Reverse discrimination challenged affirmative action; 1981–88: The Reagan administration fought affirmative action; June 12, 1995: Adarand Constructors, Inc. v. Peña.)*

1997 ◆ Proposition 187 ruled unconstitutional.

U.S. District Court Judge Mariana R. Pfaelzer ruled that parts of Proposition 187 were unconstitutional. According to this ruling, the initiative, which was designed to keep undocumented immigrants from receiving state-funded social services, called for the state to handle matters of immigration that are under federal control. Supporters of Proposition 187 vowed to appeal the decision. *(Also see entry dated November 1994: California's Proposition 187.)*

January 1997 ◆ Henry Cisneros resigned from HUD.

After four years serving as secretary of Housing and Urban Development (HUD), Henry Cisneros resigned his post amid accusations that he had lied to the FBI during an investigation into payments he made to a former girlfriend. On leaving HUD, Cisneros took a position as president and chief operating officer of Uni-

Demonstrators protest against California's Proposition 187 in New York, December 10, 1994. Three years after the initiative was passed in California, it was overturned in a U.S. District Court.

visión, a leading Spanish-language television network. Later that year, a grand jury charged Cisneros with 18 counts of conspiracy, false statements, and obstruction of justice. He paid a $10,000 fine and was later pardoned by President Bill Clinton. (*Also see entry dated 1993: Clinton named Hispanics to his cabinet.*)

January 3, 1997 ♦ Loretta Sanchez took her seat in Congress.

After a difficult campaign against a conservative Republican incumbent (the current holder of office), businesswoman Loretta Sanchez from Orange County, California, became a member of the U.S. Congress. Sanchez had switched from being a Republican to a Democrat in 1992. In the traditionally conservative southern California district, the rapid growth of the Latino and Asian populations helped to ensure her narrow victory.

November 23, 1997 ♦ CANF leader died.

Jorge Mas Canosa, head of the Cuban American Foundation (CANF), powerful lobbyist (someone who works to influence public officials and legislators), multimillionaire, and fervent opponent of Cuban dictator Fidel Castro, died. A college student at the time of Castro's takeover of Cuba, Mas Canosa joined in anti-Castro demonstrations and was forced to flee to the United States in 1960 to avoid arrest. He immediately became active in the militant anti-Castro Cuban organizations in Miami. He was also very successful in business, becoming a multimillionaire by the 1970s. He made close ties with key politicians at the state and federal level and created the organization CANF in 1980, with the initial project of broadcasting anti-Castro radio programs in Cuba. CANF grew into one of the most powerful lobbying organizations in Washington and has been behind the rigid embargoes (prohibitions on trade and commerce) the United States placed on Cuba. Mas Canosa fought throughout his life for ever harsher measures against Cuba, and many became concerned that the people of Cuba suffered more

Sammy Sosa.

deeply from the U.S. embargo than did Castro. Mas Canosa's son, Jorge Mas Santos, took over as head of CANF upon his father's death, but as a member of a younger, native-born generation, Mas Santos focused on other issues than the elimination of Castro, creating a division in the group.

February 25, 1998 ✦ Congresswoman Velázquez named Ranking Member of the Small Business Committee.

The Democratic Caucus elected Congresswoman Nydia M. Velázquez, a Democrat from New York, Ranking Member of the Small Business Committee. She was the first Hispanic woman to serve as chair or ranking member of a full committee in the history of the House of Representatives, and the third Hispanic and the ninth woman in modern times to lead her party on a full committee. Velázquez was the first woman from Puerto Rico to serve in Congress.

June 2, 1998 ✦ Ban on bilingual education in California.

California voters passed Proposition 227, which banned bilingual classroom education and English as a second language (ESL) programs, replacing them with a one-year intensive English immersion program. A federal judge denied challenges to the proposition in July, and 227 went into effect in California schools in August. (Also see entries dated 1967: Language education required; 1974: Educational reforms for non-native speakers of English.)

A demonstrator in San Juan, Puerto Rico, holds a portrait of Edwin Cortes, one of eleven Puerto Rican pro-independence activists jailed in the United States.

June 30, 1998 ✦ U.S. secretary of energy resigns.

Federico Peña resigned his position as secretary of energy, citing personal reasons. *(Also see entry dated 1993: Clinton named Hispanics to his cabinet.)*

September 13, 1998 ✦ Sammy Sosa made baseball history.

Baseball great Sammy Sosa joined Mark McGwire in breaking the 37-year-old record set by Roger Maris of 61 homeruns in a single season.

December 3, 1998 ✦ Washington State banned affirmative action.

Initiative 200 in Washington State, like California's Proposition 209, banished state affirmative action policies. *(Also see entries dated 1964: The Civil Rights Act of 1964; 1970: Reverse discrimination challenged affirmative action; 1981–88: The Reagan administration fought affirmative action; June 12, 1995: Adarand Constructors, Inc. v. Peña; November 1996: Proposition 209 in California.)*

January 5, 1999 ✦ Clinton eased travel restrictions to Cuba.

The Clinton administration approved direct charter flights from Los Angeles and New York to Cuba. Tourists were still not allowed to travel to Cuba, but humanitarian-aid workers, athletes, scholars, teachers, researchers, journalists, and government officials made up the estimated 140,000 passengers from the United States to Cuba in 1999.

April 19, 1999 ✦ A civilian was killed on Puerto Rican island of Vieques.

A stray bomb accidentally killed David Sanes Rodriguez, a local civilian security guard on the Puerto Rican island of Vieques. The U.S. Navy had been undertaking training operations, including testing bombs and playing war games with live ammunition, on Vieques for 60 years. Thousands gathered in protest.

September 10, 1999 ✦ Puerto Rican prisoners freed.

Eleven members of the militant Puerto Rican nationalist group, the Puerto Rican Armed Forces of National Liberation (FALN), which was responsible for a wave of bombings across the United States in the 1970s and 1980s, were released from federal prisons after accepting a controversial clemency (an act of mercy) offer from President Bill Clinton. The prisoners had to agree to renounce violence, avoid association with accused terrorists (including each other), and to accept mandatory (required) drug tests. Many Puerto Ricans considered the prisoners political prisoners, but the rest of the nation showed little sympathy for them, and Clinton was sharply criticized for his clemency action.

September 12, 1999 ◆ Hispanics protested under-representation on television.

Hispanic groups joined the National Association for the Advancement of Colored People (NAACP) in protesting the lack of minority roles in prime-time shows. Studies showed that 63 percent of Latinos did not feel that television represented them accurately. Hispanic groups, such as the National Council of La Raza (NCLR), urged viewers to participate in a national brownout (large decrease in usage) of ABC, CBS, Fox, and NBC television networks the week of September 12, to coincide with Hispanic Heritage Week.

September 13, 1999 ◆ The last of Proposition 187.

U.S. District Judge Mariana R. Pfaelzer approved a settlement of an American Civil Liberties Union challenge to Proposition 187, confirming that no children in California could be deprived of education or healthcare due to their place of birth, and that under the U.S. Constitution, the federal government—not the state—regulates immigration. California governor Gray Davis announced that the settlement over Proposition 187 had voided the controversial sections of the initiative. *(Also see entry dated November 1994: California's Proposition 187; 1997: Proposition 187 ruled unconstitutional.)*

November 25, 1999 ◆ Elián González rescued from seas off Florida.

Six-year-old Elián González was rescued off the coast of Florida; his mother and ten other people died trying to reach the United States from Cuba. He was placed in the home of a great uncle in Miami. In the seven months that followed, Elián became the living symbol of the Cuban exile community's passionate struggle. While his Cuban American relatives fought to keep him in the United States, the boy's father flew from Cuba to the United States to retrieve his son. Stormy protests arose in the Cuban American community in Miami, and the relatives refused to hand the boy over to officials. Armed federal agents finally raided the Miami home of the boy's relatives in order to reunite the boy and his father. Immigration officials and a series of court rulings all supported Elián's father's right to raise his son in the country of his choice. Father and son returned to Cuba after the U.S. Supreme Court refused to hear an appeal by the Miami relatives.

Elián González
being removed
from his relatives'
Miami home.

2000 ◆ The 2000 Census.

The milestone census showed that the Hispanic population in the United States had grown 58 percent, to 35,305,818. For the first time, Hispanics were the largest minority, outnumbering the African American population of 34,658,190 people. With this census, Hispanics became the fastest growing minority group in the country, jumping from 9 percent of the population in 1990 to 13 percent in 2000.

The largest group among Hispanic Americans in 2000 were Mexican Americans at 66.1 percent of the U.S. Hispanic population. Puerto Ricans were second at 9 percent, and Cubans third at 4 percent. The number of "New Latinos"—people from the Dominican Republic and a diverse set of countries in Central American and South America—had more than doubled since 1990, from 3.0 million to 6.1 million. Cubans were still the third largest Hispanic group in the United States, at 1.3 million, but there were nearly as many Dominicans, at 1.1 million, and Salvadorans, numbering 1.1 million as well.

2000 ✦ **Growth in Hispanic Web presence.**
Several Spanish-language Web sites were launched in 1999 and 2000, including Spanish versions of AOL and Yahoo! The Spanish company Terra Networks also signed a deal with Lycos to target Hispanic Americans on the Web, while Yupi.com, another Spanish-language portal, made plans to offer stock to the public. To further boost the Hispanic presence on the Internet, Gateway invested $10 million in quepasa.com and Microsoft announced the creation of a new Spanish-language Web portal in Mexico.

A section of the 2000 U.S. Census form. With this census, Hispanics became the fastest growing minority group in the country.

January 31, 2000 ✦ **Clinton and Puerto Rican Governor Rosello reached agreement on Vieques.**
As protests increased on the island of Vieques, President Bill Clinton proposed a referendum of the registered voters of Vieques, to be held May 1, 2001. The referendum would place two alternatives before the voters: (1) the U.S. Navy would stop all training on the island by May 1, 2003 and (2) the navy would be permitted to continue training, including live fire training, on terms proposed by the navy, and the United States would put $50 million into improvements on the island. Puerto Rican Governor Pedro Rosello agreed to the offer. President George W. Bush later invalidated the agreement and the referendum did not take place. *(Also see entry dated April 19, 1999: A civilian was killed on Puerto Rican island of Vieques.)*

February 22, 2000 ✦ **Affirmative action challenged in Florida.**
Florida banned race as a factor in college admissions, in another state effort to ban affirmative action. *(Also see entries dated 1964: The Civil Rights Act of 1964; 1970: Reverse discrimination challenged affirmative action; 1981–88: The Reagan administration fought affirmative action; June 12, 1995: Adarand*

Constructors, Inc. v. Peña; November 1996: Proposition 209 in California; December 3, 1998: Washington State banned affirmative action.)

May 2000 ◆ Mexico urged U.S. action against vigilante hunters at the border.

Mexican officials met with U.S. officials in Washington to discuss the abuses that had been taking place at the Mexican-U.S. border, particularly in Arizona. U.S. ranchers had formed vigilante groups, or self-appointed groups that get together to enforce particular laws without having any authority to do so, and to punish perceived crimes without giving their victims trials or due process. These groups were hunting illegal immigrants coming into the country, sometimes herding them at gunpoint. The vigilantes had been responsible for two known deaths and seven injuries to the immigrants, and possibly more that went unreported.

May 31, 2000 ◆ Tito Puente died.

Puerto Rican Latin music bandleader and percussionist Tito Puente, born Ernest Anthony Puente, Jr., in New York on April 20, 1923, died at the age of 77. Puente had recorded more than 100 albums and won five Grammy awards. A pioneer in Latin jazz, he popularized the cha cha and mambo, fusing jazz with Latin music elements. He wrote the hit song "Oye Como Va," which rocker Carlos Santana brought to fame.

July 2000 ◆ Plan Colombia, the drug war in South America.

President Bill Clinton committed more than one billion dollars to support Plan Colombia, a strategy developed by the Colombian government in consultation with Clinton officials to combat drugs and strengthen Colombian government institutions. The Plan also focused on advancing peace negotiations in Colombia's ongoing civil war. The United States provided military assistance to the Colombian government, working with military rather than police forces in the region because of the widespread corruption in the local police forces.

July 2, 2000 ◆ Vicente Fox won Mexican presidential election.

After 71 years of rule under the Partido Revolucionario Institucional (PRI), the people of Mexico voted former Coca Cola executive and governor of the state of Guanajuato Vicente Fox into the office of president. Fox ran as the candidate of the Partido Acción Nacional (PAN) on a Catholic, conservative, and democratic platform. As he took office, the Mexican economy was growing, but poverty, the drug trade, and corruption remained big problems. Fox was pro-NAFTA (North American Free Trade Agreement; which would integrate Mexico's and the United States's economies) and globalization and pro-democracy. He pledged to resolve the issues of the Zapatista revolutionaries and to end the widespread corruption in Mexico's goverment and police forces. One of Fox's

Celia Cruz, Ricky Martin, and Gloria Estefan perform during the opening moments of the first annual Latin Grammy Awards.

many campaign promises was to improve the situation of legal and illegal Mexican workers in the United States.

August 18, 2000 ◆ César Chávez Day became a state holiday in California.

The California governor signed legislation making March 31 César Chávez Day, a full, paid holiday for state employees in honor of the labor leader. Texas had the holiday on a "volunteer" status, and Arizona was working on adding the holiday in the upcoming elections.

September 13, 2000 ◆ Latin Grammy Awards.

The Latin Academy of Recording Arts and Sciences, an association composed mainly of musicians, producers, engineers, and other members of the Latin music community, presented the first annual Latin Grammy Awards show. The inaugural show presented 40 awards to various artists in many different categories. Veteran rocker Carlos Santana picked up three awards. Other awards went to producer Emilio Estefan, Mexican crooner Luis Miguel, Argentine rocker Fito Paez, Colombian singer Shakira, Dominican singer Juan Luis Guerra, and Mexican rock band Maná. Cuban singer Ibrahim Ferrer of the Buena Vista Social Club, in his 70s, was named the best new artist. Celia Cruz won for best salsa performance. Some observers in the Hispanic music industry criticized the awards show, saying it discriminated against Mexican traditions and favored singers who performed in English. The awards show took place in Los Angeles and was broadcast on CBS. It aired in 120 countries.

November 2000 ◆ California elected Latina Congresswoman Hilda Solis.

Hilda Solis was elected by an overwhelming majority as Congresswoman from the Thirty-first District of California. Prior to taking her seat in Congress, Solis had been the first Latina to be elected to the California State Senate and had served in that capacity from 1995 to 2000. She had also worked as the editor in chief for the White House Office of Hispanic Affairs and as an analyst for the Office of Management and Budget during President Jimmy Carter's administration.

November 29, 2000 ◆ U. S. Congressman Henry B. González died.

Henry B. González was the first Hispanic Representative from Texas, and served in Congress for nearly four decades, longer than any other Hispanic. González began his political career in San Antonio, where he served on the city council. In that role, he established his reputation as a firebrand when he filibustered (used extreme stalling tactics to delay or prevent an action in a legislative assembly; here, continuously talking) in the Texas Senate for a record 22 hours against pending bills designed to keep Texas schools segregated. González was elected to Congress in 1960. He fought for the rights of Hispanic Americans and worked to defeat the bracero program (the recruitment of Mexican laborers by U.S. agents). He was a moderate, however, and opposed militant protest for equal rights.

González drew attention when he called for the impeachment of President Ronald Reagan, once in 1983 because of the U.S. invasion of Grenada, and again in 1987 when he believed Reagan was involved in the arms-for-hostages scandal involving Iran. Later he called for the impeachment of President George Bush, saying he had not secured permission from Congress for the Persian Gulf War of 1991. González was named chairman of the House Committee on Banking, Finance, and Urban Affairs in 1988. He retired from Congress in 1998 and his son, Charles, took his position.

December 13, 2000 ◆ University of Michigan's affirmative action policy upheld.

In *Gratz v. Bollinger,* federal judge Patrick Duggan ruled that the use of race as a factor in admissions at the University of Michigan was constitutional. The university had argued successfully that its affirmative action program served "a compelling interest" by ensuring a diverse student body that provided educational benefits for all. *(Also see entries dated 1964: The Civil Rights Act of 1964; 1970: Reverse discrimination challenged affirmative action; 1981–88: The Reagan administration fought affirmative action; March 18, 1996: Hopwood v. University of Texas Law School.)*

2001 ✦ Hispanics won in key mayoral elections.

San Antonio, Texas, elected Ed Garza as mayor; Hartford, Connecticut, and Austin, Texas, elected first-ever Hispanic mayors. Democrat Eddie Perez, a native of Puerto Rico and president of a local community group, won in Hartford, and former city councilman Gus Garcia was elected mayor of Austin, Texas.

2001 ✦ Drug Wars continued: The Andean Regional Initiative.

The George W. Bush administration expanded U.S. support for the war against the drug trade as set out in Plan Colombia, providing additional support to Colombia's neighbors in order to guard against the likely "spillover" of refugees, armed groups, and drug traffickers as a result of the military push in Colombia. In addition to funding for counter-drug programs, the Andean Regional Initiative also included funding for social and economic programs, including judicial reform, assistance for government human rights programs, and alternative development programs that aim to provide a source of income for peasant farmers whose illicit crops have been destroyed. The initiative sparked significant debate because of Colombia's poor human rights record and persistent links to paramilitary forces, illegal right-wing death squads whose objective is to eliminate guerrillas in Colombia.*(Also see entry dated July 2000: Plan Colombia, the drug war in South America.)*

2001 ✦ A-Rod leads in the American League

Alex Rodríguez (often known as A-Rod) led the American League with 52 home runs in the 2001 season and was voted by his peers as the league's best player. He was among the leaders in almost every offensive category of the season. Aside from playing baseball, Rodríguez was the national spokesperson for the Boys and Girls Club of America and has been involved in many philanthropic (charitable) projects.

March 27, 2001 ✦ University of Michigan Law School's affirmative action policy was challenged.

A federal judge considering the University of Michigan Law School's affirmative action policy drew the opposite conclusion of the judge ruling on the undergraduate school's admissions policy. U.S. District Judge Bernard Friedman struck down the law school's affirmative action policy, ruling that "intellectual diversity bears no obvious or necessary relationship to racial diversity." *(Also see entries dated 1964: The Civil Rights Act of 1964; 1970: Reverse discrimination challenged affirmative action; 1981–88: The Reagan administration fought affirmative action; March 18, 1996: Hopwood v. University of Texas Law School; December 13, 2000: University of Michigan's affirmative action policy upheld.)*

May 2001 ◆ Deaths at the border.

Fourteen illegal immigrants attempting to enter the United States by crossing the Arizona desert from Mexico died from heat and thirst. A 2000 report by Mexico's National Commission for Human Rights estimated that more than 450 migrants had died from hypothermia and sunstroke while trying to cross the border during the period from 1994 to 2000. *(Also see entries dated October 1994: Operation Gatekeeper was launched; May 2000: Mexico urged U.S. action against vigilante hunters at the border.)*

Mexican president Vicente Fox and U.S. president George W. Bush shake hands while on a visit to the University of Toledo, September 6, 2001.

September 7, 2001 ◆ Mexican President Fox in Washington to push for immigrant workers' rights.

Vicente Fox met with President George W. Bush and delivered an emotional appeal to the U.S. Congress, urging that they consider an immigration deal granting permanent residency to some of the 3 to 4 million Mexicans living and working illegally in the United States. The two presidents agreed on the premise that both countries gain economically from the exchange of labor that occurs between the borders. While Bush ruled out the idea of a blanket amnesty for illegal immigrants, he said he would consider a program in which some "guest workers" could obtain green cards and thereby gain legal residency in the United States. Bush was not specific about any kind of criteria for workers to receive green cards. Conservatives in Congress strongly opposed easing the requirements of legal status.

November 2001 ◆ Terrorist attacks of September 11 impact Mexican workers.

The Immigration and Naturalization Service (INS) reported a huge drop in immigration from Mexico since September 11 and the return of more than 350,000 immigrants to Mexico. The economic slump in the wake of the September 11, 2001, terrorist attacks on the United States hit legal and undocumented Latino workers in the Unites States very hard. A high percentage of Mexican and other

Hispanic workers perform unskilled service jobs in U.S. hotels, conference centers, and restaurants. Thousands were laid off in the period after the attacks, and day labor was scarce. Along with the lack of work, Mexicans in the United States experienced renewed anti-immigrant hostilities. The message from the U.S. government changed abruptly in just a few weeks' time, from consideration of an amnesty or guest worker program to the U.S. Attorney General's October message to foreign residents: "If you overstay your visa—even by one day—we will arrest you. If you violate a local law, you will be put in jail and kept in custody as long as possible."

November 4, 2001 ✦ Hurricane Michelle devastated Cuba.

Hurricane Michelle, the most powerful hurricane to hit Cuba since 1926, caused significant damage to nine of the 14 provinces of Cuba. The United States and Cuban dictator Fidel Castro's government worked together for the first time to provide relief to the storm victims.

A Cuban family stands on the roof of their flooded home a week after Hurricane Michelle devastated Cuba.

December 13, 2001 ✦ Univisión and AOL announced alliance.

America Online, Inc. (AOL) and Spanish language media company Univisión Communications Inc. announced a strategic alliance, in which AOL will feature Univision.com content on several AOL Web sites. Users of Univision.com, Univisión's Web site, will have access to AOL's e-mail and Instant Messenger applications. The alliance was formed to increase U.S. Hispanic Internet use and to reach the country's fastest-growing online community, Hispanic users. *(Also see entry dated 2000: Growth in Hispanic Web presence.*

January 11, 2002 ✦ Cuban American diplomat became assistant secretary of state.

President Bush announced the recess appointment of former ambassador to Venezuela Otto Juan Reich as assistant secretary of state for Western Hemisphere affairs, the top State Department official dealing with Latin America. Bush had nominated the Cuban American diplomat the previous summer, but in Congress opposition to the nomination was so strong that confirmation hearings were repeatedly delayed. When Congress took its year-end recess without having moved to confirm Reich, Bush made the appointment of Reich on his own authority, bypassing the confirmation process for at least a year. From 1983 to 1986, Reich was the director of the State Department's Office of Public Diplomacy (OPD) for Latin America and the Caribbean. In that role, he ran a secret propaganda campaign on behalf of Nicaraguan counterrevolutionaries (contras), who were attempting to overthrow the socialist Sandanista government of Nicaragua. In 1987, after an investigation, Congress accused him of engaging in "prohibited, covert propaganda activities." Reich was also associated with a Cuban American terrorist who committed acts of violence in the name of the anti-Castro cause. Reich, too, was actively anti-Castro, and his appointment was not expected to help with any attempts to renew relations with Cuba.

January 14, 2002 ✦ New Spanish-language broadcast network debut.

Univisión launched Telefutura, its new Spanish-language broadcast network. Telefutura was created to compete with rival network Telemundo and to bring in more viewers to Spanish-language television by providing more viewing options to the large and rapidly growing Hispanic audience.

January 23, 2002 ✦ Debut of *American Family*.

American Family premiered on public television. Created and produced by Gregory Nava, it was the first drama series featuring a Latino cast ever to air on broadcast television. The series was originally financed by CBS, but the network decided at the last moment not to air it. PBS then picked up the series, which starred Edward James Olmos, Raquel Welch, Sonia Braga, and Esai Morales.

February 2002 ✦ Omar Minaya became the first general manager in the major leagues.

Senior assistant general manager of the New York Mets Omar Minaya became the first Hispanic general manager of a baseball team in the major leagues as general manager of the Montreal Expos. Born in the Dominican Republic and raised in New York, Minaya was already the highest ranking Hispanic baseball official in the nation.

February 15, 2002 ✦ Gaddi H. Vasquez became Peace Corps director.

Gaddi H. Vasquez was sworn in as the director of the Peace Corps. He was the agency's first Hispanic American director, nominated by President George W. Bush. Vasquez had previously served as the division vice president of public affairs of the Southern California Edison Company. He served in the adminis-

trations of three California governors, and had been appointed to two federal commissions, as well as serving in many national and local organizations. His parents were migrant farm workers of Mexican descent, and he was the first member of his family to earn a college degree.

March 1, 2002 ◆ Hispanics in Texas primary debate in Spanish.

In the democratic primary elections for the governor of Texas, former Texas attorney general Dan Morales ran against Laredo businessman Tony Sanchez. They held a much-publicized debate in the Spanish language, which was televised throughout the state. Sanchez won the democratic primaries.

April 1, 2002 ◆ Training on Vieques resumed.

Navy bombing on the Puerto Rican island of Vieques resumed on April 1 despite a petition by the people of the island seeking an injunction (a court order to refrain

U.S. Marshals in riot gear prepare to confront anti-navy protestors after they broke through the perimeter fence of the U.S. Navy camp in Vieques on April 28, 2001, after bombing resumed on the island.

from carrying out a particular action) against the navy. *(Also see entries dated April 19, 1999: A civilian was killed on Puerto Rican island of Vieques; January 31, 2000: Clinton and Puerto Rican Governor Rosello reached agreement on Vieques.)*

April 12, 2002 ✦ NBC bought Telemundo.

General Electric Co. (GE), as the owner of NBC, finalized its purchase of Telemundo Communications Group, a Spanish-language television network, for $2.7 billion. Telemundo was the second most popular Spanish-language network in the country, after Univisión. *(Also see entry dated January 14, 2002: New Spanish-language broadcast network debut.)*

GLOSSARY

armada fleet.

Audiencia tribunal.

Auténtico authentic.

barrio Hispanic neighborhood.

Bracero from *brazo,* literally someone who works with his arms or performs manual labor; originally applied to temporary Mexican agricultural and railroad workers, it also refers to any unskilled Mexican worker.

brazo arm.

bodega small general store.

Californio Hispanic Californian.

canción song.

caravel a small, fast ship that was ideal for trips of exploration.

caudillo chief or leader, originally of the rural poor, but today quite often said of any grass-roots leader.

Chicano derivative of *Mechicano,* the same Nahuatl word that gave origin to the name of Mexico; the term originally meant Mexican immigrant worker in the early twentieth century, but became the name adopted by Mexican Americans, especially during the days of the civil rights and student movements.

chinampas fiber mats and topsoil stacked in shallow lakes to create floating gardens—an agricultural technique.

circumnavigate to sail or go completely around, as when Ferdinand Magellan circumnavigated the globe.

conjunto a Texas-northern Mexico musical style as well as the ensemble that plays it.

conquistador conqueror.

coup d'etat the violent overthrow or alteration of an existing government by a small group.

corrido ballad.

Cortes Spanish legislative body.

ejido land parcel.

encomienda Spanish system of slavery that included forcing the slaves to become Christian.

filibustero mercenary.

flotilla fleet.

hacienda ranch.

junta committee.

maquiladoras foreign-owned assembly plants located in Mexico.

Marielitos Cubans who migrated to the United States via the Mariel Boat Lift.

Mestizo people of mixed Spanish and Native American ancestry.

Nuyorican literally "New York-Rican," a term developed colloquially by Puerto Ricans born or raised in New York.

orquesta tipica Mexican American dance music orchestra.

Pachuco a member of a Mexican American urban youth subculture during the 1940s and 1950s that developed its own style of dress (zoot suits), its own dialect, and its own bilingual-bicultural ideology.

presidio fort.

repartimientos slavery rules for dividing Indians among conquerors, discoverers, and colonists.

Tejano Mexican Texan.

teozintle corn, or maize.

uexolotl turkey.

INDEX

References to photos are marked by (ill.).

A

Acevedo, Guillermo 87
Actors/Actresses
    Arnaz, Desi 120
    Ferrer, José 119
    Gonzalez, Pedro
        "Ramirin" 97
    Hayworth, Rita 111
    Moreno, Rita 130
    Noloesca, Beatriz "La
        Chata" 97
    Olmos, Edward James
        169–70, 169 (ill.)
    Prinze, Freddie 150
    Quinn, Anthony 121
ADAL 140
Adams, John Quincy 54
Adams-Onís Treaty 54
*Adarand Constructors, Inc. v.
    Peña* 183
Affirmative action
    Florida 191
    law and legislation 183,
        184, 185, 188, 194, 195
    Proposition 209 185
    Reagan administration
        160

    reverse discrimination
        143, 160, 184
    University of Michigan
        194, 195
AFL-CIO 83
African slave trade. *See*
    Slavery
Agit-prop theater 136
Agrarian Reform Act of 1981
    153
Agrarian Reform Law 128
Agricultural Labor Relations
    Act 143
Alaminos, Antonio de 22
The Alamo, San Antonio,
    Texas 61, 61 (ill.)
Alarcón, Martín de 42
Alianza Federal de los
    Pueblos Libres 134
Alianza Hispano Americana
    79, 79 (ill.)
    segregation 118
Alianza Popular
    Revolucionaria Americana
    99
Alien Acts of 1798 47
Allende, Salvador 142 (ill.),
    144
    assassination 149
Alliance for Progress 130
Almagro, Diego de 31

Almeida, Rafael 75
Alvarez de Pineda, Alonso 27
Alvarez, Luis Walter 167
Alverio, Rosita Dolores. *See*
    Moreno, Rita
Amalgamated Clothing
    Workers of America 148
Amaru, Tupac 45
Amazon River, discovery of
    33
American Family 198
American G.I. Forum 118
American Revolution,
    Spanish support for 45
The Americas 3
    agriculture 19
    Aztecs 9, 10–11, 27
    Catholic Church 21
    Clovis culture 1
    division between Spain
        and Portugal 13
    first immigrants 1
    Incas 9
    law and legislation 22, 39
    Mayas 5, 7, 9
    newspapers 43
    Olmecs 3
    Paleo-Indians 2
    Teotihuacán 6
    Treaty of Tordesillas 14
Anaya, Rudolfo 148